Performing presence

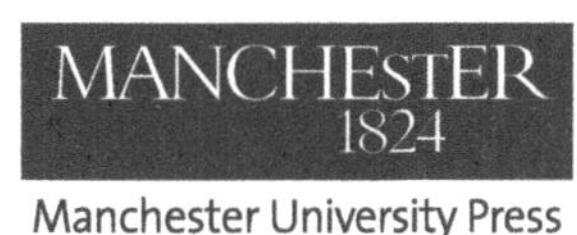

MANCHESTER
1824

Manchester University Press

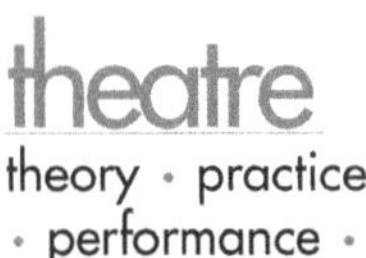

theory · practice
· performance ·

series editors
MARIA M. DELGADO
PETER LICHTENFELS

advisory board
MICHAEL BILLINGTON
SANDRA HEBRON
MARK RAVENHILL
JANELLE REINELT
PETER SELLARS
JOANNE TOMKINSON

This series offers a space for those people who practise theatre to have a dialogue with those who think and write about it.

The series has a flexible format that refocuses the analysis and documentation of performance. It provides, presents and represents material which is written by those who make or create performance history, and offers access to theatre documents, different methodologies and approaches to the art of making theatre.

The books in the series are aimed at students, scholars, practitioners and theatregoing readers. They encourage reassessment of periods, companies and figures in twentieth-century and twenty-first-century theatre history, and provoke and take up discussions of cultural strategies and legacies that recognise the heterogeneity of performance studies.

The series editors, with the advisory board, aim to publish innovative challenging and exploratory texts from practitioners, theorists and critics.

also available

The Paris Jigsaw: internationalism and the city's stages
DAVID BRADBY AND MARIA M. DELGADO (EDS)

Theatre in crisis? Performance manifestos for a new century
MARIA M. DELGADO AND CARIDAD SVICH (EDS)

World stages, local audiences: essays on performance, place, and politics
PETER DICKINSON

Jean Genet and the politics of theatre: spaces of revolution
CARL LAVERY

'Love me or kill me': Sarah Kane and the theatre of extremes
GRAHAM SAUNDERS

Transglobal readings: crossing theatrical boundaries
CARIDAD SVICH

Negotiating cultures: Eugenio Barba and the intercultural debate
IAN WATSON (ED.)

Performing presence

Between the live and the simulated

GABRIELLA GIANNACHI AND NICK KAYE

Manchester University Press

Published by Manchester University Press
Altrincham Street, Manchester M1 7JA, UK
www.manchesteruniversitypress.co.uk

British Library Cataloguing-in-Publication Data
A catalogue record for this book is available from the British Library

ISBN 978 1 5261 2304 6   paperback

This edition first published 2017

Typeset by Servis Filmsetting Ltd, Stockport, Cheshire
Printed in Great Britain
by TJ International Ltd, Padstow, Cornwall

Performing presence: Between the live and the simulated
is supported by

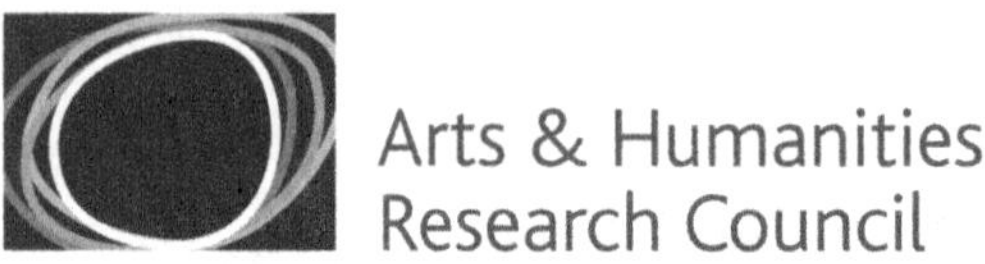

Per Claudia Romano (Fox) e Marco Trabucco (Trabu)
In ricordo di 'quel' viaggio in Spagna
and much more,
con infinito affetto

CONTENTS

ACKNOWLEDGEMENTS

A book such as this rests on the interest and support of many individuals and organizations. We would like to extend our thanks first of all to our principal colleagues and collaborators in the Performing Presence project: Michael Shanks, the Omar and Althea Hoskins Professor of Classical Archaeology, Stanford University; Mel Slater, Professor of Virtual Environments, Department of Computer Science, University College London; and Dr David Swapp, Immersive VR Laboratory Manager at University College London. It has also been a particular privilege for us to develop the book in relation to the generous contributions of time, interest and assistance by the artists whose works form the focus of the study: Gary Hill, Lynn Hershman Leeson, Tony Oursler, Paul Sermon, Matt Adams, Ju Row Farr and Nick Tandavanitj of Blast Theory; Marianne Weems, Artistic Director of The Builders Association, as well as company members and associates James Gibbs, Moe Angelos, Dan Dobson, Kyle DeCamp, Rizwan Mirza, David Pence, Tanya Selveratnam, Harry Sinclair, John Cleater and Ben Rubin. We are also grateful for the generous support of Professor Steve Benford of the Mixed Reality Laboratory at the University of Nottingham. In addition, the involvement of the artists and theatre makers Tim Etchells, Mike Brookes and Mike Pearson, Bella Merlin and Miles Anderson, Vayu Naidu, Fiona Templeton, and Phillip Zarrilli in Performing Presence project workshops, conversations and interviews has been a vital part of the formulation of this work. We would also like to thank Marco Gillies, Department of Computing, Goldsmiths, University of London, and Peter Hulton, Senior Research Fellow at the Department of Drama, University of Exeter, for their continual help and support throughout the project. During the development of the book we also benefited from the continuing invaluable assistance of Rayne Roper Wilder of the Gary Hill Studio and Claire Hellerau of The Builders Association. This project would not have been possible without the constant support and inspiration offered by our colleagues at Stanford University. Additionally to Michael Shanks, we would like to thank Henry Lowood, Curator for History of Science and Technology Collections and Film and Media Collections at Stanford University Libraries; Henrik Bennetsen, Associate Director at Stanford University's Stanford Humanities Lab; and Jeff Aldrich, Technology Director, Stanford Humanities Lab.

As a principal outcome of the Performing Presence project, this book has also received extensive institutional support. We are indebted in particular to the UK Arts and Humanities Research Council for a large research grant award to facilitate the research that underpins the volume. This award to *Performing Presence: from the live to the simulated* provided for a large-scale interdisciplinary collaboration between the University of Exeter, Stanford University and University College London from 2005 to 2009. The University of Exeter also provided extensive financial and technical support to the project.

We would also like to acknowledge the invaluable support of the staff and resources of the following libraries and institutions: the New York Public Library for the Performing Arts at Lincoln Center; the Jerome Robbins Archive of the Recorded Moving Image at Lincoln Center; Electronic Arts Intermix. We would also like to thank the staff from the Stanford Libraries Special Collections unit, especially Bill O'Hanlon, Special Collections Librarian for Manuscripts Processing and Electronic Media, for their help in locating sources at Stanford.

With regard to the figures reproduced in the book, we are pleased to acknowledge the following credits: Figures 2.1, 2.2, 2.3, 2.4, 2.5, 2.6, 2.7, 2.8, 2.9, 2.10, 2.14, 2.15, courtesy Lynn Hershman Leeson; 2.11, 2.16, 5.5, 5.6, 8.1, 8.2, 8.5, 8.7, courtesy Gabriella Giannachi; 2.12, 2.13, 2.18, 23.19, 2.20, courtesy Henrik Bennetsen; 2.17, courtesy Stefanie Kuhn; 3.1, 3.2, 3.3, 3.4, 3.5, 3.6, 3.7, 3.8, 3.9, courtesy Gary Hill and Donald Young Gallery, Chicago; 4.1, 4.2, 4.3, 4.4, 4.5, 4.6, 4.7, 4.8, 4.9, 4.10, 4.11, 4.12, 4.13, courtesy Paul Sermon. 5.1, courtesy Chris Mearing; 5.2, 5.3, courtesy David Swapp. Figures 5.4, 5.7, 5.8, 5.9, 5.10 are material and images generated through the AHRC-funded activity of the Performing Presence project. Figures 6.1, 6.2, 6.3, 6.4, 6.5, 6.6, 6.7, 6.8, 6.9, courtesy

Tony Oursler; 7.1, 7.2, 7.3, 7.6, 7.7, 7.8, 7.9, 7.10, 7.11, 7.12, 7.13, courtesy The Builders Association; 7.4, 7.5 © 2009 Estate of Gordon Matta-Clark/ Artists Rights Society (ARS), New York; DACS, London, reproduced with permission; 8.3, 8.6, courtesy Blast Theory; 8.4, courtesy Mauricio Capra.

We are happy to acknowledge that parts of Chapter 6, 'Ghosting: Tony Oursler', were developed in an earlier form as part of Nick Kaye's article 'Video presence: Tony Oursler's media entities' published in *PAJ: A Journal of Performance and Art*, 30:1 (2008), 15–31. Parts of Chapter 8, 'Pervasiveness: Blast Theory and Mixed Reality Laboratory', were published in an earlier form in Gabriella Giannachi and Steve Benford, 'Temporal expansion in Blast Theory's *Day of the Figurines*,' *PAJ: A Journal of Performance and Art*, 30:3 (2008), 60–9; Steve Benford and Gabriella Giannachi, 'Temporal trajectories in shared interactive narratives', *Proceedings of CHI 2008*, Florence, Italy April 5–10, 2008, New York: ACM; and Matt Adams, Steve Benford and Gabriella Giannachi, 'Pervasive Presence: Blast Theory's *Day of the Figurines*', *Contemporary Theatre Review*, 2008, 18:2, 218–33. The email correspondence between Giabriella Giannachi, Matt Adams and Steve Benford was previously published in Matt Adams, Steve Benford and Gabriella Giannachi, 'Pervasive Presence: Blast Theory's *Day of the Figurines*', *Contemporary Theatre Review*, 2008, 18:2, 218–33.

The interviews and correspondence extracted and published in this book were recorded and edited by the authors and corrected and approved by interviewees for publication. Gabriella Giannachi recorded interviews with Lynn Hershman Leeson and conducted e-mail interviews with Paul Sermon, Matt Adams and Steve Benford. Nick Kaye recorded interviews with Gary Hill, Marianne Weems of The Builders Association, as well as company members and associates Moe Angelos, John Cleater, Kyle DeCamp, James Gibbs, Rizwan Mirza, David Pence and Ben Rubin. Dates and locations or interviews are detailed in the extracts. Marianne Weems's pre-performance notes are reproduced with permission.

Finally, we would like to thank Maria Delgado for her interest and belief in this volume.

G.G.
N.K.

1

introduction Performing presence

Presence is a fundamental yet highly contested aspect of performance, whilst performance has come to be a key concept in a wide range of practices and discourses engaging with questions, concepts and practices of presence. In theatre theory and practice, articulations of presence invariably hinge on the relationship between the live and mediated, on notions of immediacy, authenticity and originality, and the relationship between performer and witness. Indeed, debates over the nature of the actor's presence have been at the heart of key aspects of theatrical work since the late 1950s and are a vital part of the discourses surrounding avant-garde and postmodern performance, whether in the pursuit of a transcendent or deconstructive encounter with acts and signs of performance. These debates have explored terms essential to the theatrical event, addressing the spectator's encounter with the performer, the actor's 'authenticity', 'aura', 'authority' and self-awareness and relationships between 'live' performance and its mediation, documentation or trace. Experimental theatre's engagement with video and new media has further heightened the importance of these issues. Concomitantly, in visual art, installation, media art and aesthetic and experimental engagements with new technologies, the representation and mediation of the body and the shaping of the viewer or visitor's encounters with its signs and traces have invariably aligned phenomena of presence to engagements with processes of performance and notions of performativity.

In these particular contexts, as well as in recent cultural theory, media practice and new media theory, and aspects of contemporary scientific enquiry, questions over the production and reception of presence have also gained a new significance and urgency.

Performing Presence: Between the Live and the Simulated engages with these various contexts and intersections to address a range of contemporary performance, new media and time-based visual arts practices as well as aspects of scientific enquiry that set the production and reception of presence at the centre of their concerns. In these exchanges between art, performance practice and technological experiment, in particular, an engagement with the production and enactment of experiences of 'presence' through technological means has come to the fore. The implications of such practices, in which 'presence' is invariably enacted and experienced through mechanisms in which objects, acts and bodies are encountered in their overt mediation, is fundamental to an understanding of contemporary engagements with presence: engagements with the import and impact of technological mediations on social and personal encounter; with the nature and significance of *being in* one's 'place'; and with 'being before', with the experience, enactment and definition of 'self' and 'other'. It is in these connections, too, that this book emphasizes 'presence' as both practice and experience: as phenomena realized in performative encounters with images, objects, technologies, bodies, sites, acts and events. Indeed, *Performing Presence* proposes that the advent of new media forms, and the increasing integration of contemporary performance and media, have generated new understandings of the phenomena of presence and its performance.

Here, too, the question and practice of presence have gained particular urgency in the advent of immersive, interactive and locative technologies, an urgency signalled in Paul Virilio's reflections in 'Speed and Information' (1995) on the consequences of new communications technologies for experiences of 'being there', as he writes: 'To exist, is to exist *in situ*, here and now, *hic et nunc*. This is precisely what is being threatened by cyberspace and instantaneous, globalized information flows' (Virilio, 1995). Yet although Virilio's observation suggests that the question, if not the practice, of 'presence' has gained currency across disciplines and cultural contexts in its link to the social, personal and experiential impact of these and other technologies, the matter of where, when and how presence occurs, is configured or might be experienced cannot be resolved in relation to technology alone, but needs to be addressed through analyses of the processes, mechanisms of representation and structures of experience that shape their enactment and reception. To this end, *Performing Presence* takes as its focus modes of recent and contemporary artwork, performance, locative media, pervasive games and experimental processes that, across a range of art and technological practices, have interrogated and revealed the mechanisms and implications of phenomena of presence in relation to various discourses, as well as exploring the consequences and meanings of technological innovation in relation to aesthetic and social processes and experiences.

Furthermore, while the analysis of presence may be best advanced through an exploration of relationships between such differing discourses and perspectives, this approach itself is proposed here as echoing key characteristics of the operation of presence. In this book, phenomena of presence are approached as occurring in and through networks of temporal and dynamic relationships that are in action or movement. 'Presence', in this sense, is never resolved into the settled occupation of a unique location – in a simple entrenchment of one's 'being there' – but in performative and temporary acts with regard to place, position and so relation. This concept of presence is aligned to the dynamics and motilities of experiences of witnessing and being witnessed. Such phenomena occur in an implicit unsettling of oppositions: in the uncertain divisions and differences implied in the experience of 'being before' the other or the self – and in the imbrications and tensions between perceiver and perceived.

In approach, then, *Performing Presence* begins in the convergence and exchange between performance theory, cross-media modes of art and performance and the advent of specific systems and technologies of presence, including contemporary modes of telepresence, immersive virtual reality environments, and the scientific and aesthetic discourses that have emerged across these fields. Indeed, as it is manifested in this art and performance, such a convergence and exchange of practices and discourses between visual art, performance practice and technological innovation and experiment have also implicitly challenged the broadly deconstructive, post-Derridean understanding within performance studies of the relationship between performance and technology that linked technologies of 'mediation' to the displacement and elision of the performer's 'presence' (Pontbriand 1982; Féral 1982; Fuchs 1985; Auslander 1992). In contrast, these interdisciplinary exchanges and cross-media works have tended to supersede this scepticism with a fuller engagement with various performative processes and phenomenological frameworks in which the 'presence' of the other and the self may be enacted and described. Here, too, art practice, performance theory and experiments in science and technology offer specific affinities and overlaps through interrogations of the production of presence in the apparatus and mechanisms of representation, in the complexities of site, in the multiple time structures of video installation and simulated performance, as well as in disjunctive relationships between 'real' and 'virtual' events, actions and spaces.

This proposition, which supposes that phenomena of 'presence' may be produced in counter-intuitive means and mechanisms, also reflects key aspects of the etymology of presence, in which 'presence' – 'being there' – is implicitly associated with dynamics of relation, separation and proximity as well as the opening of caesura and doubling. It is towards the production of presence in such dynamics and uncertainties, for which concepts and practices of performance and performativity provide a principal critical paradigm, that this volume directs its attention and which informs its methods and analyses. Indeed, while the convergence of specific aspects of theatre, visual art and media theory and practice as well as experimental practices in computer science and virtual reality may support this approach, it is these etymologies and definitions and their recurrence or reflection in specific phenomenologies, performativities and cross-disciplinary practices that provide the first framework within which these ideas may be elaborated. In turn, it is in the connections between these definitions and contemporary exchanges between technology, art and performance that this volume may most effectively move on to characterize specific networks, processes and acts as loci for presence.

Mapping presence

From an etymological point of view, the noun 'presence' indicates that which is *prae* (before) and *sens* (past participle of *sum*, 'I am'), suggesting 'before I am', or that which is 'in front' of me or 'in view' of me. *Sens* is present participle of *esse* (to be), which indicates 'in actual existence; opposed to *in posse*, in potentiality' (*OED* 2009). We can see from this that presence occurs in relation to a distinct tense – the present participle – which marks the present in the act of its unfolding. This suggests not only a link between the idea of presence and notions of being and 'essence' or 'essential nature' (*OED*), but also that there is an indissoluble connection between presence and definitions and concepts of 'the present'. Unsurprisingly, there is a noticeable difference between ab-*sens* (off, away, from being) and prae-*sens* (before, in front of being), though in both cases there is a clear separation between 'being' and that which is, or is not, in front of or present to it. Interestingly, *sens*, or -ence, is to be found in nouns showing state or quality (absence, diligence, elegance, temperance) (*Barnhart Dictionary of Etymology*, 1988). Thus presence indicates that which is corollary to, around and before something of quality captured at the present moment of its occurrence. Accordingly, the *Shorter OED* (1975) states that 'presence' indicates:

- 'the fact or condition of being present; the state of being before, in front of, or in the same place with a person or thing; being there';
- 'the portion of space in front of a person';
- 'the company or society of someone'.

It is significant, too, that presence can indicate both a state and its condition in space and time but also a sociality; that is, one is present to something else or in the presence of something else. In other words, presence presumes a plurality and alterity and so, arguably, it is societal and thus cultural. In turn, in the connection between 'presence' and 'the present', this etymology of presence also implies a temporal complexity. While the notion of presence evidently entails an implicit reference to temporality, the noun 'presence' is explicitly linked to the adverb 'present'. According to the *OED* (2009) this indicates:

- 'in or into the presence of someone';
- 'of the present time';
- 'in the immediate vicinity';
- 'at the present time, now; immediately, instantly, at once'.

'Being present' thus signifies a state, or condition, both in time *and* in space. It indicates 'now' but also 'in the previous moment' and so what precedes it, where we come from; so implying a temporal as well as spatial 'before'. Indeed, although presence is 'in front of I am', and so imminence, it is also what is yet to come. In other words, presence is the ecology or network that inexorably ties the 'I am' with its past and future, and that forces 'I am' to confront itself with what is other from 'it'. Yet presence is 'before I am'. It is not 'not I' or 'without me' or 'before me' but 'before I [am]'. So the subject is the 'I' that something is in front or before. In other words, presence is what appears before or in front of the subject caught in the act of its making as a subject, so implying a relational movement or change. Spatiality, temporality, sociality and being *are*, therefore, the conditions through which it occurs. Its construction is social *and* cultural, which means that our perception and reception of 'presence' vary in time and space.

Furthermore, the *Shorter Oxford* indicates that, as an adjective of relation, 'present' also:

- 'express[es] a local or temporary relation to a person or thing which is the point of reference';
- 'senses relating to place';
- indicates 'being in the place considered or mentioned';
- indicates 'existing in the thing, class, or case mentioned or under consideration';
- suggests that 'of which one is conscious; directly thought of, remembered or imagined';
- indicates 'having presence of mind, collected, self-possessed'; 'prompt to perceive or act, ready, quick'.

Presence thus also implies awareness, self-awareness, consciousness and even alertness, all of which contribute to the unfolding of the 'I am' in relation to which an object of attention is located spatially and temporally. In other words, presence represents the receptivity of the 'I am' to its own 'retention' and 'protention'. Presence of course is also related to the idea of 'presentation', which according to the *OED* indicates:

- 'the formal or ceremonial introduction of a person to another, esp. a superior; *spec.* the presenting of a person at court'
- 'something offered for acceptance; a present, a gift'.

It should be noted that *presentare* has a subsidiary in *representare* – to represent – which implies the witnessing of an act of mimesis. Annika Blunk captures the complexity of this dynamic well with respect to its significance for presence research, particularly within the sphere of technologically generated artworks, when arguing that 'to represent [*vorstellen*] means to bring what is present at hand [*das Vorhandene*] before oneself as something standing against, to relate it to oneself, to the one representing it, and to force it back into this relationship to oneself as the normative realm' (Blunk 1998: 27). For her, interactive installations thus 'reveal themselves in the dialectic of action and reaction' (Blunk 1998: 27). At least two points are crucial here: first, whereas presentation implies a positioning of presence in space and time, a positioning that forms an ecology of relationships between the 'I am' and that which is in front or before, *representation* suggests the return, or 'homecoming', of this other to oneself. Second, this 'interactive' mechanism between the 'I am' and what is in front of or before is crucial to the reading of the operation of presence in performance, as well as interactive, media and new media arts. This Introduction will return to the importance of this point later.

The fact that presence signifies 'present' suggests that implicit within presence is some idea of 'gift'. As Marcel Mauss's well known analysis (Mauss 2000) makes clear, 'gifts' carry the 'poisonous' obligation of reciprocation (*Gift* in German means both present and poison), thus the 'ecology' of presence, that is, the interaction of the 'I am' and that which is before or in front, and the environment generated by this process, is not neutral but rather charged, fraught with tension. Unlike 'aura', which comes from the Greek and indicates a breeze, wind or air, and 'charisma', which indicates grace, beauty or kindness (*OED*), presence conceals a 'poisonous' but necessary relationship between the self and that which is other. Here, when presence occurs; when the 'I am' is confronted with that which is in front or before, the 'poisonous' interaction between 'I am' and that which is in front of or before *takes place*, and an uncanniness becomes apparent. This process may be understood by recurring to Sigmund Freud's seminal study of this phenomenon. In Freud's definition of the uncanny as 'a species of the frightening that goes back to what was once well known and had long been familiar' (Freud 2003: 124), the German word *Heimlich* designates, broadly, both the 'familiar' and 'the secret'; thus, Freud notes, 'among the various shades of meaning that are recorded for *Heimlich* there is one which it merges with its formal antonym, *Unheimlich*, so that what is called *Heimlich* becomes *Unheimlich*' (Freud 2003: 132). This dynamic or tension between the *Heimlich* and the *Unheimlich*, which is ultimately a tension between that which belongs to the *Heim* (or home) and that which does not, is also implied in these etymologies of 'presence', which, as we have seen, indicate relationships between the 'I am' (the *Heim*, or home, but also that which is *Heimlich* and so secret) and that to which this is other (the *Unheimlich*). Presence thus becomes the instant or action by which that which is *heimlich* (belonging to the 'I am' but also secret to it) faces that which is *unheimlich* (which is in front or before it) and it is in the event of coincidence of these two facets that the uncanny occurs. Through this act, the uncanny, entailed by what is in front of or before the 'I am', returns to the 'I am', and thus discloses, in this movement, that which was contained in the 'I am' but was 'always already' secret to it.

This dynamic of presence is evident, too, in mechanisms of theatrical performance and is articulated, by way of example, in the playwright Samuel Beckett's overtly metatheatrical work. Indeed, the performance studies theorist Peggy Phelan captures how Beckett exploited and exemplified this dynamic in his masterpiece *Waiting for Godot* (1953). Phelan shows how in this play Beckett erases the distinction between 'stage players', meaning the actors as characters and performers, and 'stage watchers', or spectators. Here, Phelan notes, actors and spectators alike wait for something to happen and in the process of waiting their attention is continually drawn back to themselves as another interval occurs (Phelan, 1993: 14–15). It is a dynamic that suggests Beckett's exploration dramaturgically, that is, at the level of action, of what happens to presence when the before or in front of 'I am' does not manifest itself to 'I am'. For Phelan, this indicates that 'Beckett makes clear that presence is doubt' and that doubt is 'the signature of presence, rather than the security of re-presentation' (Phelan, 1993: 15). Although Phelan's reading may imply that dramatic representation is 'secure', which, as Beckett's work demonstrates, is not necessarily the case, it is correct that much philosophy and art has focused on this relationship between the 'I am' and what is before or in front, and since, as we have seen, this relationship is culturally determined, 'doubt' has come, after the Enlightenment, to represent the principal lens through which this dynamic has been enacted on stage or presented in performance. Significantly, Phelan notes that 'since Stanislavski, when actors are observed carefully and perform well, they are said to have "presence". The actor achieves presence through performing as if another' (Phelan, 1993: 117). Consistently with this, in Phelan's reading of presence on stage there is a division between the figure of a performer and that of 'another': the character they enact. This suggests that, to a significant extent, in representational theatre it is precisely a performance of the relationship between the 'I am' and what is *in front of* or *before* that constitutes the 'dramatic action' to which spectators are witness. In other words, regardless of plot and story, it is the relationship, and so the dynamic and caesura, that performers articulate between 'themselves' and their 'characters' and, to some extent, among each other as performers *and* characters that forms the 'drama' at the heart of representational theatre. An analogous tension is also a characteristic of 'non-theatrical' and experimental performance practice, and it is interesting to note here that both in dramatic theatre and in other modes of performance a focus on presence implies not so much an attention to the spectator as the actor or performer themselves, and the relationship they are able to create with their character or role as well as the dynamics they adopt to (re-)present this to their audiences.

In these contexts, too, 'presence' also implies the hybrid spatio-temporal universe that is generated by its occurrence: hybrid, because it is a zone of liminality, capturing the encounter between entities that are seemingly estranged to one another. Frank Kermode notes the effect of presence produced by the confines and requirements of a royal court, 'the king's ceremonial chamber, or simply the stated limits or area in which his person resided' (Kermode 1987: 92). Kermode concludes by pointing out how:

> certain rules of conduct, a certain etiquette, were absolutely enforced
> within these limits, not merely for security but in the interest of dignity.
> The presence could as well be a field or a ship as a palace, but the rules were
> the same. The ruler's personal presence was deemed to extend to these
> limits, ending at a particular wall or tent; this was a shared legal-ceremonial
> fiction, binding on all.   [Kermode 1987: 92]

In this sense, presence is also the ritual through which the 'I am' and
that which is before negotiate the *Gift* of their relationship. In other
words, presence is a *polis*, a space of negotiation, contention and even
suppression.

Importantly, too, these dynamics of presence engage both with a
production and performance of presence – and so the enactment of
'presence' (in the widest sense) – and the reception of presence, and
so presence as a phenomenon for the one who stands before. In this
regard, in his study of presence Craig Murray notes that whereas the
OED (1935) understands presence as an occurrence (and so act) within
an environment that is implicitly the 'object' of attention, other dic-
tionaries, such as the *Oxford Paperback Dictionary* (1979) focus on an
individual's 'subjective experience of being within a particular place
or environment' (Murray 1998: 211), thus demarcating a shift that
frequently occurs as analyses move across live, mediated and simulated
performance. Thus, whereas, in the interrogations of theatrical and live
performance, discourses around presence have tended to focus on the
presence of the actor or performer, studies of presence in simulated
environments, including those produced by telepresence and immersive environments, including CAVE, have tended to focus on the user
or participant's capacity to 'feel present' within a simulation. This not
only marks a shift of emphasis from spectatorship to participation and
even performance, with affinities to critical discourses in time-based art
and installation as well as contemporary work falling under the broad
definition of mixed reality performance (see Benford and Giannachi
2011), but it is also indicative of a broader phenomenon, namely the
inclusion within the mechanisms of presence of a *technology*. Murray
thus notes that while, historically, the body has been configured as the
'locus of presence' (Murray 1998: 213) and in connection with this
demonstrates how questions of presence have been intrinsic to constructions of 'our phenomenal body' (Murray 1998: 214), these debates
have turned towards questions pertaining to the post-human and even
cyborg, to which technologies, and concomitant overlaps between 'real'
and 'virtual' bodies and identities, are integral.

Phenomena and signs of presence

That such dynamics, differences and separations may be loci for 'presence' is also reflected in phenomenological accounts of the emergence and experience of the presence of the self and its relationship to otherness and alterity. Indeed, in the context of phenomenology, which as a philosophical method implies the study of structures and acts of consciousness through analyses of experiential phenomena rather than autonomous or discrete objects, 'presence' may be configured as both 'emergent' in time and as the medium and means by which encounters with alterity and so the experience of one's own identity and limits are sensed. Thus, in his address to *The Hospitality of Presence* (2008), an examination of 'the problems of otherness in Edmund Husserl's phenomenology', Daniel Birnbaum's point of departure is an equation between 'presence' and Husserl's founding turn towards phenomenology in the early twentieth century, which leads him to propose that:

> The phenomenological reduction implies a radical shift of attitude, from a focus on objects – typical of the 'natural attitude' – to a focus on the *modes of givenness* of objects. To thematise the modes of givenness requires a close inspection of the modes of consciousness through which the objects in question are made to appear . . . To scrutinize the givenness of things thus implies a close investigation of the correlative forms of consciousness, and of 'presence' as the very medium through which things present themselves to consciousness.   [Birnbaum 2008: 13, original emphasis]

This notion of presence as a 'medium' provides for a further extension of aspects of these etymologies of presence. Suggesting, again, an unfolding of the 'I am' in relation to which an object of attention is located spatially and temporally, the notion of 'presence' as the 'medium' through which the objects 'present themselves to consciousness', suggests the 'presence' of things is a phenomena conditioned by the delays and deferrals implied in acts of presentation and discovery. Presence, here, is an experience linked also to the performance of subjectivity; to the realization of a consciousness of the self *in* and so *before* the 'presence' of objects and acts emergent in time. As Birnbaum emphasizes, such an implicitly processual understanding of presence departs from the dualities in which objects are placed in simple opposition to a discrete subject. He notes that:

> In post-Cartesian philosophy, the thing in question is usually taken to be an 'object' standing over against a 'subject', and the ideal situation – in which

the thing is given in a true manner – is that of immediate self-evidence. This, in turn, is generally taken to mean that the object is given in the temporal present, that is, as 'now'.   [Birnbaum 2008: 20]

In this context, not only the notion of the autonomous 'object' and 'its' qualities comes into question, but so too does the notion a discrete moment of the 'present-tense'. Thus, Husserl's phenomenology presents a core questioning of the 'now' point, or 'the present', as a singular immanent or stable moment, and articulates instead 'the present' as always subject to a direction of travel. Following Husserl's analysis of the subjectivity of temporal perception and his vision of time as a flow of presence, rather than a succession of measurable successive 'now' points, the philosopher Francisco Varela elaborates a three-part temporal structure constituted of 'now', 'retention' and 'protention'. Retention is described as belonging to the past even though it is happening 'now', whereas protention is 'the expectation or the construction of the future' (Varela 1999). Extending the implications of such a temporal structure towards his concept of the 'hospitality' of presence, and, by implication, 'the present', Birnbaum proposes that in this temporality:

> The present is permeated by absence and otherness; only when letting in what is other than itself, can it remain what it is. Thus, it can hardly be interpreted as a principle of exclusion, closing the ego off from that which is foreign and different. Given the fundamental role of alterity, presence must instead be seen as a principle of hospitality.   [Birnbaum 2008: 181]

Integral to phenomena of 'presence', here, is the notion of a *being before*, spatially and temporally, and consequently a relationship and definition of the self in *co-presence* with that which is other to itself; and so a presence characterized in process and alterity. Such a reading of presence echoes, too, an ethics of encounter that has been constructed in phenomenologies of presence subsequent to Husserl and which have, at times, explicitly influenced articulations of presence and relation in art and performance. Thus, with regard to the experience of the presence of the self and other in performative encounters, a processual emphasis is evident in Martin Heidegger's notions of 'neighboring nearness' (Heidegger 1971: 103), a concept which the artist Gary Hill has directed attention to, noting that specific aspects of his own thinking and practice 'resonate with Heidegger's notion of living in time or being face to face' (Hill in Sarrazin 2000: 222). Set out in Heidegger's series of lectures, 'The Nature of Language' (1959), these concepts describe presence arising as acts of persistence, defined, with regard to the self, in the experience of 'neighborhood', meaning 'dwelling in nearness' (Heidegger 1971: 93) to

the other; an encounter implicitly defined in a co-performance of identification, association and difference. For Emmanuel Levinas, extending
both Husserl and Heidegger's positions in *Totality and Infinity* (1969),
the realization of the self in relation to the other presents an ethical
choice between self-containment, an 'I' defined as 'totality', or a realization of self defined in otherness, an 'I' defined in 'infinity'. Indeed, it is
Levinas's projection towards the presence of 'I am' defined in an openness to the other that Birnbaum's articulation of the 'the hospitality
of presence' specifically echoes. In this context, Levinas proposes, his
project in *Totality and Infinity* 'will present subjectivity as welcoming
the other, as hospitality', for 'in it the idea of infinity is consummated'
(Levinas 1969: 26–7). Indeed, in this 'mode of being', where '[s]epara-
tion is the very constitution of thought and interiority, that is, a relationship within independence' (Levinas 1969: 104), Levinas emphasizes that,
with regard to the definition of the self, 'it is impossible to place oneself
outside of the correlation between the same and the other' (Levinas
1969: 36). Thus, Levinas directs attention toward a 'mode of being' and
realization of 'I am', and so a presencing of the self, whereby '*alterity*
is thereby reabsorbed into my own identity as a thinker or possessor'
(Levinas 1969: 33, original emphasis). Such a choice, act and mode of
being, Levinas argues:

> is produced in the improbable feat whereby a separated being is fixed in its
> identity, the same, the I, nonetheless contains in itself what it can neither
> contain nor receive solely by virtue of its own identity. Subjectivity realises
> these impossible exigencies – the astonishing feat of containing more than
> it is possible to contain.   [Levinas 1969: 26–7]

Indeed, it follows that not only is the position of 'the I' and so the
presence of the self, articulated in 'hospitality' towards the other, but the
experience of the other is itself a function of this separation and so a self-
presence. Levinas thus emphasizes that:

> the radical heterogeneity of the other is possible only if the other is other
> with respect to a term whose essence is to remain at the point of departure,
> to serve as *entry* into the relation, to be the same not relatively but abso-
> lutely. *A term can remain only at the point of departure of relationship only
> as I.*   [Levinas 1969: 36, original emphasis]

It follows, finally, that it is in '[t]he presence of the Other' (Levinas
1969: 99), and in the act of 'containing more than it is possible to
contain', that that the self is defined *in relation*, so echoing the 'return'
or the 'homecoming' of the other to the 'I am' implied in the etymology

of presence. Indeed, in his reading of presence after Husserl, Birnbaum proposes a mechanism of alterity within the experience of presence that functions at the level of both the temporal ('living') present and an identity of consciousness defined in an openness to the other. He concludes that:

> the living present, far from being a self-sufficient atom, involves a fundamental form of alterity . . . Husserl, when reaching the most fundamental level of consciousness – the living present – simultaneously discovers the impossibility of reducing that which is 'other' than presence, since presence in itself appears as a form of 'othering'. On the most primitive level, the identity of consciousness presents itself as an 'othering of the same'.   [Birnbaum 2008: 152–3]

Consistently with an etymology of presence that presumes plurality and alterity, these accounts of phenomena of presence articulate relation, division and movement. It is here, too, and particularly in the notion of the production of presence in a being *in front of* or *before*, that phenomena of presence may be related to the operation and mechanisms of the sign, which is conventionally associated with the absence of the 'object' of attention. Indeed, these phenomenological accounts of the definition of 'presence' in dynamics of otherness – and of the performance or realization of 'self-presence' in and as *alterity* – may also be read in relation to Jacques Derrida's celebrated project that would reveal the operation of the supplement or trace – of delay, deferral and difference – within 'writing', and thus within any claim to the presence of original, 'authentic' or transcendental meaning or position. Indeed, no study of the performance and reception of presence in contemporary art, performance and technology can proceed without engaging with the consequences of this critique. Here, too, a consideration of Derrida's deconstructive turn may provide for a further articulation of a performance of presence always already enacted in division and alterity.

In Derrida's project, aimed at a deconstruction of concepts of 'presence' and its concomitant oppositions and hierarchies within Western metaphysics, the claim to 'presence' is treated as a suppression of the uncertainties in which signifying systems function. Specifically, in his critique of Ferdinand de Saussure's structural linguistics, and adopting the proposition that the sign functions in a relationship between signifier (the mark or sound) and signified (the concept or unit of meaning), Derrida follows Saussure's description of language as an entirely conventional construction that enables our thinking of the world, even as he works to reveal the instability that underlies the oppositions upon which this account rests. In doing so, Derrida observes that, despite Saussure's description of meaning as entirely a function of self-regulating linguistic structures, his very account of the functioning of these systems in oppositions between a signifier (which is recognized by the reader only in its difference from all other signifiers within the system) and the signified (which, in the recognition of the signifier, manifests the unit of meaning) implies a realm of the 'transcendental signified', of originary or 'authentic' meaning, beyond the differential operation of the signifier and so the functioning of the linguistic system itself. Indeed, only by gaining access to such a realm could the play of differences between signifiers that defines the self-contained linguistic system result in the 'presence' of meaning. In response, Derrida proposes a collapse of the binary opposition between signifier and signified, thus simultaneously restoring Saussure's proposition that meaning is a function of the linguistic system alone, while directing attention toward the consequence of this move; that, within any self-contained linguistic system, 'meaning' must be finally 'undecidable', as it is always already subject to the differential operation of the signifier. Thus 'meaning' (and the sign itself) can never be 'self-present'. It follows that the 'import' of the sign is never final or autonomous, but rather a function of the difference and deferral in which the linguistic system (of which it is a part) operates. It follows, too, that where any linguistic system strives to operate as 'a system regulated by an *internal* necessity, and that in a certain way its structure be closed . . . for it must be believed that there is an *inside* of language' (Derrida 1976: 33, original emphasis), the oppositions on which this claim to interiority rests become themselves a focus of Derrida's questioning. Indeed, such 'interiority' rests again on the claim to self-presence: on the linguistic system's unbreachable opposition to exteriority.

In Derrida's deconstruction of Saussure, then, the 'presence' of meaning, and so the immanence of the 'transcendental signified', can never be achieved in any final sense, for meaning is always already subject to motility; to an 'undecidability' that is the condition of the functioning of language itself. Indeed, it follows that where all positions are produced as a function of others, then the very claim of any linguistic system to 'interiority' is an unstable position, for, as Derrida proposes: 'The Outside ~~is~~ the Inside' (Derrida 1976: 44). Here, with regard to 'presence', then, and consistently with this critique of Saussure, Derrida's 'deconstruction' works to reveal the contradictions, the play of *differance*, in which implicit claims to a transcendental, final or foundational 'presence', and, similarly, to the genuine, the real, or the authentic – to that which would *precede* or *transcend* the functioning of the sign – necessarily suppress. Under Derrida's paradigm, the claim to presence is *discursive*, made in a suppression of linguistic, and so cultural, historical and political contingency and contradiction. In the absence of the 'transcendental signified', then, the claim to 'presence', to the unique occupation of *this place*, has no final foundation but can only be 'performative', in the sense that it 'enacts that to which it refers' (Pearson and Shanks 2001: 69).

This paradigm, of course, has had profound consequences for the understanding and critique of presence in theory, criticism, art and performance, while Derrida's critical practice, which exemplifies his elaboration of this paradigm, has also provided a fundamental influence on engagements with the performance of presence. In the introduction to her translation of Derrida's *Of Grammatology*, Gayatri Spivak describes Derrida's 'structure of writing' as 'the sign under erasure', noting its '[t]race-structure, everything always inhabited by the trace of something not itself' that 'questions presence-structure' (Spivak in Derrida 1976: lxix). It is this practice, too, which shadows the deconstructive turn in art and performance, influentially characterized by the performance studies theorist Philip Auslander, in *Presence and Resistance* (1992), as strategies effecting an interruption, or, he suggests, 'a deconstruction of presence and of the structures of authority in performance', which, under the tactics of postmodernism, may be 'coupled with a refusal to offer "alternative" representations' (Auslander 1992: 47).

Yet, under this paradigm, and with regard to phenomena of presence, there is no necessary contradiction between the experience of presence and the absences – and deferrals – in which the sign operates. Thus, following Derrida's proposition that '[f]rom the moment that there is meaning there are nothing but signs' such that '[w]e *think only in signs*' (Derrida 1976: 50, original emphasis), there can be no perception of 'presence' beyond the operation of the sign itself. It is on this basis, of course, that the deconstructive turn, which is to say, the critical habitation of texts (in the widest sense) in such a way as to reveal the *operation* of signs and the *construction* of presence, is not necessarily antithetical to the phenomenon and so the experience of presence. Indeed, it is in this context that Auslander, in his association of the deconstructive turn in media-based performance with a politics of postmodernism, emphasizes, after Derrida, the ambivalence of any deconstructive project, which, he suggests, always runs the risk of confirming or reinstating the very 'structures of authority' it seeks at once to inhabit and critique (Auslander 1992: 25–6). With regard to the phenomena of presence and the sign, however, this complicity between the absences of the sign and the production of experiences of presence runs deeper. Thus, with regard to the phenomena of presence, and specifically in connection with Charles Sanders Pierce's elaboration of phenomenology in his *Principles of Philosophy* (1931), Derrida remarks that:

> *manifestation* itself does not reveal a presence, it makes a sign … There is thus no phenomenality reducing the sign or representer so that this thing signified may be allowed to glow finally in the luminosity of its presence. The so-called 'thing-itself' is always already a *representamen* shielded from the simplicity of intuitive evidence. The representamen functions only by giving rise to an interpretant that itself becomes a sign and so on to infinity.   [Derrida 1976: 49, original emphasis]

It follows that there is no necessary contradiction between the indeterminacies of the sign and the effect, illusion and enactment of presence, which, in the absence of the transcendental signified, 'is' the phenomenon of presence 'itself'. Indeed, where, with regard to the sign and linguistic system, 'The Outside ~~is~~ the Inside', so, by analogy, and after Spivak, one might propose that with regard to presence as phenomenon, 'presence-structure' ~~is~~ 'trace-structure'. Indeed, such a structure of trace and division is reflected in phenomenological accounts of presence as the experience of the self in the trace of the other and of movements toward and returns from exteriority. In these instances of and relationships with alterity, the mechanisms of presence are those of the sign itself: of trace, emergence, movement, difference, of 'The Hinge' (Derrida 1976: 65) or *difference*. Here, phenomena of presence are produced in *movement* and *difference*, rather than *as* transcendence or *in* the confines of 'interiority'. It is an effect reflected, too, in the etymological roots of 'presence' and their dramatization: in the relation between 'presence' and 'presentation'; in Phelan's assertion of 'doubt' as the operating trope of 'presence'; in the production of presence in zones of liminality; in the uncanny return of the other. Indeed, Derrida, and his influence, reveal, perhaps, first of all, that there is no 'normative' state or phenomena of presence (nor a transcendent one) nor one necessary, unified or stable means of its provocation.

Such assumptions and tactics are evident, too, in recent experimental practices as well as performance theory and artworks that make an overt address to the practice and performance of presence, whether from the perspective of its production or reception. Thus, Alan Dix's paper 'absenT Presence' (Dix *et al.* 2004) outlines a series of experimental projects testing the perception of 'past presence' or 'absent presence' in virtual, physical or cyberspace environments, thus resting the production of presence as a phenomena in signs and experiences of 'absence'. Dix records that:

> The absent presence challenge was to create a system that for some environment, virtual or physical, where visitors are normally alone or have few people around, can in some way sense the presence of those who have gone before . . . and also the visitors' own presence in some way is taken forward.   [Dix *et al.* 2004]

Lev Manovich provides for an analogous characterization of telepresence systems, noting that, despite articulating a relationship of absence and distance, telepresence allows the subject to control not just the simulation but 'reality' itself. Telepresence thus provides the ability to 'remotely manipulate physical reality in real time through its image', leading him to conclude that 'the essence of telepresence is that it is antipresence. I don't have to be physically present in a location to affect reality at this location' (Manovich 2000: 175). Such a dynamic is evident, too, in interactive art installations. The Milan-based group Studio Azzurro, who have been developing media-based interactive 'videoenvironments' since 1995, have thus noted the paradoxical effect of producing motilities between the 'virtual' and 'real' objects and images, in which the viewer's actions and interactions, to which these virtual 'objects' and images respond, effect a passage between 'real' and 'screened' spaces (Kaye 2007a: 123–8). In this context, Paolo Rosa, one of the founding members of the group, notes, in effecting the 'disappearance' of the object's materiality into mediation, but the return of its functionality in interaction: 'I had become aware how paradoxically the more objects tend to lose their material essence, dissolve their physical nature into flux and data, the more they tend to disappear, the more their "presence" gains ground' (Rosa in Valentini 1995: 160). Analogously, in performance studies, Jon Erickson describes another mechanism of absenting in which presence as phenomenon is articulated and amplified, arguing that:

> Presence seems to be most evident in silence, since it resists the disembodying proclivities of discourse. One is holding back the articulate meaning that the audience is expecting. Presence of the body is stronger when linguistic desublimation is absent; more precisely, not absent, but not yet manifested.   [Erickson 1998: 63]

As Erickson implies, such a theatrical presence is underpinned in a performance of the 'now' point as flow, and so an overt articulation of the theatrical sign as subject to the temporal structure outlined by Husserl, in which the experience of 'the present' is enacted in the traces of what was and what will be. Erickson concludes that:

> 'Presence' in the theater is physicality in the present that at the same time
> is grounded in a form of absence. It is something that has unfolded, is read
> against what has been seen, and presently observed in expectation as to
> what will be seen. It means that the performer is presenting herself to the
> audience, but at the same time holding something back, creating expecta-
> tion . . . In other words, not only does the notion of presence in perform-
> ance imply an absence, but that absence itself is the possibility of future
> movement; so paradoxically, presence is based not only in the present, but
> in our expectation of the future.   [Erickson 1998: 62]

Such perceptions of the articulation and amplification of presence
in states and processes of liminality differ from those ascribed within
performance theory to a postmodern turn in art and performance since
the early 1980s. In this highly influential discourse, a critique of 'presence' in performance practice has been linked to the 'technical means'
by which a construction of the 'live' 'presence' of the performer might
be exposed and denuded. Thus for Chantal Pontbriand (1982), Josette
Féral (1982), Eleanor Fuchs (1985) and, in response to these articles,
Philip Auslander (1992), a critique of 'presence' in performance has
been linked directly to the deployment of technologies of 'mediation' in
the work of multimedia artists and performance groups such as Laurie
Anderson and The Wooster Group, as well as in popular cultural forms.
In advancing this influential thesis, Auslander cites Pontbriand, who
proposes that:

> [t]he more performance is expressed by technical means, the more chance
> it has of being removed from the theatre or theatricality; the more it
> withdraws from representation into simple presentation; the more it
> draws away from aura into simple actuality; the more it withdraws away
> from classical presence to assert a new and different presence, a radical
> presence.   [Pontbriand 1982: 156]

In contrast to this, but implicitly positioning itself within the same
opposition between the 'now' of performance and an elision of presence effected in mediation, Erika Fischer-Lichte's subsequent elaboration of presence in performance has sought to restore the 'now' point
and so self-presence and authority of the performer. Writing in *The
Transformative Power of Performance* (2008), Fischer-Lichte thus proposes that 'What the spectators see and hear in performance is always
present. Performance is experienced as the completion, presentation,
and passage of the present' (Fischer-Lichte 2008: 94). Setting out a taxonomy of presence in performance that ranges over the '*weak concept of
presence*' offered in the 'presentness' of 'the sheer presence of the actor's

phenomenal body' (Fischer-Lichte 2008: 94, original emphasis), the *'strong concept of presence'* asserted in 'the actor's ability of commanding space and holding attention' (Fischer-Lichte 2008: 96, original emphasis), and the '"real" presence' called for by performance art, in which '[w]hat occurred in an action or performance always really happened in the present' (Fischer-Lichte 2008: 97), Fischer-Lichte proceeds towards a *'radical concept of presence'* (Fischer-Lichte 2008: 94, original emphasis). This final practice offers a 'presence' in a 'constant process of becoming . . . a transformative and vital energy' (Fischer-Lichte 2008: 94). In each case, however, Fischer-Lichte valorizes the 'real' body in the 'present moment', thus arriving at a position which must, she emphasizes, 'exclude products of technical and electronic media' (Fischer-Lichte 2008: 100), for:

> While they might simulate effects of presence, they are unable to generate presence itself . . . They create the *impression* of presentness without actually bringing forth these bodies or objects as present . . . Human bodies, their fragmented objects, and landscapes are made to seem present in a particularly immediate manner but they remain constituted only of moving lights or pixel arrangements on a screen. Real human bodies, objects, or landscapes actually remain absent.   [Fischer-Lichte 2008: 100, original emphasis]

Echoing Pontbriand's notion of a 'radical presence' to be revealed in a stripping away of theatre and theatricality, and so of extraneous layers or representations, Fischer-Lichte's model seeks to restore the 'aesthetics of performance as the aesthetics of presence' (Fischer-Lichte 2008: 100) in opposition to the 'presence effects' produced in electronic media. Yet these trajectories towards a 'radical presence' rest on oppositions between mediated and unmediated presence while privileging in this binary opposition, as Fischer-Lichte asserts, the event of 'presence itself' which would realize the 'completion' of the present, the 'now'. Such oppositions between 'presence effects' and 'presence itself' plainly risk the installation of a normative (and privileged) mode and state of presence: a 'real' (radical) presence that would escape or transcend acts and processes of signification.

As Derrida's paradigm suggests, however, performance, like any medium, is locked into its signs. Furthermore, in so far as any phenomena are produced in the apparatus and mechanisms of representation, there is no *a priori* opposition between media (theatrical, electronic or other) with regard to 'presence'. Within this perspective, presence may be best considered as performed, as produced *in the act*, rather than as a function of a particular medium or in relation to the 'intrinsic' value of certain modes of presentation – or simply as a term privileged and so *in opposition to* absence. Indeed, where presence is produced *in difference*, both at the level of the sign and in the phenomenological encounter with the other, so the phenomena of presence may emerge in layering, in veiling, in the very operation of the sign and representation. Thus, where representation implies the 'gap', the 'delay'; where representation is implicitly 'before' or 'after' 'itself', in the sense that representation functions in the difference announced by its absent object, so *this difference* is also a locus for presence. 'Presence', in this sense, is *in* the theatrical relation: a function of representation (or the sign) itself, rather than a ritual transcendence, a moment available in opposition to technologies, or a transcendence of the mechanisms by which it is produced or received. It is in these senses that phenomena of 'presence' emerge in unfolding acts or processes. Here, presence is necessarily a function of being before or after 'itself', a *taking place* within temporary networks and ecologies. Experiences of presence may thus be associated with dynamic and shifting relationships that incorporate and imply liminality, tension and contestation and that function in approaches to and withdrawals from 'self' and 'other'. Such phenomena are produced and received in the uncertainties and slippages *in* the experience of 'being there' and 'being before': in *temporary acts* implicated in the production of the networks in which they take place.

Technologies of presence

It is for these reasons that this book is concerned, first, with the performance of transitions, movements, displacements and changes in which phenomena of 'presence' are produced, whether those acts are encountered as 'live', 'mediated' or 'simulated', or in moves across this continuum. Within this forum, *Performing Presence* focuses on phenomena of presence performed in movements between trace and event, image and action, proximity and distance, simulation and 'the real', between the mediated and the 'live', in the uncanny return, and in the pervasiveness and layering of networked place and location. Here, it is in the dematerialization of the performing body, too, that presence is resurgent in these various movements and events: as a theme, a question and as an aesthetic practice.

In advancing these questions, this volume also approaches the performance of presence both as a set of practices and theoretical elaborations, a juxtaposition and dialogue presented in the interpolation of interviews with the artists whose work provide the principal foci of this study, as well as key statements and textual and visual documentations of works. Here, too, and in exploring connections, conjunctions and overlaps between art practices, performance, art and new media theory, and also discourses and outcomes of experimental practices in science and technology, *Performing Presence* implicitly reflects the character of the broader research project in which this book was formed and of which it is one culmination. Developed over four years from 2005, 'Performing Presence: from the Live to the Simulated' provided for a sustained collaboration between the University of Exeter, University College London and Stanford University through major funding from the UK Arts and Humanities Research Council. Spanning performance and new media theory and practice, computer science and archaeology, the project proceeded in dialogue and collaboration with artists whose practices utilize a range of technologies to explore the performance and reception of presence. Thus the artists whose work is examined in our articulation of concepts and practices of presence engage variously with virtual worlds, video and video installation, telepresence, television, projection, multimedia theatre, locative media and ubiquitous computing. In doing so, the various modes and forms of their work exemplify modes of engagements with key themes and questions concerning contemporary experiences of presence and the implications and consequences of technology's operation within the everyday. Lynn Hershman Leeson's work thus interrogates constructions of identity in representation, and through this the operation of site, trace, memory, mediation and repetition in experiences of presence. Gary Hill's work elaborates the phenomenological complexities of a presence provoked in encounters with 'the other' in the multiple times and spaces of video installation. Paul Sermon's telepresence works position the participant at a distance from others – and frequently the 'live' image of themselves – in installations that facilitate their intervention into multiple and remote locations, posing questions over the link between experiences of 'presence' and the integrity of place and position. Tony Oursler's installations incorporating video projection and the animation of objects and 'media entities' explores the viewer's definition and experience of self-presence through their investment in media forms and practices. The Builders Association's multimedia performances enact and thematize contemporary experiences of networked social relationships and places while articulating and modulating the presence of the performer through simultaneous 'live' and electronically mediated channels of address. Blast Theory, in their collaboration with Nottingham

University's Mixed Reality Laboratory, provoke and articulate experiences of 'pervasive presence', of the simultaneous occupation of multiple positions produced in the interweaving of 'fictional' landscapes and interactions with the participant's experience of their everyday life. Finally, and complementing these analyses, the Performing Presence project facilitated a series of experiments in CAVE, an immersive virtual reality environment, to elaborate and test a cross-over and transposition of practices between art, performance and experimental methods in presence research. It is in this conversation between the critical analysis of these artists' work and the outcomes of this experimental practice, too, that this book defines its method, definitions and conclusions.

As these various foci suggest, the method and character of the book, like that of the Performing Presence project itself, is strongly interdisciplinary and ranges across performance studies, new media theory, visual art and discourses in computer science, as well as other areas of work. The differing approaches and inflections these discourses and objects of study imply also shape the chapters that follow. Lynn Hershman's Leeson's work is approached in the context of recent ideas around site specificity, archaeology and performance, and the transposition of acts and experiences into virtual worlds. Gary Hill's video installation is analysed in relation to early video art's affinity to experimental musical practices and implicit links with the conceptual turn in art that informs his analysis of language, time and experience. Where chapters foreground technologies whose development and application in the sciences have been overtly linked to definitions and concepts of presence, so we set out pertinent histories and uses. Such contextual analyses provide a necessary introduction to Paul Sermon's use of telepresence, to the analysis of the experience of CAVE and explorations of mixed reality performance and ubiquitous computing. In contrast, there is no equivalent link between video as a technology, video installation or the broad development of multimedia theatre and discourses and definitions of presence. Instead, in approaching these practices, we consider the experiences and concepts of presence elaborated in these artists' integration of technology into their work, while referring to defining discourses within performance studies, new media theory and other relevant debates. Yet, in these various engagements with phenomena of presence, the work addressed in *Performing Presence* continually returns to the enactment of these phenomena in analogous and related movements and processes. In this context, the book foregrounds a series of implicitly related figures, tropes and tactics that these artists' works exemplify with regard to presence, and configured here as 'tracing', 'emergence', 'distance', 'simulation', 'ghosting', 'disjunction' and 'pervasiveness'. Across these 'case studies' it is in the emphasis on 'presence' as an emergent phenomenon, as always *before* or *in advance* of itself, that these otherwise diverse engagements and practices converge – and it is at this convergence that *Performing Presence* directs critical attention.

Performing Presence begins, then, in an exploration of Lynn Hershman Leeson's work and its dynamic of location and non-location, and evidencing of present and past acts and events, that provoke encounters with signs of personality, identity and relation. This first chapter, 'tracing', analyses Hershman Leeson's early site-specific work *The Dante Hotel* (1973–74) her performance and construction across a range of forms and diverse works of the persona *Roberta Breitmore* (1974–78) and, more recently, *Life Squared* (2006). Developed under funding of the Langlois Foundation, and in conjunction with the Performing Presence project, *Life Squared* consists of the reconstruction and archiving of *The Dante Hotel* and *Roberta Breitmore* in the persistent virtual community of Second Life. This chapter, then, explores these works with Lynn Hershman Leeson, analysing the processes that led to the construction of an 'animated archive', and considers how the electronic traces of which it primarily consists at once reoccupy and uncannily depart from the original live performance and its sites.

Chapter 2, 'emergence', focuses on Gary Hill's engagement through video-based installations with a phenomenology of presence and an interrogation and enactment of philosophical positions stressing a processual engagement with the image and its subversion in evocations of the body. Addressing, in these contexts, ways in which the experience of these installations over time may provoke a sense of 'visceral physicality' (Hill in Sans 1999: 73) that seems to exceed the video image's evident status as a visual sign, Hill's work emphasizes a phenomena of presence articulated and interrogated in relation to the viewer's temporal and spatial displacement from the image.

In turn, in Chapter 3, 'distance', Paul Sermon's installations, in which participants interact through teleconferencing and telepresence systems from remote sites, provides an investigation of how Sermon's work multiplies and extends the spatial distinctions Hill's work articulates between performance, mediation and reception, provoking a further fragmentation and overlapping of the subject's spaces and positions, which becomes an engine for the amplification of experiences of presence. Focusing on Sermon's principal works in this medium from 1992, this chapter closely analyses Sermon's *Headroom* (2006), an installation created at the time of the Performing Presence project, within which Sermon published a dialogue on the development of this work, parts of which are excerpted here.

Punctuating these extended examinations of artists' engagements with presence in meetings and combinations of performance, site and technology, Chapter 4, 'simulation', examines the immersive virtual reality environment CAVE, introducing the discourses of presence around this technology and focusing, in particular, on two experiments in performance and presence developed within the Performing Presence project in conjunction with the Department of Computer Science at University College London in 2008 and 2009. Exploring the transposition and mediation of performative practices into scenarios involving virtual agents, human performers and interactivity, these processes emphasize overlaps between discourses in science and technology and practices and thinking in performance studies and visual art, to offer dialogue between the bodies of work that this book as a whole addresses.

Chapter 5, 'ghosting', focuses on the artist Tony Oursler's development of work that overtly addresses the construction of experiences of presence in cross-media installations in which the video image is relocated as a projected and screened image on or within three-dimensional objects, dummies, forms and sites. Engaging with and playing on experiences of the uncanny, and challenging the viewer's relationships with media forms and practices, Oursler's works question the limits of self and media to place the viewer in multiple positions in relation to their perception of the 'presence' of 'media entities'.

Chapter 6, 'disjunction', and Chapter 7, 'pervasiveness', explicitly return to the dilemmas articulated in the citation from Paul Virilio at the opening this Introduction: the transformation of place and location in the context of new technologies and communications systems and its implications for the experience of presence. In The Builders Association's multimedia theatre, presence is configured within disjunctive relationships between co-dependent real and virtual systems that performers traverse, and whose operation may be read after Derrida's figure of 'The Hinge' (Derrida 1976: 65), and architectural notions of disjunction while thematizing issues of liveness and mediation, presence and place, network and identity. In a radically different mode of work, the media and performance company Blast Theory, in their collaborations with the University of Nottingham's Mixed Reality Laboratory, have developed pervasive performance works that investigate the 'social and political aspects of technology' (Blast Theory 2005) and that operate in a conjunction of aesthetic and scientific experiment and enquiry. In doing so, and as exemplified in *Day of the Figurines* (2006), the company have created locative and performative structures for participant players whose experiences of their presence to themselves, within and to their roles, and to others in the unfolding game, challenges the association of phenomena of presence with the occupation of a particular, singular, unique or unified location.

Finally, we offer conclusions around an understanding of presence defined in the performance of relation and network, in which an articulation of transition, of temporal and spatial shift, of multiplication and disjunction, offers tropes and tactics for the production and reception of phenomena of presence. Indeed, as these examinations of artwork, technologies and experimental practice suggest, where phenomena of presence are realized in doubling, division and movement, in relation and caesura, and within an 'ecology' or 'network' of actions, then experiences of presence will be closely tied to states of liminality, and so to relationships and acts *between* the live, the mediated and the simulated. Presence, here, is practised and received in counter-intuitive and contingent ways, an experience produced and articulated in contingent relationships and slips between experiences of 'being there' and 'being before'. Such experiences of 'presence' are produced and received in unstable and changing encounters: as phenomena realized in ephemeral acts, events and configurations, and so in a performativity in process and in view.

2

---

tracing Lynn Hershman Leeson

Lynn Hershman Leeson's work investigates performances of identity and experiences of encounter through networks of traces and remains of 'acts' and events that have implicitly occurred 'elsewhere,' both temporally and spatially, and are now available to a viewer or visitor only in their mythology, or as documentations of sets of past social interactions (Dinkla 2001: 136 ff.). In doing so, Hershman Leeson's work engages with the enactment, realization and experience of the 'presence' of places and identities through processes that expose and utilize the gaps, caesura and absences inherent to acts of representation. Frequently elaborated through processes of doubling and multiplication, and articulated across radically different forms, Hershman Leeson's strategies also engage with the effects of memory, repetition and layering and so the experience of presence as a function of time, transformation and mediation. In these various processes, Hershman Leeson's performance and production of presence foregrounds mechanisms of 'difference': differences between the various personae that constitute her female *alter egos*; between the multiple places and times of her work's occurrence; and between the traces through which these personae and places are encountered in a tracing of activities now past.

Hershman Leeson's engagement with the affect of the relic or trace in relation to experiences of presence is evident in her earliest performance art presentations. In her first site-specific and performance work, *The Dante Hotel* (1973–74), visitors to a 'real' run-down hotel in San Francisco encountered 'evidence' evoking fictional guests and events in the form of personal belongings abandoned in two rooms. Subsequently, for *Roberta Breitmore* (1974–78), Hershman Leeson constructed a semi-autobiographical persona met primarily in 'documentation': in evidence of Hershman Leeson's largely 'unseen' performances conducted and recorded over a four-year period and made available through exhibitions and publication that included correspondences, newspaper announcements, dental records, psychiatric assessments and receipts of financial transactions. In both *The Dante Hotel* and *Roberta Breitmore*, Hershman Leeson's tactics interrogated the sign or trace as a prompt to experiences enabled and made more complex by the viewer's role as participant in the realization of the work – and by their literal and metaphorical occupation of 'the place' of the work. Such strategies also overtly articulate her protagonists' and viewers' 'presence' to 'the work' while emphasizing a dislocation and removal from an implied 'original' 'live' occasion or performative process. In her specific engagement with technologies, too, Hershman Leeson's work has tended to amplify the unfolding of a network or ecology of positions, events and times in which the viewer is implicitly positioned as an agent of presence, as the 'animating' subject who stands before and yet enacts the work and its places. In the 1990s Hershman Leeson reconfigured the character of Roberta as *CybeRoberta* and, more recently, in *Life to the Second Power*, or *Life²* or, in its final form, *Life Squared*, or *Life^n* (2006), in processes that overtly elaborated a layering of 'past' and 'present' acts, traces and sites. Where in *CybeRoberta* Roberta became an engine navigating the internet, in *Life Squared*, which, with *The Dante Hotel* and *Roberta Breitmore*, forms a principal focus of this chapter, Roberta was reconstituted as a bot living in the persistent virtual community of Second Life. In these reappearances and reworkings Hershman Leeson advanced her address to the signs and experiences of presence in the complex relationships between 'real' and 'virtual' sites. *Life Squared*, developed under funding from the Langlois Foundation by the Stanford Metamedia Lab, directed by Michael Shanks, Stanford University Libraries, Stanford Humanities Lab, then co-directed by Shanks and Henrik Bennetsen, in collaboration with Linden Lab and Pulse 3D Veepers System, and in conjunction with the Performing Presence project, thus consists of the 're-production' of *The Dante Hotel* and *Roberta Breitmore* in Second Life. This piece, exhibited in 2008 at Montreal Museum of Fine Arts and the San Francisco Museum of Modern Art, not only re-stages and 're-mediates' some of Hershman Leeson's most influential works, but investigates how this electronic medium at once extends, re-presents and uncannily departs from an 'original' 'live performance' to constitute, again, a 'presence' enacted by the visitor in the traces of events past.

Sites for presence

Hershman Leeson's articulation of her work as a network of differentiated images, actions and events dispersed in space and time, in which the viewer might act simultaneously as witness to and agent of the work, is evident in her earliest installations and performances. Here, too, the complexities of site and the experience, occupation and enactment of place formed an integral part of her work and served to define key aspects of a provocation and interrogation of experiences of presence. Hershman Leeson's first site-specific installation and performance, *The Dante Hotel* (1973–74), took place in the 'real' Hotel Dante, a then dilapidated hotel in the North Beach area of San Francisco with earlier associations with the Beat poets. Here, with her collaborator Eleanor Coppola, Hershman Leeson rented two rooms: No. 47, which was open for the duration of the work and within which an installation was set, and No. 50, which Coppola kept open for one week. Furnished with the 'personal belongings of an invented tenant', visitors to room 47 were allowed 'to explore these objects to flesh out the inhabitant's identity, past and present' (Tromble 2005: xvi). By contrast, room 50 was sub-let to a friend, Tony Dingman, who had been hired for the occasion to 'live' in the room and be observed by visitors to the work (and to the hotel). Here Hershman Leeson and Coppola's installations played overtly between signs of representation and the real, so prompting speculation from their visitors over the nature of their experience, their place and presence 'within' or 'before' a work and the limits and exchanges between the artists' activities and decisions and its various sites. Indeed, it is toward the visitor's encounter and occupation of the multiple tenses and spaces of this 'found' site that *The Dante Hotel* is most clearly directed. Room 47, then, was decorated with peeling wallpaper of repeated photos of the room, while in room 50 small Polaroid photographs had been positioned next to objects they documented to show 'the subtle changes made through time'. Using, she has suggested, 'a real hotel room to examine the context of occupants of the hotel in real time' (Tromble 2005: 20), and open twenty-four hours a day for nine months, or, in the case of Coppola's room, for one week, *The Dante Hotel* thus approached a 'found environment' (Tromble

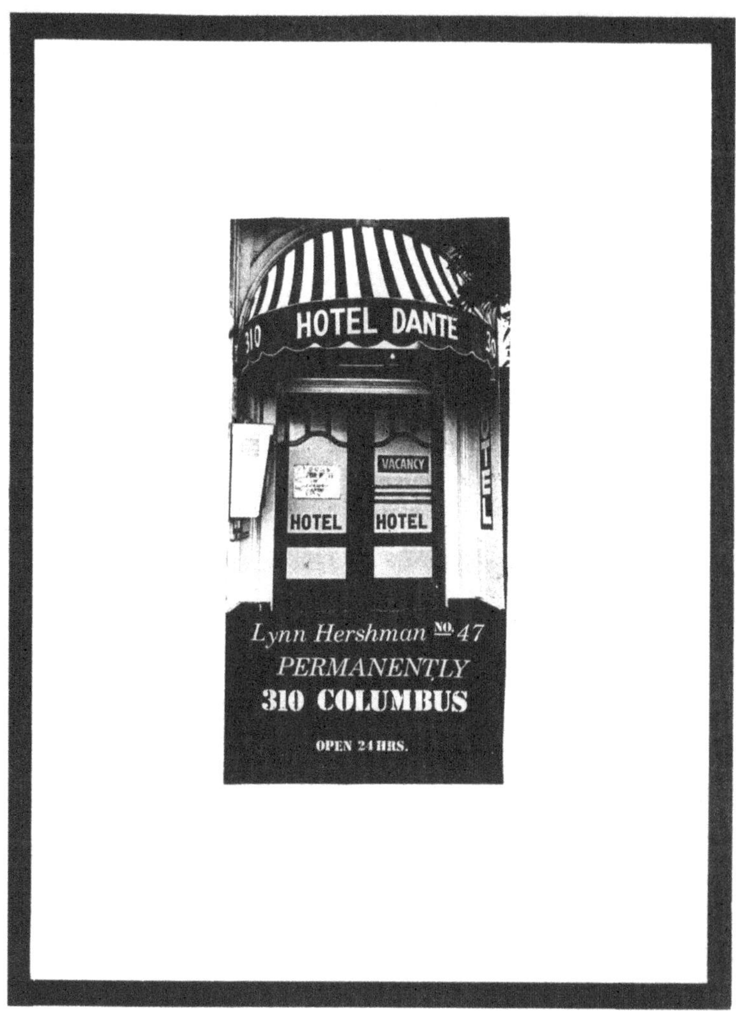

Figure 2.1 Lynn Hershman, *The Dante Hotel* (1973–74)

2005: 23) in such a way as to mark the difference of site from 'itself', articulating, through a series of doublings, the Hotel Dante's temporary reconfiguration 'within' Hershman Leeson's work. In this context, Hershman Leeson's interventions into the site served to evoke the ambience and traces of those who might occupy the room by deploying found material from the local area, including everyday objects and clothes. Counterpointing Hershman Leeson's residence in the room as artist and

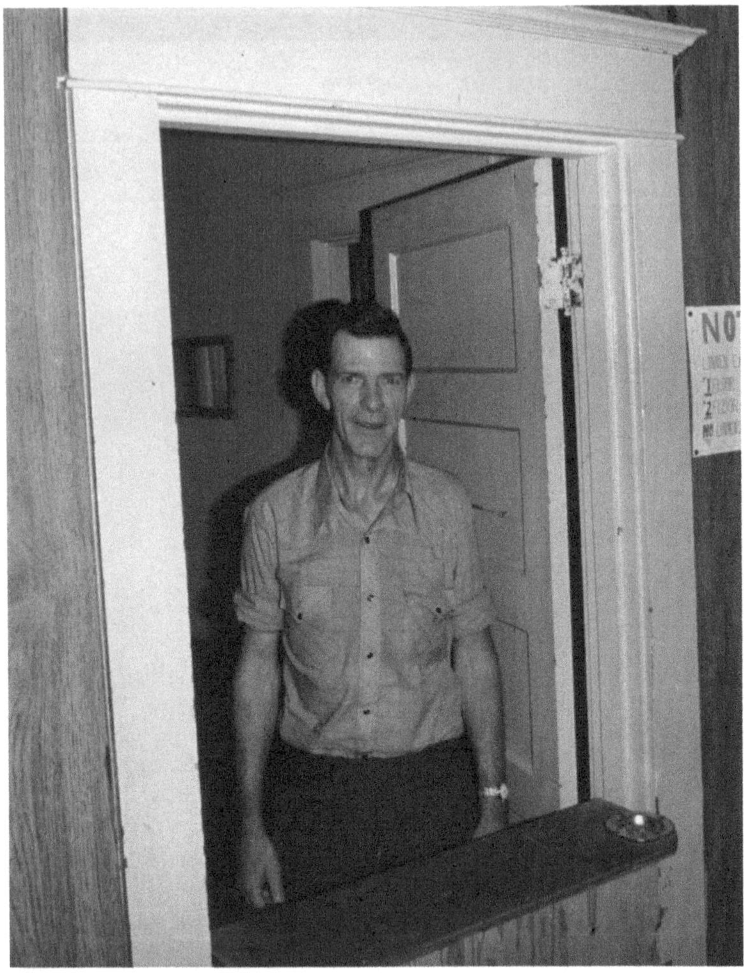

Figure 2.2 Lynn Hershman, *The Dante Hotel* (1973–74)

guest, and doubling the visiting subject, two life-size dummies were also placed around the space and in the bed.

GABRIELLA GIANNACHI What is the importance of site in your work?
LYNN HERSHMAN LEESON I began to explore the idea of site in 1972 because my work was shown in an incomplete way in museums. I found a site that was just a hotel room. I liked the name. It was only twenty dollars a week and it was in a location that was central and dealt with transience. This seemed a more appropriate way to show

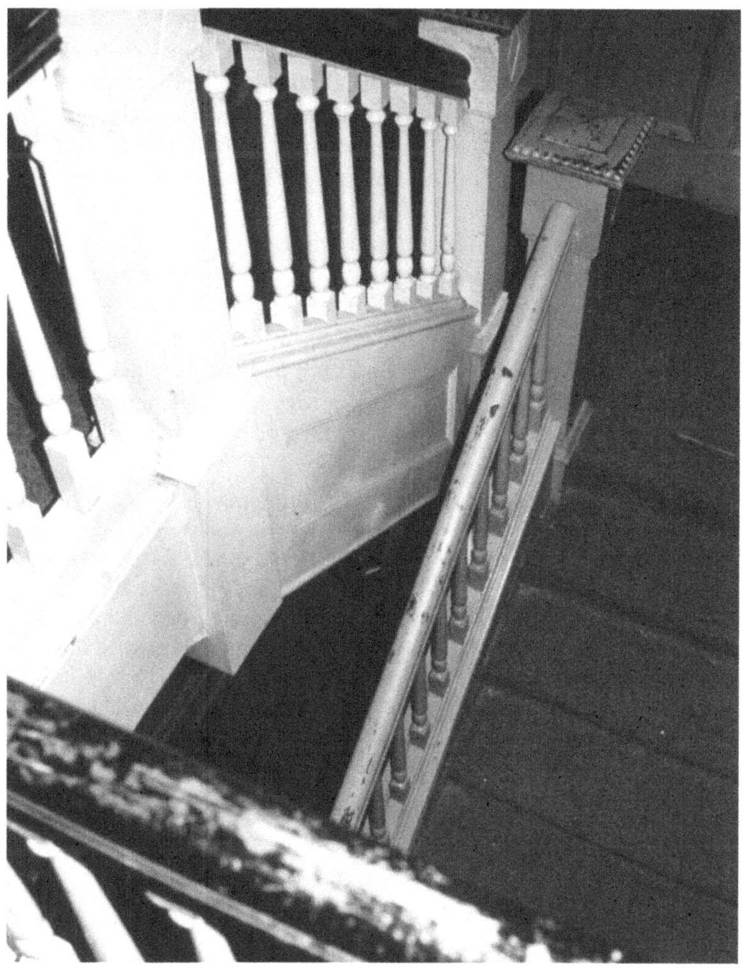

Figure 2.3 Lynn Hershman, *The Dante Hotel* (1973–74)

this particular piece because it was indigenous to the Bay Area, to its neighbourhood, and I wanted to explore the social structure of that environment as seen through an anonymous identity. The place required a pre-architecture of being in the environment, of walking through the building, just like a flow chart, which allowed you to trespass into a space that is not yours and presume what the relics or the discards meant that were left throughout, which were really clues to the identity of the occupant.

[San Francisco, November 2008]

In occupying and framing the visitor's presence in these ways *The Dante Hotel* begins on entry to the Hotel Dante, when visitors, Hershman Leeson notes, 'signed in at the desk, and received keys', then walked up the stairs to the designated rooms. Through this initial interaction Hotel Dante not only becomes co-present to Hershman Leeson's 'work' but its residents unwittingly 'became part of the exhibition' (Tromble 2005: 23) as their 'real' activity becomes the object of *The Dante Hotel*'s representations. Indeed, while, as an 'artwork', *The Dante Hotel* was generated in encounters with signs and traces of possible past activities, and so in evocations of the recent or nearby presence of a guest or guests, these remains were articulated in the viewer's simultaneous occupation of the 'real', everyday and implied (or imagined) contexts within which they were placed, and whose elements changed over time. An early review describes room 47 and the journey to it as follows:

> faint odours of cooking and disinfectant that always hang in the corridors of cheap hotels, the long lonely walk to the door and the finality of passing through it . . . The room is shrouded in a heavy, pale, silverish light that filters through a Venetian blind hanging listlessly in a window overlooking Columbus Avenue. On the pillows of the bed are two women's heads, death masks in wax with real hair; the blankets are dishevelled in such a way that two emaciated bodies might be underneath. A disarray of cheap lingerie spills out of partly opened dresser drawers, a pair of boots sprawls across the floor. On top the dresser, an old radio, lipstick, nail polish, Vaseline. On the corner wash-basin . . . a murky fish bowl, a pair of reading glasses on top a paperback novel abut the adventures of a Mafia moll; from within a built-in closet, the muffled voice of a woman reciting on a recording.   [Albright n.d.]

Such details suggest *The Hotel Dante*'s porous relationship with its sites, while Hershman Leeson herself portrayed the dressing of the room as a complex process of juxtaposing 'reality against reality, like layers of veils and skin that invite incision' (Hershman 1973a). Such acts work to augment the visitor's sense of presence in and before *The Hotel Dante*, which simultaneously acts as both the work and defers to the 'real' hotel. Referring to this process as acts of 'adding and subtracting', Hershman Leeson offered a detailed account of her construction of a room within a space already implicitly occupied:

> A green light bulb in the corridor of the room gives the impression I want. I scatter clothing about and rearrange the ladies in bed. The ladies are the strongest aspect. The wallpaper makes it look too artsy, too much like an exhibit. I plan to strew orange and green and black clothing in and out of

the drawers. It is like painting a picture. The record on the table will be my signature. I will buy two live goldfish for the table. Seaweed so they can eat. The goldfish poetically refer to the women. Both will be female. I bring in a book I think the woman would like to read. I am becoming these women, acting out this fantasy. . . . LESS IS MORE. The space is the sculpture. Anything I put into it takes away from it.   [Hershman 1973a, original emphasis]

Later, Hershman Leeson also incorporated goldfish into *Lorna* (1982), one of the earliest interactive environments that engaged with non-linear film narrative. Yet whereas in *Lorna* the 'virtual' bowl in the film contained a fish that was absent from an identical – and so mirroring – real bowl located in the room from which the viewer was experiencing the work (Dinkla 1997: 191), in *The Dante Hotel* the goldfish constituted, alongside the viewer, the *liveness* of the work itself. Thus while, in *Lorna*, the real and the virtual 'faced' each other in opposition, in *The Dante Hotel* the 'real' and 'virtual' were contained within one another. For the visitor, the found environment of the Hotel Dante amplifies this, becoming, in its relationship with *The Dante Hotel*, a site to which they are present and yet which is differentiated from itself. Here, distinctions between 'art' and the 'everyday' cannot be resolved – and the doubles (two dolls, two goldfish, two rooms) do not coincide with each other. In this uncertainty Hershman Leeson's 'guests' find themselves unable to easily occupy a single, stable position 'within' or 'outside' the work, but are directed, instead, toward their traversal of sites and possibilities.

Analogous dynamics occurred in Coppola's room. A reviewer notes: 'when Tony opens the window and looks out into Columbus Avenue [the hotel is at 310 Columbus Avenue], Columbus Avenue rushes in and becomes as much part of room 50 as the rumpled bed or shaky dresser, as much part of the work as Tony himself' (Minton n.d.). Observing the contaminations between 'art' and 'life' occurring through the work, the reviewer goes on to draw attention to a note stuck to the dresser mirror, in which Coppola says: 'I realize that I want to aestheticize all kinds of ordinary acts . . . elevate them to consciousness, therefore art' (Minton n.d.). Hershman Leeson describes the difference between the two rooms as follows:

[Coppola] took Polaroid shots of the objects in the room and noted the almost invisible changes that took place daily. She documented the process through which time showed itself. . . . My room, on the other hand, recreated the ambience of the presumed former inhabitant through props that defined fictional identities. Books, glasses, cosmetics and clothing were

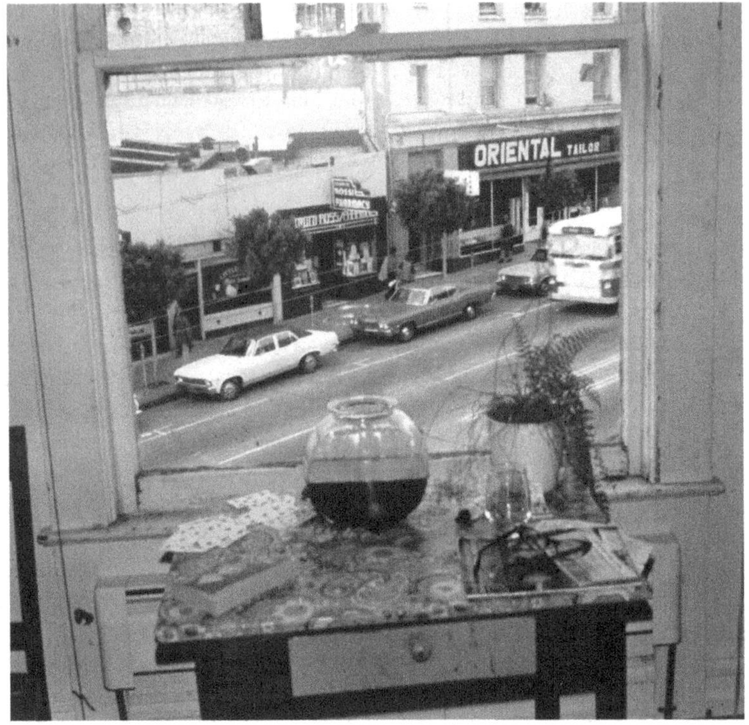

Figure 2.4 Lynn Hershman, *The Dante Hotel* (1973–74)

selected to reflect the education, socio-economic background of the occupants. A radio was turned on to broadcast local news in counterpoint to the sound of gentle breathing installed beneath the bed. Pink and yellow light bulbs cast faded shadows that draped themselves like forgotten cadavers over the lonely walls . . . Residents of this transient hotel became 'curators' and cared for the exhibition.   [Hershman 1973b]

By articulating the different places in which its identities are formed *The Dante Hotel* also amplifies uncanny divisions and displacements in the 'real time' location and activity of its visitors and participants. It is in this approach, too, that Hershman Leeson captures the presence of the visitors 'within' the work as, she proposes, they become ultimately responsible for 'curating' the room. Some visitors to *The Dante Hotel* chose to intervene directly into its 'real' location, leaving traces by adding graffiti on the dresser of Hershman Leeson's rented room. In inviting such interventions *The Dante Hotel* worked to amplify these visitors' experiences of presence *in* and *before* this environmental work,

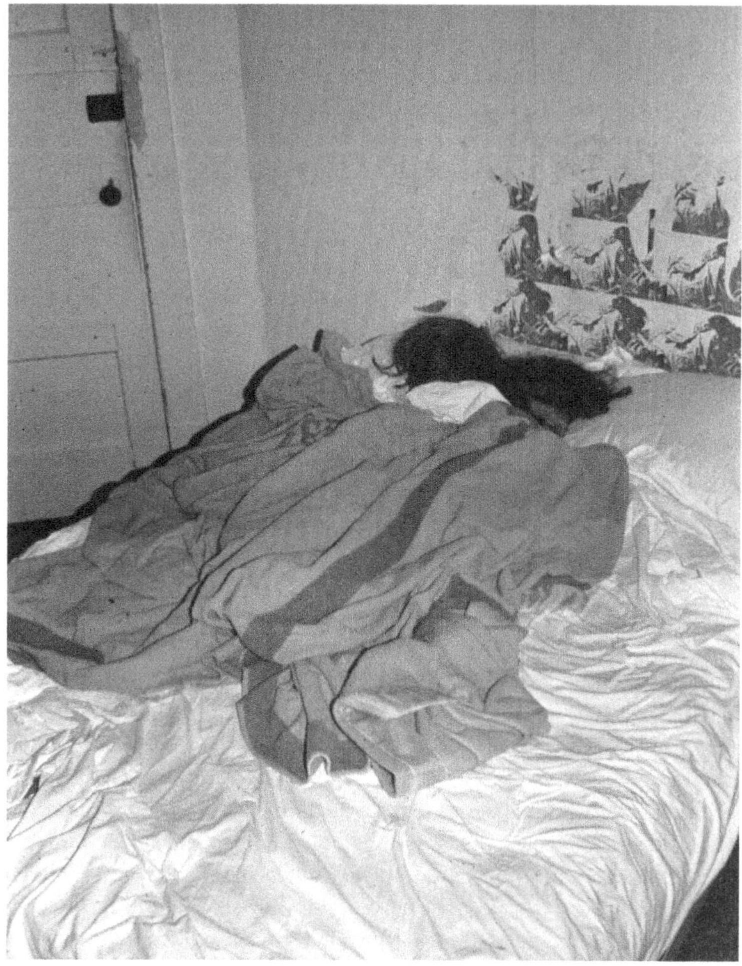

Figure 2.5 Lynn Hershman, *The Dante Hotel* (1973–74), detail of room 47

prompting them to *act out* and confirm their performance of its sites. Indeed, in enacting their own 'additions' or 'subtractions' *The Dante Hotel*'s occupants perform various aspects of their presence to its sites, at once occupying the work and leaving traces as part of its process, its accumulating spatial and temporal layering.

Following *The Dante Hotel*, Hershman Leeson's site-specific pieces further elaborated such engagements in which the actions of both protagonists and visitors occupy multiple positions and meanings in a way that informs and affects the occupation of a specific site. Thus, in *Forming a Sculpture Drama in Manhatten* (*sic*) (1974), consisting of three dispersed site-specific installations occurring simultaneously, multiple actors of Hershman Leeson's 'identity' were bound conceptually by a single fictional narrative, while *Re:Forming Familiar Environments* (1975) mapped a live interactive game over its visitors' journey through a private home, in this case Eleanor Coppola's private house.

GABRIELLA GIANNACHI Could you talk about the theme of the 'Private I' that runs through your work?

LYNN HERSHMAN LEESON We are all our own investigators of our life as we travel thought time trying to find out essentially what life means, what we are here, or what the essence of being is. Those are things we all consider. We set up problems for ourselves to solve. We become detectives, finding the clues, and the clues all lead us to who we are essentially. It is what Mary Shelley made Frankenstein ask: who am I, where did I come from, what is my destination – these are the key questions that we all think about in our life.

[San Francisco, November 2008]

Announced in a commercial broadcast on ABC (Tromble 2005: 34), *Forming a Sculpture Drama in Manhatten* operated between three New York hotel rooms – at the Chelsea Hotel, the Plaza, and Central YWCA – which were conceptually linked 'through a fictional narrative about three women who simultaneously arrived in New York and checked into separate rooms' (Hershman n.d. a). In contrast to *The Dante Hotel*, each of the rooms contained clues that revealed information about the occupant's identity, such as smells, sounds and clothing. 'Each environment,' Hershman Leeson's contemporaneous notes state, was 'composed of hallway smells, rug tears, window sounds, key shapes, the feel of air,' such that the 'boundaries of real time and space as related to linear time and space will be tested as a constant shift between the planned virtual reality and the spontaneous actual life and interceptions' (Hershman n.d. a). In this work, for which most materials were locally drawn, the installation was again comprised in a layering of 'real' and 'virtual' sites that served to heighten the question of the participant's position within an installation and event whose location and elements seem multiple or mobile. Hershman Leeson's contemporaneous notes state that:

The physical and sociological ecology of each environment will be respected. Salient energies may be amplified, but the general balance will remain intact. Sounds, recordings, and temperature changes act as symbolic extensions of colour. Walls may be softened by light bulbs in varying hues and intensities while their intrinsic glow may be neutralised or distorted by nearby recordings or television programs. Everything is taken into consideration: the sockets, shadows, nail holes, number of steps to and across the room. Every aspect of the space participates in the composition. … Of course there are problems in defining the boundaries of real time and space as related to linear time and space. There will occur a constant shift between the planned virtual reality and the spontaneous actual life reality that intercepts (changes outside the windows, extraneous noises, shifts in lighting at various times of the day). 'Real' items will serve as symbolic ones. Letters, books, eyeglasses, etc. will be real and token objects at the same time. The ambiguity is appealing.   [Hershman n.d. b]

Here, too, each installation became subject to accidents and events that threatened to breach or confuse the limits or parameters of site and performance, and which in retrospect Hershman Leeson 'accepted' into the work. Hershman Leeson had intended room 111 at the Chelsea Hotel to be occupied by an actor throughout its duration and to be available to visitors at any time, day or night. In order to reflect 'the sociological and economic quality of the neighborhood' (Hershman n.d. a), Hershman Leeson had set two wax casts of the actor's face in the room, one of which had been coloured white, the other black. Yet, although it had been leased for a year, the actor experienced anxiety 'at being subject to voyeuristic scrutiny' for such a prolonged period of time and the room was shut shortly after the piece commenced (Tromble 2005: 37). Room 903 at the Plaza, by contrast, was a re-enactment of the Eloise myth in an installation that created the 'feeling that a child had been left there' (Tromble 2005: 37), while spectators were prompted to move through its spaces by the sound of running water from a bath. Finally, the room at Central YWCA included a male mannequin 'wrapped in plastic and then shrouded by another, heavier plastic sheath, standing over an enigmatic female form that appeared to sleep in the bed' (Tromble 2005: 37). This third installation ended after only two days when a hotel maid inadvertently cleaned the room, wrapped its components in brown paper and stored them in a lobby closet, where they remained, unclaimed (Hershman n.d. a). The acceptance of such incidents implicitly works against oppositions between that which falls 'within' and 'beyond' the artwork, so amplifying the permeability of installation, performance and site.

In the subsequent *Re:Forming Familiar Environments* members of the collective COYOTE were hired to 'perform tableaux throughout Eleanor Coppola's house, doing simple everyday tasks such a taking a bath, sleeping, or peeling potatoes. A few prostitutes simulated patrons during the six-hour interaction' (Tromble 2005: 44). The event was documented by Hershman Leeson, who several weeks after the work ended placed adverts in newspapers showing 'photographs of patrons with members of COYOTE and the caption "Cultural exchange"' (Tromble 2005: 44). After *The Dante Hotel*, this piece operated in a contamination of the signs of 'art' and its everyday contexts, sites and objects. Hershman Leeson noted: 'we were interested in converting ordinary and often overlooked spaces into extraordinary sites for expanded awareness. Floor plans of the house were designed into game boards' (Hershman 1975). To this end Coppola's house was mapped and potential audience trajectories were designed through it. The game's objective was 'to (as minimally as possible) transform an inhabited dwelling; to alter perceptions about the potential uses of familiar environments' (Hershman 1975). The rules were as follows: 'visit each area on the plan that has either a circle or a triangle; a monitor outside each area will give you a letter; put the letters together to form three words; bring entries to the dining room where prizes will be awarded' (Hershman 1975).

GABRIELLA GIANNACHI How would you describe audience trajectories in *Re:Forming Familiar Environments*?

LYNN HERSHMAN LEESON The piece took place in Eleanor Coppola's home. Two museums wanted us to do something in her house and we just decided that instead of giving them a tour we would turn the entire house into a game board. So we used the floor plan as a kind of Monopoly, drove people into the rooms in order to find something, though at the end there was no real prize. We were in one room and we projected the game's instructions to the groups who were in the living room. We engaged a union of prostitutes to be in the rooms doing various things, like interacting with the patrons, so that you did not know who was real and who was not, who was a prostitute and who was not. This created a blur over the whole population who came that evening.

[San Francisco, November 2008]

In each of these works the visitor is positioned as if in occupation of multiple locations produced in contaminations between signs of the artwork and the everyday, the quotidian and the undetermined. In turn, in its structuring and articulation of the visitor's experience of presence, Hershman Leeson's tactics emphasize not so much a *being before* or *being in* the work as a traversal of positions: a simultaneous *being before* and *enactment of* the work and its various places. Indeed, this is a tactic and experience exemplified by *The Dante Hotel*, in which the visitors occupy and their activities mediate the hotel room and its double: the gallery, the installation. In such mechanisms as these, the visitor to

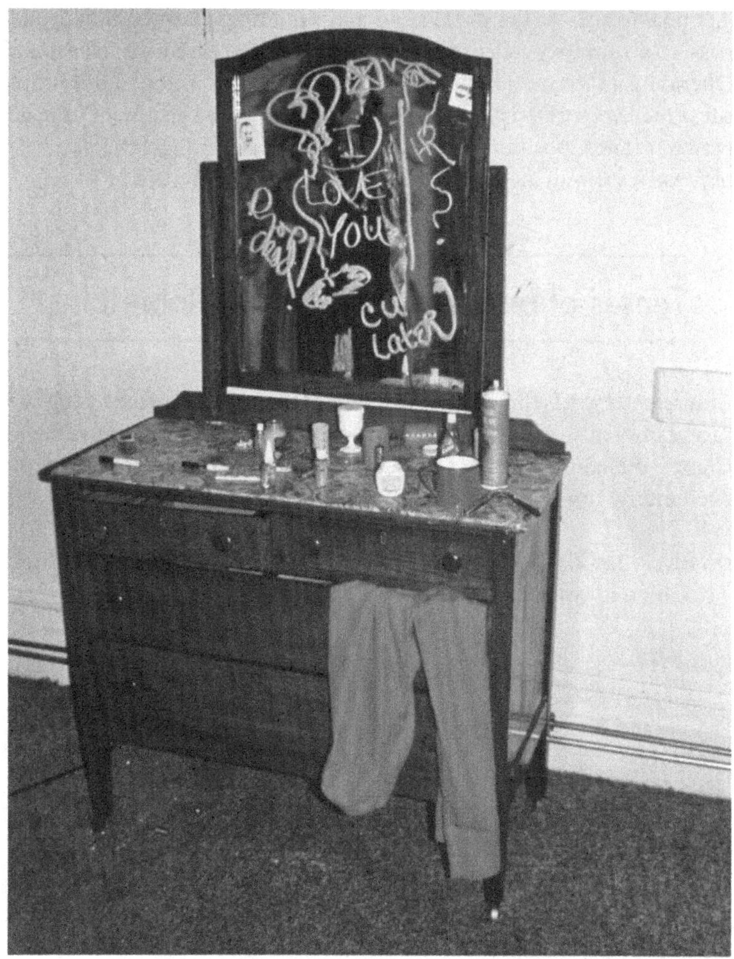

Figure 2.6 Lynn Hershman, *The Dante Hotel* (1973–74)

The Dante Hotel are present as participant, object of attention, curator and subject or protagonist within an emergent work and process they 'act out'; at once the auditor of the installation and the trespasser, the intruder into the private space and time of which it consists.

In this context the presence in the Hotel Dante of life-size heads and dolls amidst the clutter of functional and everyday objects served to amplify the dialectic between sites and possible confusions over the 'place' of the work and its signs. In response, one visitor, nine months after the opening of the installation, perhaps conflating the 'real' and 'fictional' places of the installation and becoming alarmed by the stillness of a dummy, called the police, fearing the discovery of a body. Operating in provocations and invitations to act across its multiple sites, *The Dante Hotel* provokes performances, by the visitor, of passages between states, positions and times, producing contingent experiences of presence simultaneously within and outside of the work.

Tenses of presence: performing Roberta

Consistently with this notion of the performance of presence in passages between sites and positions, Hershman Leeson's subsequent work aligned the complexities of place with the location of the subject and encounters with the signs and proofs of identity.

GABRIELLA GIANNACHI What is the role of doubling and multiplication in your work?

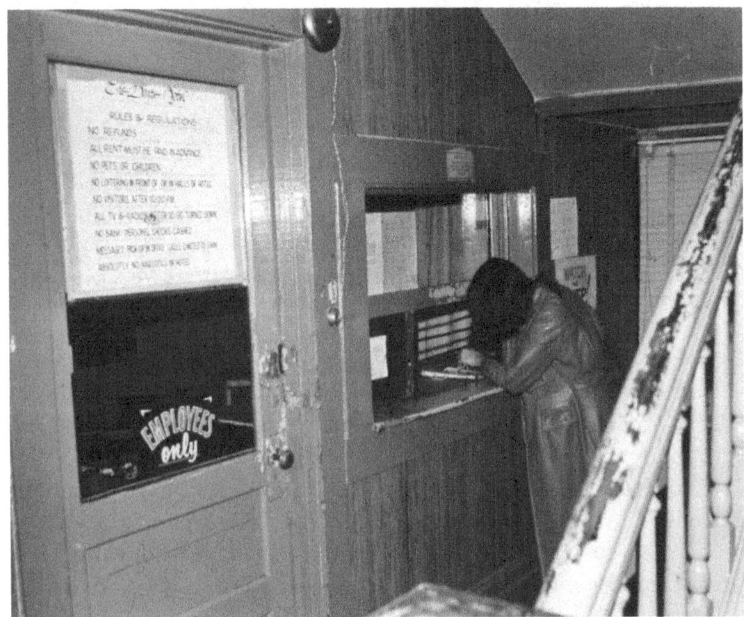

Figure 2.7 Lynn Hershman signing in at *The Dante Hotel*, San Francisco, November 1973

LYNN HERSHMAN LEESON The doubling and tripling was for me a scientific approach in the work. If you could prove something several times, there would be a factor of validity. So, for instance, when we had three Robertas in addition to the original one, their experiences contributed towards the understanding of what Roberta's own experiences meant. The number three constitutes the proof of validity of an assumption. I am told that in science you have to prove something three times. Hence we have three rooms, three Robertas, three cyborgs and three critics.

[San Francisco, November 2008]

Roberta Breitmore (1974–78), which combines photo, video and performance, has been described as 'an early excursion into virtuality, straddling the boundary between fiction and reality, or art and life' (Rötzer in Schwarz and Shaw 1996: 136). Here Hershman Leeson constructed the role of, and at various times and locations performed, 'Roberta Breitmore', donning a costume, wig and make-up to enact the signs of a persona, identity and a 'physical embodiment' consisting of 'a set of individual gestures, needs and fears' (Rötzer in Schwarz and Shaw 1996: 136). Yet even as Hershman Leeson's various enactments and multiplications of the signs of Roberta evoke 'her' persistence across various contexts and media, so they also disperse the signs of presence and identity to create a field of differentiated signs and elements. It follows that 'Roberta' is available to those who traverse this field, to be animated by the viewer or reader in perceived or assumed differences and differentiations from 'Lynn', who enacts, hosts and composes these various signs and events.

Hershman Leeson claims that the character of Roberta was 'born' when 'she arrived in San Francisco on a Greyhound bus' (Hershman Leeson in Tromble 2005: 25), reputedly checking into the first hotel she saw, the Hotel Dante, because, she reported, 'she likes the name' (Roth n.d.). Echoing *The Dante Hotel*, and so provoking, in retrospect, a collocation and networking of various occasions and recollections of Hershman Leeson's works, Roberta then registered in room 47 and followed 'the worn path to its door' (Roth n.d.). Carrying with her $1,800, her entire life savings, Roberta subsequently became involved in a series of social interactions: she picked up two credit cards, a driver's licence, rented an apartment, placed an advert in the *San Francisco Progress* to advertise for a room-mate, and met with each respondent to the advert three times in an implicit play between a 'proof' and persistence of Roberta's presence to the applicant and the repetition staged by 'performance'. Meetings were documented photographically and each event tape-recorded so that the people who replied to the advert became part of her 'fiction' (Hershman Leeson 1996: 330). For Hershman Leeson, Roberta acted as a kind of 'barometer' that 'reflected the values of her culture' (Roth n.d.). Thus she penetrated 'trends such as EST, WEIGHTWATCHERS' and experienced alienations, which led her to correspond with a psychiatrist. An excerpt from Roberta's confidential psychiatric evaluation states:

> While awaiting the therapist's availability she wrote him two brief notes of moderate despair but avoided telephone contact, which had been offered. Spelling and word usage suggested mild disorganization, borderline intelligence or limited education. Reason for seeking evaluation was severe alienation and inability to find a room-mate or steady employment. Mental status revealed a tall, heavy woman. Her childlike appearance was exaggerated by her soft voice and naiveté. She was dishevelled, particularly at the first interview, when her long blonde wig was improperly placed. She wore dark glasses throughout both interviews, sat sideways to avoid looking directly, and hid her face behind her hair. She wore a mini-skirt and knee-boots to both interviews. She was totally unaware of her seductive posture and recognized anxious body movements, such as pulling at her skirt, only when they were pointed out. She was unable to recognize how her appearance, incongruent posture and mannerisms might interfere with object relations, and insisted she looked like everyone else. Her affect was constricted and immobile and masked her mood of depression and fear. She asked if the therapist would give her shock treatments. She described

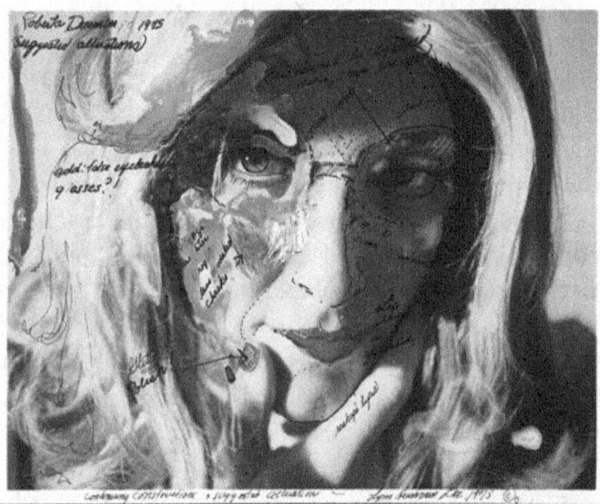

Figure 2.8 Lynn Hershman, *Roberta's Construction Chart # 2* (Roberta Breitmore series) (1975)

> feeling separated from the world by a glass box and having difficulty distinguishing dreams from reality.   [Roth n.d.]

Described as the 'private performance of a simulated persona', Roberta was 'at once artificial and real' (Hershman Leeson 1996: 330). Encountered as traces and evidence of incidents and activities in 'real places' at 'real times' performed, variously, by Hershman Leeson and others, Roberta's activities were almost exclusively encountered in their remains: a checking account, a driver's licence, the psychiatric report and her credit ratings. Met as 'evidence' of past activity over whose veracity, significance and connection the viewer or reader is invited to speculate, 'Roberta' is animated by 'her' viewer's or reader's various engagements with the traces of a 'fictional' past that lays claim to the 'real'. Such a process also positions the performance of Roberta's 'presence' as subject to a direction of travel, in which the various times and tenses of 'Roberta' suggest a flow between Hershman Leeson's (and others') 'past' performance of her signs and fictions and her audience's present reception.

By the notional end of her performance, Roberta Breitmore, whose name, Hershman Leeson notes, was derived from a Joyce Carol Oates short story 'about a woman who tracks celebrities through letters she places in newspapers' (Hershman Leeson in Tromble 2005: 33), had accumulated forty-three letters from individuals and had twenty-seven adventures (Hershman Leeson 2003). Eventually Hershman Leeson hired three additional women to enact Roberta: Kristine Stiles, Michelle Larsen and Helen Dannenberg. The three performers wore wigs and costumes identical to the ones worn by Hershman Leeson when performing: 'Each had two home addresses and two jobs – one for Roberta and one for herself – and each corresponded with respondents to the advertisement and went on dates that were obsessively recorded in photographs and audiotapes' (Tromble 2005: xiii). Thus all four 'Robertas' existed simultaneously for a short time, until Hershman Leeson ceased performing as Roberta, leaving the three hired performers on their own (Tromble 2005: xiii).

GABRIELLA GIANNACHI What was the role of the three critics?

LYNN HERSHMAN LEESON I wrote criticism under the pseudonym Prudence Juris, who wrote academic formalist criticism for *Artweek*, Herbert Goode, who wrote intuitive criticism for *San Francisco Progress*, and Gay Abandon, who wrote in both styles on a number of papers. They wrote for maybe four or five years during the mid-seventies. Once in a while one of them writes even now, but not very

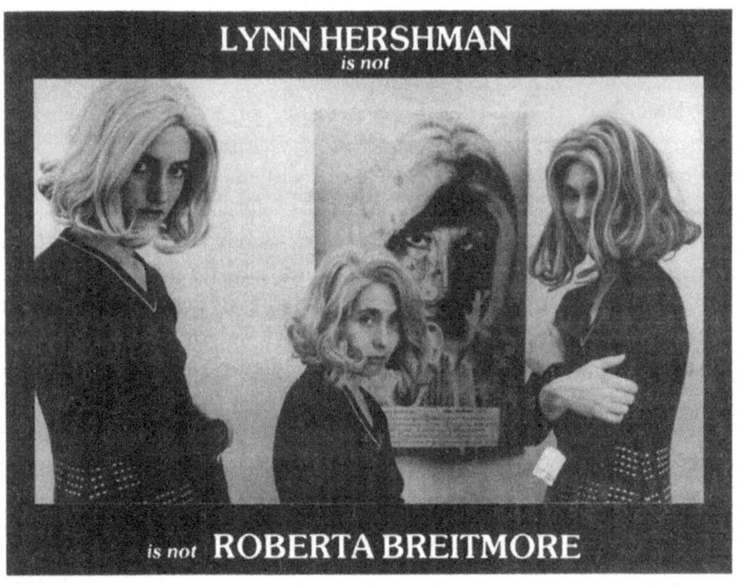

Roberta Look Alike Contest
April 30, 3-5 p.m., de Young Museum

If you look like Roberta, or know someone who does, enter the Roberta Look-Alike Contest. Judging will take place 4:00 Saturday April 30, M.H. de Young Memorial Museum, Golden Gate Park. Winner will receive a signed portrait of Roberta.

Roberta's Room: Room 111, Bakers Acres, 3000 Jackson Street, April 1-30, 4-6 daily. Roberta's Multiple: April 1, Square, April 15, #55 bus. Roberta Look Alike Contest: Judging: M.H. de Young Memorial Museum, April 30.

M.H. de YOUNG MEMORIAL MUSEUM, GOLDEN GATE PARK, SAN FRANCISCO, CALIFORNIA, APRIL 1-MAY 14, 1978

Figure 2.9 Lynn Hershman, *Roberta Look Alike Contest Poster* (1978)

often. One of them wrote some 'letters to the editor' while I was away last year, but they didn't get published. They wrote mainly about my work and sometimes fought with each other over interpretation. I critiqued the idea of critics and critiqued the fact that women artists were only shown when critics had validated their work. It was a kind of subversion of the very restricted infrastructure of the art world. Unless you were credible you had no chance to show your work. If two critics argued with each other, taking completely different views, the artists would benefit. It was kind of an 'in' joke with myself. Nobody knew about it at the time.

[San Francisco, November 2008]

Roberta also made a number of further appearances over an extended period of time. In 1976 Hershman Leeson accepted an invitation by the critic Moira Roth to participate in a series of performances she was curating at the University of California, San Diego. For this, she stayed at Roth's house. In the event, this became Roberta's 'first and only' live 'official gallery/museum engagement', an appearance that in Roth's account invited a further unsettling of perceived relationships between 'Roberta' and 'Lynn'. Roth describes the emergence of Roberta out of Hershman Leeson's room as follows:

> The first morning Hershman emerged from her room dressed as Roberta – booted and mini-skirted, wearing a blonde wig, and with her face heavily almost crudely, cosmetically painted. It was an unsettling encounter. She did not behave quite 'in character', but neither did we talk with our usual degree of comfort. After she left my house, she spent the day – the first of several – meeting a variety of people, including a group of men who wanted her to join a prostitution ring.   [Roth n.d.]

In another elaboration of this aspect of Roberta's definition, in 1978 Hershman Leeson presented an exhibition of Roberta artefacts entitled *Lynn Hershman is not Roberta Breitmore/Roberta Breitmore is not Lynn Hershman* at the de Young Museum in San Francisco. Here, Hershman Leeson prompted a Roberta look-alike competition, attracting 'transvestites, gay men, women, young girls and even a set of elderly female twins, all in blonde wigs, costumes and make-up' (Roth n.d.). Photographs of the contestants then entered the same process Hershman Leeson's own images had been subject to and were thus rephotographed, painted, collaged together, drawn on and annotated (Roth n.d.).

Roberta was finally exorcised in a 1978 performance at the Palazzo dei Diamanti in Ferrara. Today we are left with her effects, photographs, artefacts and ashes. The choice of Ferrara was, seemingly, to reveal the link between Roberta and Lucrezia Borgia, whose crypt is in the Palazzo, and who, like Roberta, had suffered from the 'trauma of early incestuous relationships' (Tromble 2005: 30).

GABRIELLA GIANNACHI How did you prepare for working on Roberta?

LYNN HERSHMAN LEESON I spent three years studying towards a PhD in psychology to get Roberta's background to be a creative composite of stereotypes for the particular traumas that she under-went. I did that to think about the facets that make a personality or an identity or something as fleshed out as possible. So *Roberta Brietmore* was trying be as unaffected as possible, not an obvious performance, but more an invasion of an alien personality.

[San Francisco, November 2008]

Roberta is survived by and persists in engagements with the documentation of her making, such as *Roberta's Construction Chart #2* (1975) and *Roberta's Body Language Chart* (1978). In the former series the nine stages of the construction of Roberta are indicated. These instructions accompanied a photograph of Roberta's face transformed into a map that, quite literally, indicated the routes of its make-up, which in turn were part of the process of the making of Roberta (Tromble 2005: 117). In an implicit extension of Hershman Leeson's earlier engagements with 'real' sites, these 'maps' trace processes of addition and subtraction in the form of make-up and incision. In the latter series, shot during a psychiatric session, Roberta is seen in a series of behaviours, including 'Americans show greater differences gesturally', 'A hand to the face may serve as a barrier', 'Covering legs reveals frigidity, fear of sex' (Tromble 2005: 109), which again function as a map of her behaviours and were also recorded by the psychiatric evaluation as 'evidence' of her mental state. Finally, among the numerous photographic documentations, *Roberta Aged by Weather and Time* (1976) consists of Roberta's image

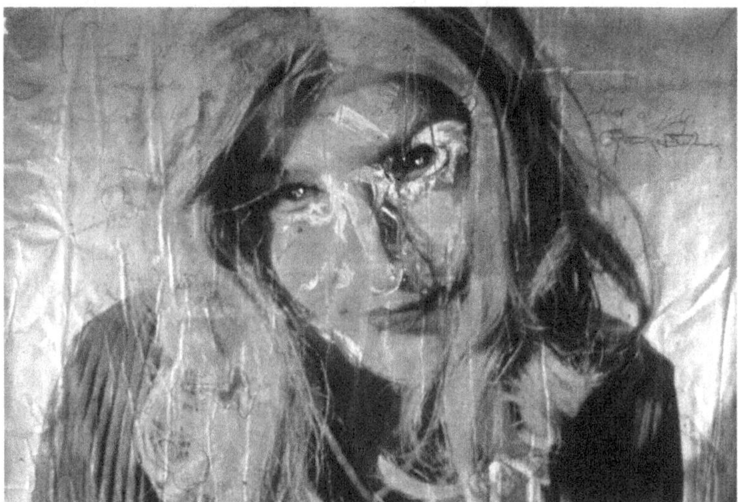

Figure 2.10 Lynn Hershman. *Roberta Aged by Weather and Time* (1976)

printed on crumpled paper, then rephotographed and painted over as if to indicate that even the various documentations of Roberta's making and behaviour act as further traces, constructions and so layers of Roberta Breitmore's performance.

GABRIELLA GIANNACHI How would you describe the role of time in your work?

LYNN HERSHMAN LEESON Time is really important in all these works. They do not just live in the time that they exist, but they expand or become reincarnated in various forms that are more appropriate to that particular point in time. So the end of something is not really the end, it is just is a phase, just as we as humans go through various phases in our maturation, so the chronology, as it shifts, gives a different sense of being to that particular work at that particular time, but it is not the only one.

[San Francisco, November 2008]

Roberta Breitmore presents a field of interrelated objects and signs marked by gaps in time and evidence. For Hershman Leeson, Roberta Breitmore belongs to 'a collective culture' and is 'a blend of persona and environment' living in the '"found environment" of San Francisco', where she operated 'as a sociologist, interviewing people, noting their reactions' (Hershman n.d. c). Constituted as the location of Hershman Leeson's work, and formed in a collocation of actions by various agents, Roberta Breitmore is encountered *as* palimpsest: as a rewriting by 'her' performers, viewers and readers in specific and multiple times, places, locations and identities. It is in these rewritings and so differences that the uncanny experience of 'Roberta's' 'presence' is produced and received, as that which appears to persist in or traverse these traces as a function of the 'viewer's' engagement. In these various respects, *Roberta Breitmore* is also the site of a work never complete, or *always to be completed*, whose operation is analogous to the performance of a 'real' site: a place that evidences itself in traces of what has happened and is to be read and realized by those who encounter, enact and so occupy 'its' signs. Indeed, the 'production' of Roberta Breitmore in these encounters with her traces exemplifies the performance of presence in an ecology or network of past and future possibilities. In this work, Roberta Breitmore gains a proximity to the viewer or reader precisely through their investment (and so 'her') movements across the relics and the promises of her appearance and in the gaps and slips between locations and tenses.

Archival presence

Nearly twenty years after the exorcism of *Roberta Breitmore*, Roberta was re-mediated as *CybeRoberta* (1995–98), a figure dressed identically to Breitmore and whose fictional persona was, in Hershman Leeson's words, 'designed as an updated Roberta' (Hershman Leeson 1996: 336) and so an implicit variation and thereby extension of Hershman Leeson's earlier tactics. Navigating the internet, but also a creature of the internet, a cyberbeing, Hershman Leeson points out that: 'surveillance, capture and tracking are the DNA of her inherently digital anatomy. They form the underpinning of her portrait' (Hershman Leeson 1996: 336). *CybeRoberta* was conceived of simultaneously and occasionally exhibited with *Tillie, the Telerobotic Doll* (1995–98), a work in which participants could see the world through the eyes of Tillie or, by standing in front of her in the gallery, see their reflection in her eyes, thus seeing how others would catch sight of them on the internet. Here, Hershman Leeson presents a technological extension of the viewer's enactment (in reading) of Roberta's signs and so perspective and identity. When the two works were exhibited together this multiplication and shifting

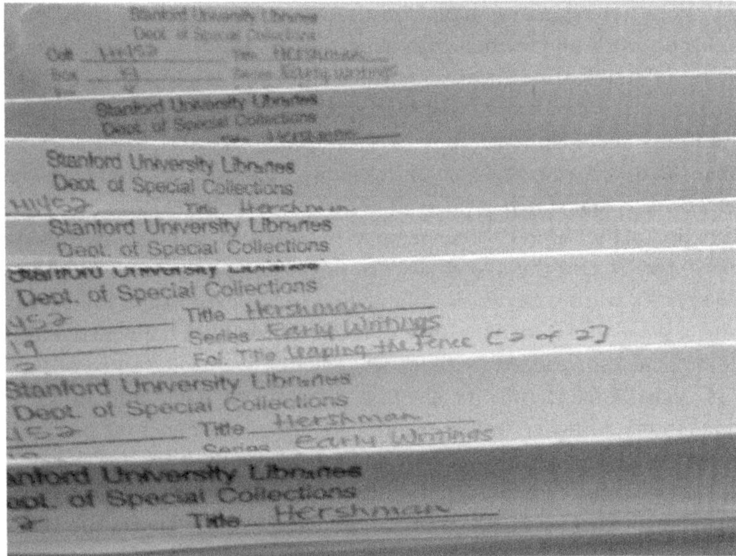

Figure 2.11 Box 19. Lynn Hershman Leeson papers, M452, BOX 24. Department of Special Collections, Stanford University Libraries, Stanford CA

of positions was amplified as they pirated each other's information, so causing a further 'blurring' of positions and identities. *CybeRoberta* and *Tillie, the Telerobotic Doll* were thus, Hershman Leeson notes, 'the first robotic Net works with a humanoid presence' (Hershman Leeson in Tromble 2005: 87 and 89). In a further layering, Roberta also presented similarities to the character of the bio-geneticist Rosetta Stone, the protagonist of *Teknolust* (2002), who, by combining her own DNA with computer software, bred three self-replicating automatons named Ruby, Marine and Olive, all performed by Tilda Swinton. Subsequently, Roberta appeared again in *Life Squared*, a work comprising in part an animated version of Hershman Leeson's archives hosted at Stanford University Libraries Department of Special Collections. As a re-animation and re-mediation of her work, *Life Squared* also represents an interrogation and extension by Hershman Leeson of her own earlier engagement with site and presence, in part through the persistence of her earlier works in a new form and medium. In these respects, *Life Squared* directly extended Hershman Leeson's engagement with the performance of presence in the repetition and variation of signs of actions and events now ostensibly past.

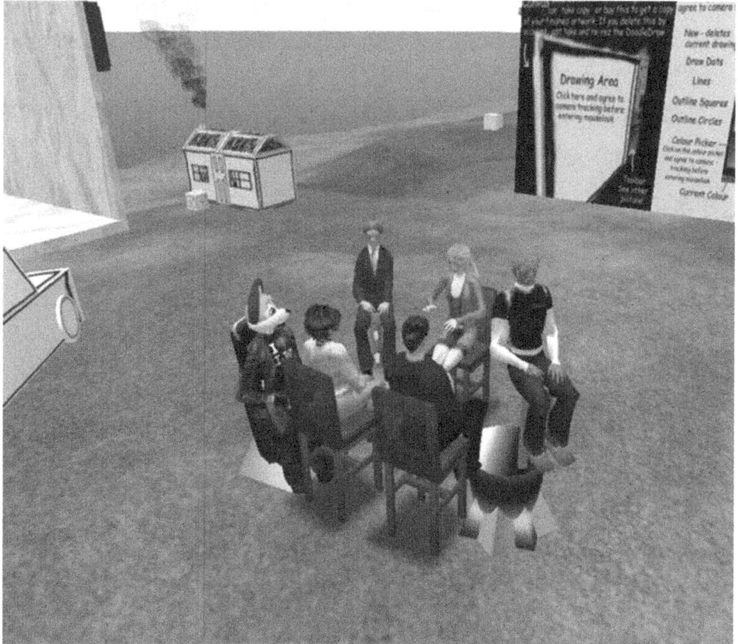

Figure 2.12 An early *Life Squared* meeting

GABRIELLA GIANNACHI How was *Life Squared* generated?

HENRIK BENNETSEN Henry Lowood, Michael Shanks and Lynn Hershman Leeson had been working with the idea of an animated archive of Lynn's work. I joined the team a little later. Originally we thought of doing a game, but I felt that we should look for a space that would enable us to do something else. I went to an art opening in San Francisco and met a guy that worked for Linden Lab and he said: 'I think Second Life is exactly what you are looking for' because 'it is an empty desert where you get the power to populate things with geometry and textures, and computer code to make the space come alive'. So I looked into Second Life, which was pretty small at the time, and we started to dabble around in it. We were absolutely new in there. And it was funny. I remember the early meetings [in SL] were so crazy. We were sitting in a circle and Lynn was there, and Michael and Henry, and I remember I had got a new car and I was riding over everybody. It was anarchy and we really started thinking about how profoundly different this space was to our regular meeting space where I had never yet ridden anyone over by car.

[San Francisco, October 2008]

The original aim of *Life Squared* was to create 'an overarching metanarrative and gamespace' within the online world of Second Life

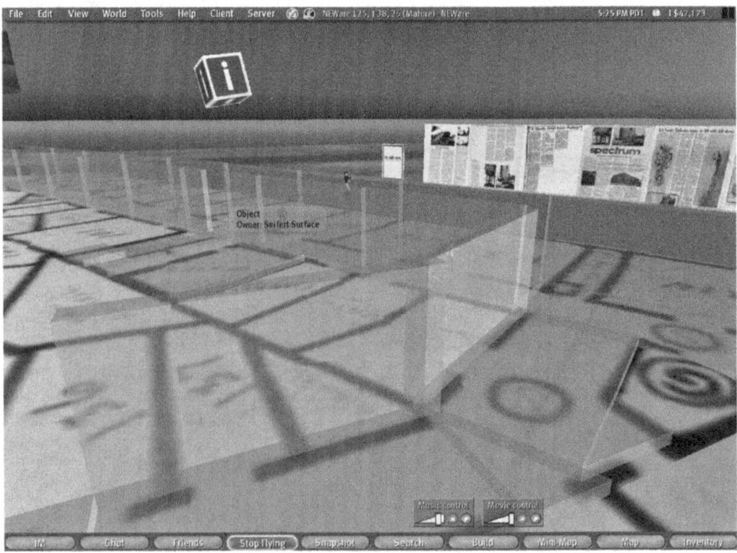

Figure 2.13 Early design experiments for *Life Squared*

Fragmented Journal from 1973

(a partial chronicle of events)

Lynn Hershman

February 9, 1973 The "Works in Spaces" exhibit opened tonight
at the San Francisco Museum of Art. Eleanor Coppola and
I are particularly intrigued with Robert Irwin and Dorthea
Rockburne's transformations, their subtle concern for the
intrinsic character of space. Yet each applied their own
sensibilities. Just as certain papers have proclivities
towards absorption of inks, so too individual spaces co-
alesce energies. A perceptivity to the differences can be
acquired, just as one can train herself to feel the varying
surfaces when a pen is dragged over an alternately rough
and smooth surface. I would like to practice this, so
would Eleanor.

March 22   The air is soft and salty, drizzling the frothy rain
of a San Francisco spring. I absorb the air like a sponge
sops up wet nourishment. Over Orange Blossom Tea at the
Cafe Trieste, Ellie and I discuss renting a space for a
three day exhibit.
        Ellie knows of a dance studio with a skylight that
causes marvelous shadows each afternoon which we plan to
visit as well as an abandoned doughnut shop and an empty
dime store.
        My exhibition in Los Angeles took two years between
the first contact and the eventual show. The time lag
bothers me, but what are the alternatives?

April 10   Working with non-commercial ideas is as hazardous
as it is liberating. Galleries won't lend spaces for
ephemeral ideas, so to exercise new notions one has the
intriguing option of creating his own space.
        Neither of us know what we will really do, but feel
committed to this project. There is a responsibility that
goes along with having an idea. It becomes your obligation
to see it through, to make it a reality. Carl Andre has
said that just thinking things isn't enough, you have to
keep putting them into the world. One grows by meeting
an idea's physical consequences.

Figure 2.14 Extract from Lynn Hershman, *Fragmented Journal from 1973*

that would integrate real and virtual architectures, character avatars, artefacts, somatic characters and, in a later phase, situational components such as site tagging and GPS locators. Using content from the Hershman Leeson archive at Stanford Libraries Department of Special Collections, such as the *Fragmented Journal from 1973*, in which Hershman Leeson recorded her preparations for *The Dante Hotel* with Coppola, but also numerous images, receipts, letters, interviews and notes, fragments of information embedded within the storyline of a

```
        The lady in bed at the University Art Museum, for instance,
        was the same lady in a coffin (without the feet) at the Jodi
        Scully Gallery in Los Angeles.  The feet were moved to be
        part of my Mills Show.
                So, in an F.A.O. Schwartz shopping bag, I insert two
        heads, various arms and legs, and drive to #47.  I meet Mike
        Neil (Ellie's brother) who photographs my lady in bed plus
        the building.  An ad in ARTWEEK is cheaper and more effective
        than sending out announcements.
                Both women seem better in bed. The combination has
        more electricity and comes closer to getting the energy of
        the room I want.
                As I am leaving, the deak clerk informs me that the room
        was formerly occupied by two lesbians.


November 5      Ellie selects room #50, but is unsure about her conclusions.
                She is interested in repainting the furniture in the color it
                already is, like a wood grain on a wood grain; or of painting
                the shadows cast by the nails and chairs.  She is also thinking
                about blocking out a window with a bathroom frosting, allow-
                ing only a center square to be clear.


November 8      Although I like the way the film turned out, it is too
                much of a departure from the tableau that evolved.  A sad
                sacrifice.  Have to be careful of overkill.


November 10     Photograph of my ladies  Xeroxed 24 times makes wall
                paper.  As the show will be opened for 24 hours, I paint
                a drawing on the wall in phospholuminescent paint that
                while invisible in the daylight, glows in the evening.


November 15     Surprise.  Ellie says she has rented a friend who
                alternates his life between flop houses and Pacific Heights.
                He buys Brooks Brother shirts for $.25 at Goodwill and
                throws them away when they are dirty.  He will live in her
                room during the two weeks as she feels he fits into the
                context.


November 20     Both of us are working things out in our room.  Adding
                and subtracting.  We are glad that we have gone through with
                this, actualized our idea.  The freedom we developed to
```

Figure 2.15 Extract from Lynn Hershman, *Fragmented Journal from 1973*

crime scene, the team aimed to 'reveal layers of clues, each of which [would] propel a search for lost identity'. In conception the *Life Squared* environment was to be based on the 'Private I' theme and motif that recurs through Hershman Leeson's work, except that, in this instance, a 'missing person' would be 'traced through a trail of artefacts and partial or even erased information. Finally, a new 'bot' character was to be created to 'incorporate deviance' within three works (Shanks *et al.* 2009).

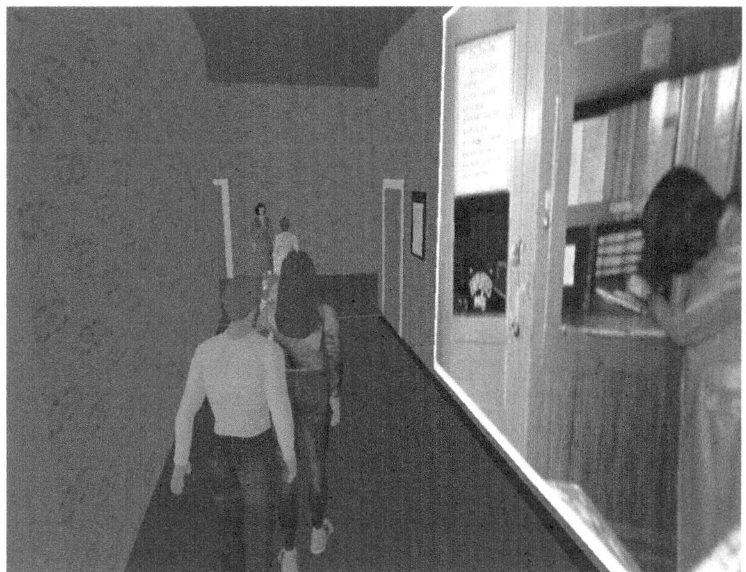

Figure 2.16 An early demonstration of *Life to the Second Power* to the project team and other invited guests

Life Squared was modelled on the floor plan of Hotel Dante, in a restaging of the site specificity and interactivity of Hershman Leeson's 'original'. Visitors were thus invited to sign in a blue box to enter the project and a red one to enter the room, in which documentations from room 47 at *The Dante Hotel* were reproduced. In place of a clerk, visitors would encounter a bot, named 'Dante', who would guide them through a door. They would then climb a staircase and walk down a narrow corridor from which they could enter room 47. Hershman Leeson describes the resultant piece as 'a remix of original photographs from the archive of *The Dante Hotel* with virtual avatars trespassing, changing things, and leaving their trail' (Hershman Leeson 2009: 14). Just as the visitors to the 'historical' work, *The Dante Hotel*, frequently left traces of their presence in the rooms, here visitors to Second Life could impact on aspects of the installation. More broadly, too, *Life Squared* consisted of a series of interrelated sites, including a gallery space, a Roberta bot as well as the re-enactment of *The Dante Hotel*, all in SL, and as a whole the piece encompassed a display of virtual representations of materials from the Hershman Leeson archives. In a further elaboration and multiplication of its sites, when the piece was exhibited at the Montreal Museum of Fine Art in 2008 and San Francisco Museum of Modern Art in 2009, 'real' archival and documentary materials were displayed alongside terminals allowing access to the Second Life installation, while the virtual counterparts of these 'real' objects were also displayed in the navigable SL environment. Finally, the traces left by the visitors in the virtual installation were captured over time by machinima and as still images.

GABRIELLA GIANNACHI Why was the Dante Hotel chosen as the starting point for *Life Squared*?

LYNN HERSHMAN LEESON I consider *The Dante Hotel* as my first work. It grew all these other parts. It grew Roberta. We decided to start with *The Dante Hotel*, then use Roberta and after that to see what would happen. We were interested in being able to manipulate time, in looking at the past as a context to reconsider the present, in being able to participate with strangers in a non-geographic space, in looking at social networks in 3-D virtual worlds as to what they can re-represent to a completely different audience. We were interested in reviving an earlier exploration of space, and migrate this into a more contemporary form. It was not really the island itself, or Second Life, that we are dealing with, but rather the programming. We were trespassing, expanding and creating a morphing into the

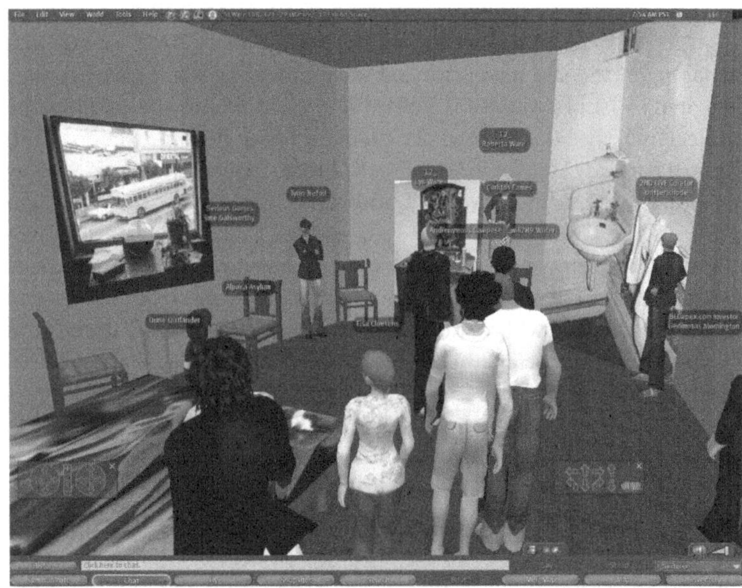

Figure 2.17 An early demonstration of *Life to the Second Power* to the project team and other invited guests

way that programme allows you to interact with people, with other individuals much in the same way that *The Dante Hotel* did.

[San Francisco, November 2008]

In *The Dante Hotel* the visitors' practice, their realization of Hershman Leeson's work in the mobility implied by this installation's occupation of the 'real' time and space of the Hotel Dante, unsettled both the site of the hotel and its realization as a site-specific work. Indeed, this 'original' event occupied multiple locations, where *the question* rather than *resolution* of 'its place' animated its engagement with site, identity and presence. *Life Squared* re-stages this disturbance of a 'real' site by proposing and articulating the persistence of *The Dante Hotel* in the performances of its SL participants. In this respect, Hershman Leeson's site-specific works, including *The Dante Hotel*, set out an agenda in which site is perceived as always already subject to its performance and so contingent on the temporary practices of occupation, habitation and narrative that animate it. This is an agenda echoed in later articulations of place, performance and presence, in which the experience of 'being there' is necessarily contingent on the enactment of site. Thus, for the performer and director Mike Pearson, and former Artistic Director of the influential Welsh performance company Brith Gof, who created large-scale site-specific performances between 1981 and 2003, site specificity rests in an articulation of precisely such complexity, whereby:

> site specific performances **recontextualise** site: they are the latest occupation of a location where occupants are still apparent and cognitively active. They are extremely generative of signs: the **denotative** and **connotative** meanings of performance are amended and/or compromised by the **denotative** and **connotative** meanings of site. Such performances are a complex overlay of **narrative**, historical and contemporary, a kind of **saturated space**, or a scene-of-crime, where, to use forensic jargon, 'everything is potentially important'.   [Pearson in Kaye 1996: 214, original emphases]

Where 'the site' – and correspondingly the site's claim to personal, social and cultural 'place' – is layered and contingent, so too 'presence', the act and experience of 'being there', is rendered mobile and transitory: an 'act' performed *in* the complexities, and overlappings of times, spaces and contexts in which 'this place' might be realized. In this regard, the stabilities and effect of 'presence' in *The Dante Hotel* are perceived and constructed in retrospective narratives – in response to that which remains – which becomes the anticipation of a future act and occupation. Here, the engagement with presence 'in' *The Dante Hotel*, like that produced in this work's persistence through *Life Squared*, mirrors and articulates the complexities of the site it enacts. It is in this approach to 'presence' that *Life Squared* plays across the distinctions between documentation and 'score' or 'notation', deploying its visitors' attention across past and an imagined future places; toward the possibility of their 'being present' 'in' a site in which they traverse and enact that which is *remembered* and *anticipated, recorded* and *produced.*

GABRIELLA GIANNACHI How was the design of *Life Squared* developed?

HENRIK BENNETSEN There was lot of reproduction in Second Life. We talked about how we should try to do something that could really only happen in Second Life. We started with *The Dante Hotel* and recreated the walk through the hotel with the picking up of the key, the walking down to the room, that was as much part of *The Dante Hotel* as the room itself. If you had walked down to the room of the original installation, you would have seen a bunch of shady characters and all of a sudden you would have felt out of the safe space that you normally experience in an artistic context. It was vital to reproduce this feeling in Second Life. We stripped away all the non-essential parts, like the other levels of the hotel, but chose to maintain the experience of entering the hotel, going to a reception, walking down a hallway. There were some technological constraints about what we could do in the actual room. *The Dante Hotel* allowed for a level of interaction, and people, for instance, changed the writing on the mirror in the room. Lynn always talks about the increasing amount of dust in the room. But there is no dust in a virtual world and it was hard to wipe out a virtual lipstick and draw on a virtual mirror, so the constraints of the platform certainly played into how the work ended up being. We could, however, do other things. So we built avatar radar sensors which could track how people moved through the space and we built the hypergallery where people could just ask for the next set of pictures and they had came up on the wall.
[San Francisco, October 2008]

For the architect Peter Eisenman, in his questioning of 'traditional geometries and processes in architecture' (Eisenman 1986: 4), site is precisely a function of such a dynamic between presence and absence. Observing that 'absence is either the trace of a previous presence, it contains *memory*; or the trace of a possible presence, it contains *immanence*' (Eisenman 1986: 4–5, original emphasis), Eisenman reads site as complex and multiple, always subject to processes and rhythms of disappearance and appearance. It is a characterizing of site, too, in

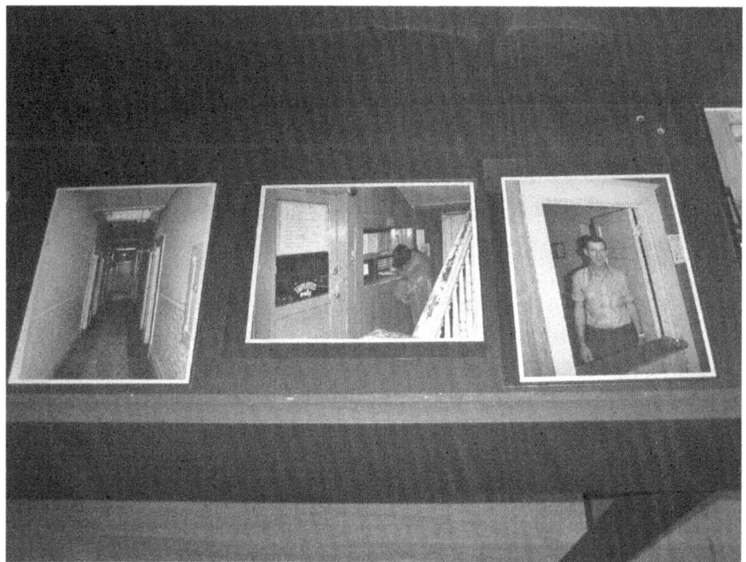

Figure 2.18 Lynn Hershman's work displayed at the Montreal Museum of
Fine Art, 2008

which the occupation of place – and so the experience of presence – is
implicitly configured as an act rather than a state or condition. Whereas
in architecture, Eisenman proposes, 'a presence is a physically real form,
whether a solid, such as a building, or a void, such as a space between
two buildings' (*ibid.*), site 'can be thought of as non-static' (Eisenman
1986: 5–6). In understanding this effect, Eisenman suggests, we may
consider:

> the difference between a *moving arrow* and a still arrow . . . if a picture of
> each were taken and compared, they would be virtually indistinguishable.
> What distinguishes the moving arrow from the still one is that it contains
> where it has been and where it is going, i.e., it has a memory and an imma-
> nence that are not present to the observer of the photograph; they are
> essential *absences*.   [Eisenman 1986]

In this formulation, a site is neither that which it *was*, a stable a
point of origin, nor that which it *will be*, a specific, 'knowable' point of
destination. It follows that the temporality of site and so the experiences
of 'presence' integral to it will be congruent with Husserl's description
of time as 'flow', in which the 'now point' – and so the occupation of this
place – of 'being there' – is always already subject to a direction of travel.

Indeed, it is in this movement, and in the participant's occupation of their *own* place and *the place of others*, that Hershman Leeson articulates the formation of identities in transpositions between location, site, identity and agency. In this movement, too, Hershman Leeson's work explicitly engages with and evokes transitory acts of presence produced in these shifts: in the enactment and occupation of places formed in the ephemerality and layering of site, and in the performance of their multiple spaces and times.

GABRIELLA GIANNACHI What was the role of the various interactive objects that formed the installation in Second Life?

HENRIK BENNETSEN Each object had its function. The scrapbook, which was populated with scanned images of the original scrapbook that Lynn had built for *The Dante Hotel*, was a vehicle for transporting knowledge. The doorway was the icon for entering into a new space. Through the book, people could read extracts from Lynn's diary and so understand what the original experience was like. We wanted to use Dina and Ruby and wire them into the space. We had a working version where people could walk up and talk to a robot. The little bot we finally used was like the tour guide inside the hotel. It just showed the way down to the room, so people did not wander off in some other random direction inside the hallways of the hotel. [We used the image of] the original receptionist in *The Dante Hotel* for that bot. When people came in and signed into the guest book to get the key, the little bot came out. You signed in by touching the bell and then wrote your name in the guest book – and so you are given the keys to the room by this guy who then says, 'Follow me down to the room.' We ended up with four arrow keys so you could walk the virtual Roberta through and she could watch the space unfold. Looking back, I would have loved the technology platform to capture more metadata about how we built things. So we could have a time slide rolling back the island. Imagine that you could go to the Second Life space and pull a slide and see how the whole space was built.

[San Francisco, October 2008]

Yet in relation to this notion of presence not only is *Life Squared* constructed in the persistence of *The Dante Hotel*, and so in multiple tenses, but this layering has been extended in its exhibition as a form of 'mixed reality'. In its presentation at the Montreal Museum of Fine Art a two-way mirror was integrated into the work to produce a further multiplication of perspectives and spaces to be traversed by the visitor. For this installation a large monitor was hung on the wall both

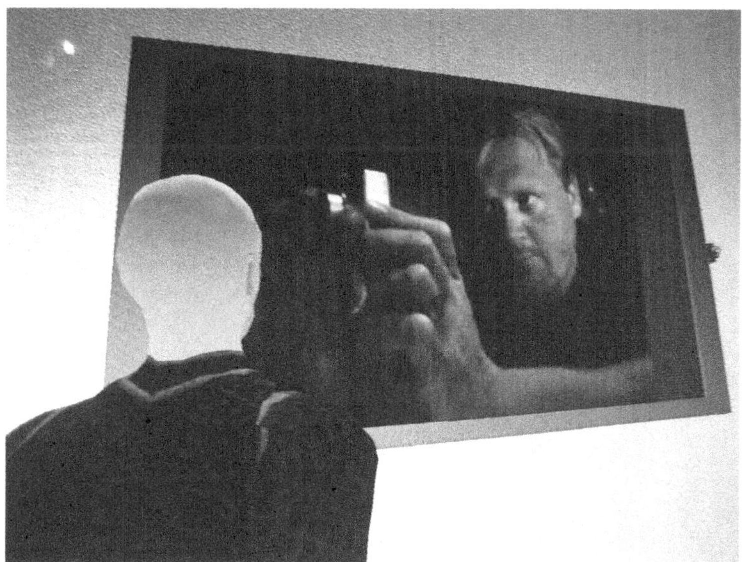

Figure 2.19 Lys Ware (a.k.a. Henrik Bennetsen) taking a photograph of
Henrik Bennetsen taking a photograph of Lys Ware in *Life Squared*

in the museum and in Second Life. The museum monitor permitted a
view from the physical space into the contained space in Second Life
and, vice versa, the Second Life monitor mediated the physical space
into SL via a webcam. Visitors could thus explore Hershman Leeson's
documentations displayed in the museum and then re-explore them
in their digitised form as displayed in Second Life. Here, and just as
in its first manifestation, the performance of *The Dante Hotel* through
Life Squared generated a layering of spaces and locations that amplified
the viewer's simultaneous roles. Indeed, 'the viewer' in this elaboration
of *Life Squared* may discover themselves occupying various positions:
they may scrutinize the documentation of Hershman Leeson's work
in the physical gallery site; watch over other participants' interactions
in Second Life; while simultaneously acting out their avatar, to observe
'themselves' from Second Life. It is in the visitor's mobile perspective,
too, that *Life Squared* amplifies the doubling in which the visitors to
The Dante Hotel discovered themselves acting out the multiple place of
Hershman Leeson's work.

   Life Squared, in its recollection, re-enactment and transformation
of the Hershman Leeson archive extends the artist's earlier engagement
with the performance of site and presence toward a dynamic 'mixed

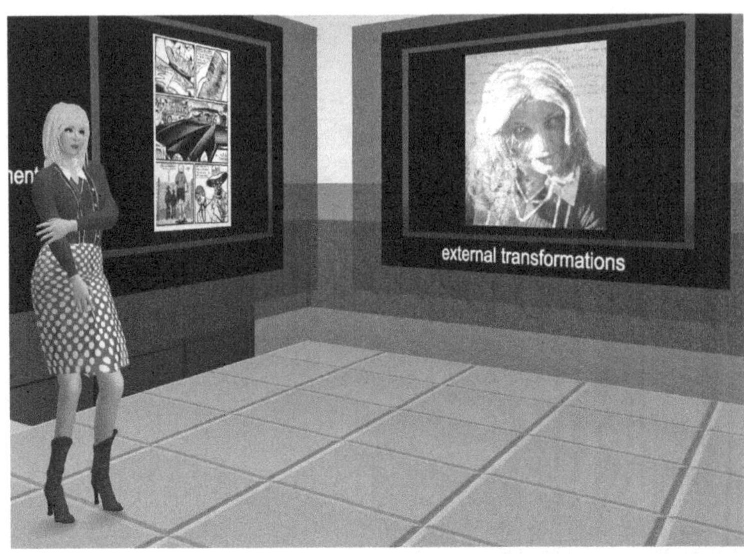

Figure 2.20 The Roberta bot in *Life Squared*

reality' experience where visitors may co-create works as well as explore digital reproductions and fragments of the 'original' archive. In these respects, *Life Squared* exemplifies Hershman Leeson's approach toward the 'presence' of 'real' sites and 'performed' identities, further amplifying the porous relationships in her earlier work between the viewing subject and the signs and evidence of the 'presence' of others. Indeed, *Life Squared* re-animates the tactics of trace, evidence and evocation that structure and shape the viewer's encounter with both *The Dante Hotel* and *Roberta Breitmore*, to produce a participatory 'documentation' of works that explicitly operate in the visitor's enactment of place and presence. In this sense, too, *Life Squared* re-produces and restages experiences of presence produced *in* action. Here, experiences of 'being there' are amplified in the visitor, viewer or reader's 'performance' across the multiple sites and tenses of the places and works they 'act out,' in the articulation and realization of experiences of presence produced in simultaneous acts of *anticipation* and *recollection*.

3

emergence Gary Hill

Developing and deploying video and video projection in ways that challenge expectations around the primacy of the visual image, Gary Hill's works raise questions around the functioning of representation, electronic mediation and video itself in the performance and perception of the body's presence. Frequently constructed toward paradoxical encounters with overtly mediated and so 'absent' figures, Hill's work engages with a phenomenology of presence explored in an articulation of signs of the body in the multiple spaces and times of their performance and encounter: in the intertwining of 'real' and 'recorded' times articulated in video's replay; in the performative acts of viewing; and in relation to Hill's physical engagement in generating the work. Implicitly engaging, in this context, with the mechanisms and means by which the sense of the image's 'presence' seems to exceed its status as a visual sign, Hill's video installations provoke counter-intuitive experiences of a body or bodies whose materiality is self-evidently of other times and spaces, yet which assert an uncomfortable or uncanny physicality. Emphasizing his work's expression of a 'visceral physicality' through de-materialized, mediated, and fragmented images of the body, Hill notes that, with regard to the political charge of his work: 'it has to be fully embedded in something that is visceral and happening against the will of your desire to be cognitive. I want the body – literally and metaphorically – in your face' (Hill in Sans 1999: 73).

It is toward these paradoxical senses of an emergent presence, too, that Hill's work frequently unfolds in a disturbance of the elements that his images appear at first to offer. Indeed, where the visual image may provide an overt starting point for an engagement with his work, Hill's deployment of the imperatives and characteristics of video – and especially his shaping of the viewer's experience over time – frequently come to articulate differences and uncertainties between image and language, appearance and sense. As this suggests, in its address to the body and the image, and implicitly in his various approaches to 'presence', Hill's work purposely evades being locked into the 'medium' of video or its visual aspect, but rather incorporates video and its images in the course of challenging and extending its terms. In keeping with this, and remarking in 1993 that 'I don't see myself as a video artist' (Hill in Furlong 2000: 205), Hill has consistently stressed that 'virtually all my work in one way or another has something to do with putting into question the hierarchical position of the image' (Hill in Quasha and Stein 2000: 253). Here, rather than resolve his practice into its visual representations, Hill's images are articulated, challenged and transformed through attention to the multiple spaces and times of their performance and encounter in which this sense of presence is produced and questioned.

Time and the body

In the development of Hill's work as a whole, this displacement of the image and phenomenological address to presence first emerges in installations in which relationships between fragmented, dispersed or obscured signs of the body are articulated in the 'real' space and times of viewing. Thus, in installations such as *CRUX* (1983–87) and *Inasmuch As It Is Always Already Taking Place* (1990), Hill introduces caesura into the image of a body whose signs seem, nevertheless, designed to uncannily occupy the spatial and temporal co-ordinates of the figure they represent. Yet it is in the very exposure and so subversion of these images' attempt to occupy these places and spaces of the 'real body' over time, and so in an unfolding sense of their absence, or lack, that the subject of Hill's work appears.

GARY HILL Video is not so much a medium as a space. If we think about it in relation to film it becomes very apparent. Film is very much a medium. If you hold the 'object' of film up to the light you can see what it is – a sequence of still images that create the illusion of movement. Whereas video, even though it has a set of sync signals to produce a similar illusion, remains significantly different, since it's a continuous stream of pixels taking place one at a time – something akin to weaving, perhaps. An image/object never really exists at once (in ONE time). So it's difficult for me to think of video as a medium of images; it's more akin to a cybernetic space to think from and within. Working with electronic media seems to always bring up a number of Zeno's paradoxes. I find myself running into the dichotomy paradox in which one has to get to the half-way point before completion, and no matter where you are on the way there is always a new half-way point. I used this notion to structure the work *Accordions* (*The Belsunce Recordings, July 2001* [2001–02]). Without getting too technical, as the camera zooms in on a subject, more and more black frames are inserted between video frames – the closer the zoom gets the slower the image moves, as if one will never arrive or that the image will become a still [point] before you reach it. So it's complicated . . . Yes, I use images, and many times that translates literally into thousands of images, but almost without exception the context is one of deconstruction: of negating images as the given place.

[London, July 2007]

In tandem with this, Hill also counters a resolution of his work into its images by approaching video's mediation and operation in time as a 'cybernetic space to think from and within,' a space in which he has engaged with, and frequently disturbed, philosophical premises and discourses. It is an aspect of his practice evident in his collaborations with writers and philosophers, including Jacques Derrida, as well as his work's affinity and dialogue with writings of the late existentialist thinker Maurice Blanchot, among others. Here, Hill's work emphasizes and amplifies video's hybrid character, while his staging of the de-materialized body has referenced practices of conceptual art, performance, and music, as well as video's differential relationship to film, practices that have themselves frequently been antithetical to the resolution of an artwork into its visual or material aspects alone.

In these various respects, Hill's early installations engaging with the mediated body's placement in 'real' space marked a key moment in his overt engagement with issues and practices of presence. In doing so, these installations also signalled a moment of change, building as they do on Hill's earlier development of an 'electronic linguistic' in his single-channel video works while providing the basis for his subsequent

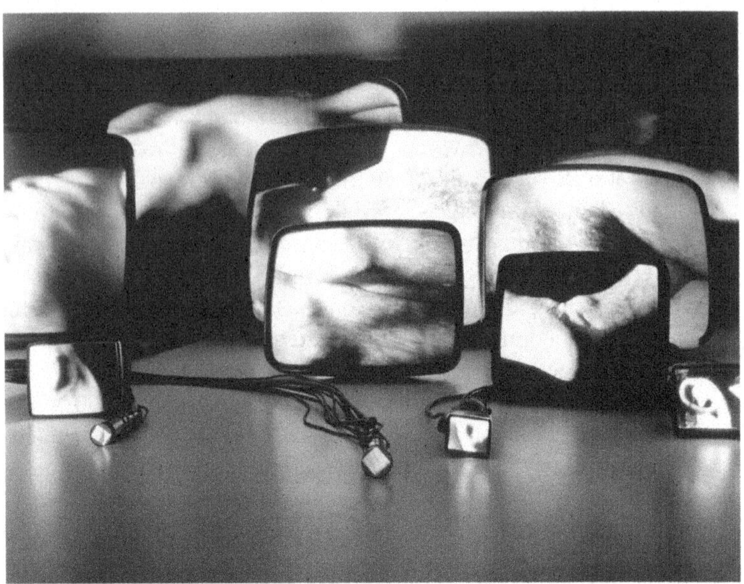

Figure 3.1 Gary Hill, *Inasmuch As It Is Always Already Taking Place* (1990). Details. Sixteen-channel video/sound installation. Sixteen modified ½ in. to 23 in. black-and-white video monitors (cathode ray tubes removed from chassis), two speakers, sixteen DVD players and sixteen DVDs (black-and-white; one with stereo sound). Dimensions of horizontal niche: 16 in. high × 54 in. wide × 66 in. long (41 cm × 137 cm × 167 cm). Edition of two and one artist's proof

investigation of media and the phenomenological presence of the body integral to his later projective installations.

Exemplifying, along with the earlier *CRUX* (1983–87), a fragmentation of the image across the real space of the gallery or site, *Inasmuch As It Is Always Already Taking Place* (1990) presents sixteen modified black-and-white video monitors ranging in size between ½ in. and 23 in. Separated from their outer casings, the monitors are placed into a deep horizontal cut inset into the gallery wall a little over a metre from the floor, scattered variously before and next to each other. Hill's *catalogue raisonné* records, '[t]heir arrangement as such is one of accumulation, a pile-up. They appear as a kind of debris – bulbs that have washed up from the sea or perhaps stones that have broken down to smaller and smaller particles' (Hill 2002: 147). In this arrangement, each monitor brings a quality of its *objectness*, emphasized here by their stripped casings and the gallery setting, into coincidence with the fragment of a mediated body. Collectively, these screens seemingly map the surface of the skin, such that:

> a one-inch monitor displays a portion of a palm of a hand, or an unrecognisable terrain of skin; a four-inch monitor displays part of a shoulder or an ear; a fifteen-inch monitor emits the stomach, and so on . . . In each image there is little movement, suggesting a wavering gaze or the murmur of the body, yet ambiguous. The movement and sound (barely articulated phrases, rustling papers, skin being rubbed) objectify themselves as a collection of closed loops with no beginning and no end.   [Hill 2002: 147]

As this account suggests, *Inasmuch As It Is Always Already Taking Place* explicitly plays between the monitor-as-object, these mediated signs of the body and video's shaping of the time and experience of the image, including the *return* and objectifying effect of time-looped video. It is in these relationships, too, that Hill's installation implies, at one level, a movement of its various elements toward unity or wholeness – and so a direction of travel – just as it articulates an open-ended unfolding over time. Indeed, in many ways, this installation's gesture consists of a continual *coming closer* or *being before*. Amplifying this, the various aspects of its arrangement seemingly amplify an approach toward the viewer. Thus the outer casings of the monitors are stripped to foreground the surface of the screen in what seems an attempt to press the skin to its surface. Simultaneously the 'real time' recordings of these fragments emphasize their 'shared' time, rhythm and movement before the viewer, just as they mirror the real time in which the viewer looks. In turn, these scattered signs are placed within a niche whose dimensions echo those of the hypothetical 'whole' body to which they refer. Yet in inviting the perception of a coming closer – and the promise of a coming together – of these various mediated signs of the body, this installation, like many of Hill's works, foregrounds a sense of movement and experience of process over and above any final resolution. Indeed, in its link to presence, this is a movement and unfolding addressed, as in many other of Hill's works, in the wordplay of its title. Evidently, *Inasmuch As It Is Always Already Taking Place* at once refers to the act of 'placing' or 'placement', in which images of the body are seen to be 'taking their place' before the viewer in this perpetual approach to and identification with the viewer's body. At the same time, the act of approaching itself is caught in the ephemeral event in which such a time-based work 'takes place'. Here, *Inasmuch As It Is Always Already Taking Place* engages with the idea, practice and effect of the body's presence by emphasizing this perpetual approach and so *being before*. In this sense, Hill's title implies that it is the unresolved *performance* or *act* of placing that claims these images' uncanny presence, as this body's continual 'arrival' before the viewer effects a physicality felt *in* rather than despite its mediation.

Yet, as well as the implicit link in Hill's work between image, process and an evocation of the body's 'visceral physicality', *Inasmuch As It Is Always Already Taking Place* also reflects Hill's interest in relationships between language, speech acts and the functioning of the image. It is this engagement with language, performance and mediation, too, that is at the root of Hill's approach to questions and experiences of presence. In this context, and as Hans Belting suggests, in its approach to the body *Inasmuch As It Is Always Already Taking Place* might also be read after the strongly linguistic turn in Hill's work, such that:

> the images are like single syllables, out of which our consciousness assembles words and sentences. This body seems to exist 'between' the various images, because no single image can adequately represent that peculiar 'Being' that literally stands before us.   [Belting 1995: 48]

More precisely, the fragmentary images of *Inasmuch As It Is Always Already Taking Place* may be considered to be 'like single syllables' in so far as they operate as 'utterances', and so as events in time. Indeed, this treatment of the body rests directly on Hill's earlier development of an 'electronic linguistic' expressed in his single-channel tapes, in which the composition of image sequences was bound to the utterance of sounds, syllables and words, and which is transposed here towards a 'speaking' of the body. In this context, too, Hill's early single-channel video provides a further means of articulating the time structures of his later installations and their direct evocation of the body and presence. Here, and while sharing Hershman's focus on the enactment of presence and its relationship to time as 'flow', Hill's work explores the performance of presence in unfoldings and modulations of continuous time-based processes rather than in responses to traces and representations of acts and events ostensibly 'absent'. Thus, where Hershman locates phenomena of presence in responses to and investments in the traces of events past, Hill's work looks toward the emergence and modulation of experiences of presence over extended times.

Indeed, the importance of process and emergent experiences shaped through an address to the performative qualities and time structures of video is evident in Hill's earliest works. Thus, where Hill's early single-channel tapes from 1976 and 1977 were evidently aligned to other contemporaneous investigations in video art of the technical properties of the medium, Hill's particular interrogation of the functioning of the visual image in time was aimed not at uncovering a core language of video 'as a medium' so much as realizing structures that would resist and affect, modulate and produce change in the emergent visual and sonic languages at play. Hill thus observes that his early approach to time in video served to assert differences from the 'real time' of watching in order to produce dislocations between image, time and experience, and dissonances in the viewer's *sense* or experience of time, noting that:

> Many of the early single-channel video pieces were in a sense 'system performances' that generated their *own* time in relation to *real* time. There are really so many folds in time involving media, feedback, delay, writing, speaking and the body. Time becomes more like a Möbius band or Klein bottle without an absolutely 'real' side.   [Hill in Quasha and Stein 2000: 244, original emphasis]

Consistently with this articulation of video's functioning in relation to incongruent processes and states, many of Hill's early single-channel tapes used video and live feedback or applied 'camera and image processing devices' (Hill 2002: 66) to explore the transformation of 'real world' images and scenes into increasingly abstract colours and shapes. In this context, early tapes such as *Mirror Road* (1976), *Bathing* (1977), *Windows* (1978) and *Objects with Destinations* (1979) played out the electronic malleability of recognizable images of everyday scenes and objects: a car journey seen through a mirror; a woman bathing; an exterior landscape framed by a window; the visual overlaying and transformation of everyday instruments and objects. Prompted by Hill's sense that 'in some ways linguistics seemed related to electronic phenomena' (Hill in Furlong 1993: 189), these early 'system performances' provided for a structural engagement with video's transformation of the times and appearance of the 'real world' and existing pictorial and painterly conventions, as well as the experience of those auditing the tape. In these respects, Hill's 'electronic linguistic' engages with and foregrounds video's 'performativity', a sense that, in producing its images and affects, this electronic medium is neither neutral nor transparent but implicitly 'enacts that to which it refers' (Pearson and Shanks 2001: 69). Such a notion of 'performativity' supposes that video *transforms* that which it re-presents: video has its own 'voice'; it 'speaks' the image. In turn, these strategies came to form the basis of Hill's later engagements through installation with phenomena of presence.

In this development, then, Hill's early *Electronic Linguistic* (1977) and *Sums and Differences* (1978) provided the clearest treatment of image, sound and time structure generated electronically, and in doing so emphasized this performative aspect of Hill's early work. Suggesting

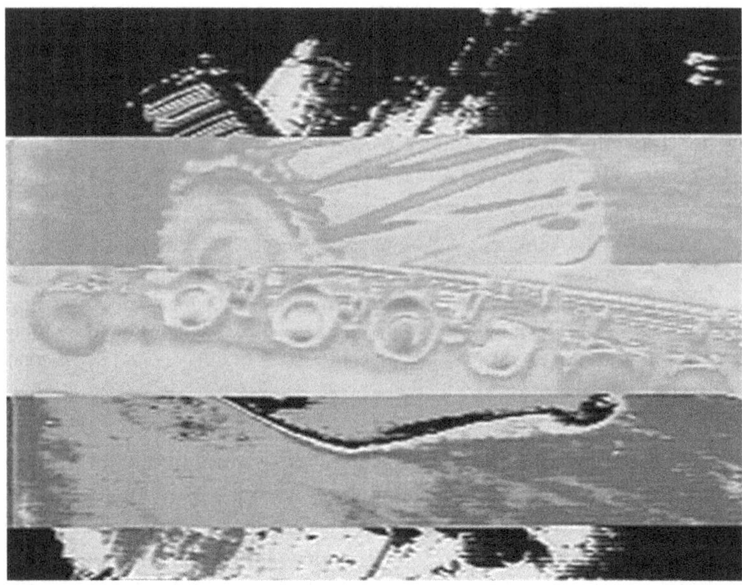

Figure 3.2 Gary Hill, *Sums and Differences* (1978). Detail still. Video (black-and-white, stereo sound); 8:00 min.

the 'utterance' or 'speaking' of the video image, *Electronic Linguistic* returns to black-and-white imagery to offer 'visualizations of electronically generated sounds' (Hill 2002: 68) and so a 'performance' generated entirely from within the system itself. In contrast, *Sums and Differences* superimposes sounds and images of musical instruments, with increasing and intense rapidity, in order to 'play' image and sound over and through one another. Beginning with the perceptible alternation of images with their corresponding sounds, and culminating in an alternation so rapid as to produce one composite sound and seemingly unstable and fluctuating image, the final oscillation 'speaks' an image/sound composite, transforming the perception of both the instruments and their musical purpose. Indeed, this video synthesis, in which the auditor of the tape finds their experience shaped by the evolving 'electronic linguistic' over and above its constituent images and sounds, foregrounds the musical influences acting on Hill's approach to time structures.

Hill's subsequent work extended this engagement with video's 'voice' or 'speech' towards explorations of 'the structure of a linguistic phenomenon at a visual level' (Hill 2002: 79) in, for example, the single-channel *Picture Story* (1979) and the further 'synchronisation of visual and linguistic elements' (Hill 2002: 81) in *Equal Time* (1979). However, in the subsequent *Around & About* (1980) and *Primarily Speaking* (1981–83), a work expressed both as a single-channel tape and multichannel installation, Hill engaged explicitly with a 'co-performance' of utterance and image, so deferring attention to the interplay of separate or distinct visual and aural elemets in their shaping of the performance and experience of the work's time.

GARY HILL I think my notion of time expanded dramatically after reading Kunio Komparu's book on Noh [*The Noh Theater: Principles and Perspectives*, 2006]. He discusses several concepts, and split time and reverse time in particular come to mind. I was working on *URA ARU (the backside exists)* [1985–86], which involved performers speaking in Japanese and the tape being played forwards and backwards – rocking back and forth over phrases to 'reveal' other words and phrases. I wrote a little paper on it called *Origami Time*. There are also a couple of works in which I edited images to the syllabic structure of speech [*Around & About*, 1980, and *Primarily Speaking*, 1981–83], which produced another kind of time – something like 'word time' with images. What I discovered in doing this was the idea that a word can have time. Since each word, or at least those with multiple syllables, would generate multiple images, one experiences the words taking time – opening up, as it were. The words stopped being mere objects and kind of opened up time – one's relationship to it became dynamic; you are not simply *in* time but *thinking* time – making time thinking through the language as it spits out images.

[London, July 2007]

Comprised of rapidly changing images prompted by the syllabic sequence of Hill's reading of an extended, self-reflexive text, in *Primarily Speaking*, Hill notes, the 'existence' of the image 'is directly tied to speech', for 'unless I speak the image does not change or move' (Hill in Sarrazin 2000: 217). Rigorously foregrounding the performance and experience of this 'speech act', and seemingly resisting any sustained or final synthesis, this work, George Quasha and Charles Stein suggest, comes to be 'endlessly at variance with itself' (Quasha and Stein 2001: 1) as utterance and image are continually subject to the changing performative affect of each others' position and occurrence. Emphasizing 'self-difference and antithesis' (Quasha and Stein 2001: 1) in conjunctions of speaking and seeing, *Primarily Speaking* becomes an exploration of the variability and malleability of utterance, word and image over time, while resisting any single or stable position *outside* of this performance. As a result, Hill proposes, this work 'really puts one inside the time of speaking since every syllable produced an image change; suddenly words seem quite spatial and one is conscious of a single word's time' (Hill in Sarrazin 2000: 217). In these ways, *Primarily Speaking* further foregrounds 'performance' and 'performativity', and an ebb and flow of sense, over a resolution of the tape or installation into the import of specific images or combinations of words and images, so implicitly subjecting each of its elements to the notion of a 'present' – or 'now' point – that is contingent on a flow, direction or act. In this mode of work, Quasha and Stein thus propose:

> *utterance and image should be co-performative* in the way that they inform each other in the very moment of the combined video and verbal gesture: a configuration of lines in motion may 'click in' as an image of an object just after the word for that object is uttered or appears on the screen. Or, conversely, an ambiguous phrase may condense toward a single meaning as an image for that meaning comes into view.   [Quasha and Stein 2001: 1]

Such tactics have significant implications for video's 'performance' of the body and this body's 'presence' before the viewer. Where for *Primarily Speaking* the time of speaking becomes an engine of *difference* between word and image, for *Inasmuch As It Is Always Already Taking Place* Hill's 'accumulation' of a 'collection of closed loops' serves to emphasize these images' differential operation in time. Conjoined by their function as an index of 'the body' and the coincidence of their 'real time' recording and playback, each of these video fragments nevertheless evidently operates *in its own time* even as it approaches the time and space of the viewer; that is, in *differentiation* from both the time of viewing (and of the viewer's body) and the times and repetitions of the other nearby tapes. It is in this visual association and yet temporal dissonance, too, that this 'pile-up' of time-based images become *co-performative*; each affects the import and position of the others in this 'body,' affecting in turn the viewer's experience *before* them, while, in combination, emphasizing differential relationships, process, variability and change. As a result, and as Gottfried Boehm suggests, the body in this installation is at once in a state of action and resists resolution into a static image of the body, so presenting a 'quality of perpetually coming into being, of becoming a representation *with time* rather than in time' (Boehm 1995: 37, original emphasis).

This is a presentation of the mediated body, too, that reflects the premises and explorations of earlier 'Body Art' events and documents that Hill's works implicitly reference, and which was also rooted in a phenomenology of the body. Thus for Dennis Oppenheim and Vito

Acconci, developing body-based artworks through live performance, video and photographic documentation in the late 1960s and early 1970s, the body provided a 'de-materialized zone of psychological topology' (Oppenheim in Kaye 1996: 66) that would evade the limits of the 'object' precisely because of its processual and excessive nature. '[O]ne of the most catalytic aspects of Body Art,' Oppenheim later recalled, 'was this connection to the real world' (Oppenheim in Kaye 1996: 66), one in which the body was revealed as permeable and quintessentially active and *in activity*' (Kaye 2000: 159). Reflecting the phenomenological emphasis of these modes of work, Acconci similarly emphasized that '[o]ne thing I learned through working with the body is that you can't think of it as an object' (Acconci in Nemser 1971: 21).

Hill's presentation of the body is made in an analogous refusal of the object. Thus these monitors' articulation of a resistance and difference to the *times* of the surrounding video loops as well as the time in which it is viewed presents a body whose images are in process. Indeed, *in time*, and in their *repetition*, these images neither 'arrive', to cohere as the body they would apparently represent, nor do they become 'arrested' as fragmentary images of a body that is simply absent. It is an operation integral to the equivocal sense of 'presence' Hill's installation produces, and which is evident in responses to this work. Thus the writer and theorist Lynne Cooke emphasizes this installation's production of a disturbing relationship with those who watch, proposing that here:

> Each monitor is thus the site of the body which appears on the screens as immutably present and yet outside actual time. Its impregnable solitude reduces the viewer's role to that of mute witness at what Hill describes, disquietingly, as 'the incessant, however fragmentary, anatomical site'. Presence is brought to betray a haunting absence.   [Cooke 2000: 139]

The 'taking place' to which Hill directs attention implies, in this context, absence from the place itself, and so the phenomena of a spatial and temporal *being before*; an event in which the 'presence' of the body is approached in the promise of its arrival, in the process of its images' *coming before* the viewer. In this respect, *Inasmuch As It Is Always Already Taking Place* emphasizes a *restlessness* and *difference* with regard to the 'place' of a body 'always already' in the process of being enacted. It is a process and focus evident, too, in Hill's other early large-scale installations directly intertwining place, presence and signs of the body. *CRUX* (1983–87) articulates the persistence of the body in its 'failure' to fully 'take its place' before the viewer. Originally conceived as a performance, and produced by fixing four small cameras and microphones to his

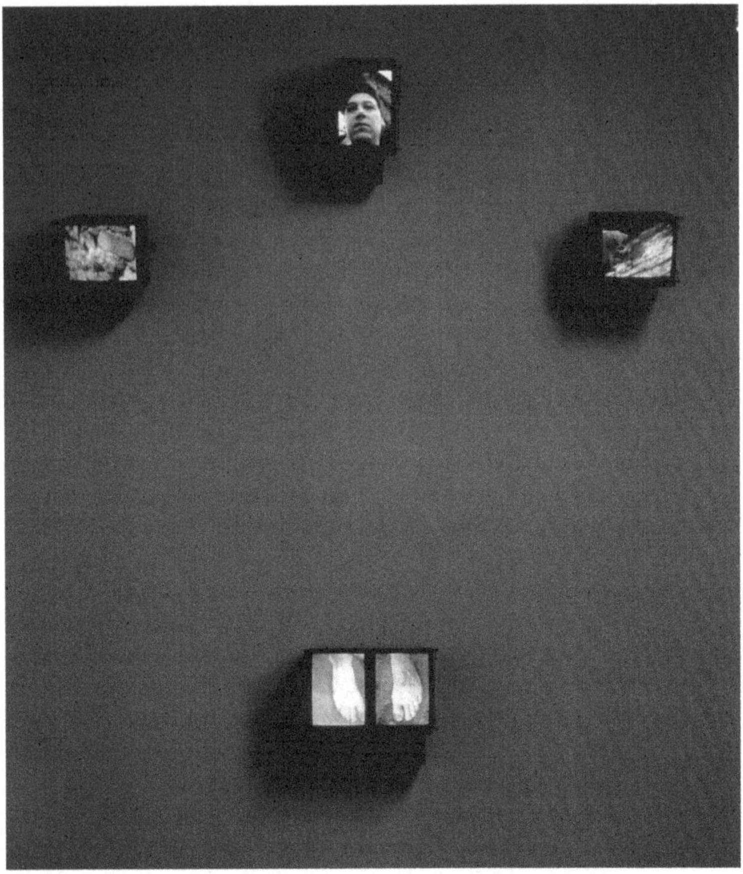

Figure 3.3 Gary Hill, *CRUX* (1983–87). Five-channel video/sound installation. Five 20 in. colour video monitors, four monitor mounting brackets, five speakers, five-channel synchronizer, five laser-disc players and five laser discs (colour; mono sound). Dimensions: as installed, approx. 144 in. × 144 in. (365 cm × 365 cm). Edition of two and one artist's proof

ankles and wrists, with a fifth camera directed towards his head, *CRUX* fixes the 'object of seeing' to Hill's bodily extremities such that:

> In effect, [my] body films its own absence, metaphorically pinning or nailing its extremities to the cross with the camera's 'objective' view (dis)embodying the 'video' . . . Only extremities of the body are seen, a body crucified and impassioned by the cameras that have entered it.   [Hill 2000a: 303]

Re-presented through the positioning of five monitors in the form of a cross, *CRUX* plays fragments of a body in action, seeming to bring the body closer even as it explicitly emphasizes the various absences in which its recordings, representations and arrangement function.

In these various respects, too, Hill's play on the persistence of the body exemplifies his approach to video as a medium grounded in time rather than the image; a medium in which 'acts' or 'events' inhabit the 'image' to delimit it or effect its disturbance. Indeed, in advancing Hill's address to 'the incessant, however fragmentary, anatomical site' these two installations operate in the promise that the body *will be here*, posing the question of the body's persistence in the absence of its materiality and the disruption of its appearance.

In this context, too, Hill's sceptical and demanding approach to the visual character of video has been read in its affinity to aspects of French literature and theory. Bruce Ferguson, writing in 'Déjà vu and Déjà lu (already seen et already read)' (*sic*), thus observes a link between Hill's method and philosophical critiques of the loss or betrayal of presence in representation's erasure of its object. He notes that:

> French texts exude a resolved class of rage at the betrayal of language to *not* be able to capture completely and accurately the world as it is known through experience. To be (monstrously) contained by inescapable metaphors (endless relays of substitutions of one thing for another in the way that Barthes describes metaphor as making '. . . an infinitely ambiguous object out of a simple, literal object'). To only know 'presence' by virtue of an absence (the always and forever unlocatable referent . . . [Ferguson in Hill 1994:16]

More specifically, Hill has himself frequently directed attention through his work and commentary to the importance of the writing and philosophy of Maurice Blanchot (1907–2003). While the relationship of Hill's later work to Blanchot's creative writing is pervasive, intimate and subtle, Hill's method of work obtains an affinity to Blanchot's identification of a radical scepticism with the identity and operation of literature, set out in his supposition that: 'literature begins at the moment when literature becomes a question', such that it is emergent in 'its own negation' (Blanchot 1999a: 359–60). Analogously, Hill's practice is frequently directed toward a questioning of the emergent identity, meaning and elements that would constitute the work itself, a process clearly reflected in his rigorous questioning of the status and import of the image through patently visual modes of work: a tactic in which the experience of presence is invariably placed at the fore. Indeed, for Blanchot, the 'arrival' of the image defeats a rhythm and processual movement between absence and presence, in which the phenomenon of that which is represented once came into being. He asserts that:

> The thing was there, we grasped it in the living motion of a comprehensive action – and once it has become an image it instantly becomes ungraspable, non-contemporary, impassive, not the same thing distanced, but that thing as distancing, the present thing in its absence, the thing graspable because ungraspable, appearing as something that has disappeared, the return of what does not come back   [Blanchot 1999c: 418]

Hill's video installation evidently approaches the image in relation to this 'living motion' whose erasure Blanchot describes, and so in the promise or potential of *coming closer* to presence. Indeed, if the experience of 'presence' is provoked by that which is emergent, then video's capacity to traverse real and virtual, near and distant, live and recorded, may itself constitute rather than defeat its 'performance of presence', a position reflected in Hill's observation of the paradox of video's 'simultaneous production of presence and difference' (Hill 2000b: 292). It is in precisely such an operation – in a movement between binaries – that Hill's work addresses the articulation of 'presence' *in process*: as a temporal and spatial 'taking place'; as an act or a mode of *becoming* subject to delays, hesitations and mobility. It is this operation too that can be seen to underpin Hill's most overt engagements with the performance and perception of the presence of the figure in video installation.

Enfolding images: 'tuning is a function of time'

In his series of projective installations, initiated with the interactive *Tall Ships* in 1992 and subsequently extended in a series of works created from 1995 to 1996, Hill's shaping of the viewer's engagement through the time structures of video installation were extended and amplified in a further diffusion of the image into 'real' spaces. Here, too, and while these installations invariably operated in silence, the implicitly musical basis of Hill's early work was turned further towards the shaping of the image's 'taking place' and, in doing so, towards the viewer's implication in these works' articulation of the emergent sense and signs of presence over an extended time.

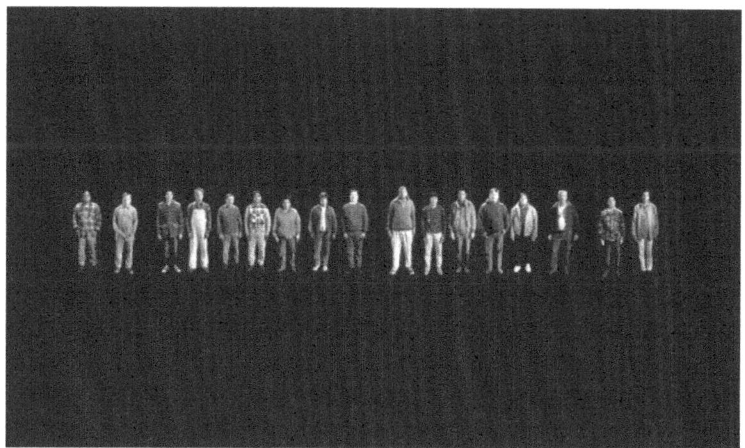

Figure 3.4 Gary Hill, *Viewer* (1996). Five-channel video installation. Five video projectors, five-channel synchronizer, five DVD players and five DVDs. Edition of two and one artist's proof

NICK KAYE Are there specific works where the experience of time is linked to an interrogation of presence?

GARY HILL A number of the multi-channel projection works like *Tall Ships* [1992], *Viewer* [1996] and *HanD HearD* [1995–96] contain a kind of self-conscious presence through the viewer being reflexively folded into the works and in some sense completing the work. These works are also about estrangement from presence – that is, one feels like somewhat of a stranger, an other, perhaps like being in the wrong place at the wrong time. So it's not an easy presence, as one's being is kind of 'on alert' and up for questioning. These works play with the double meaning of projection – the images are projected and we project ourselves forth into the relationship.

[London, July 2007]

Mirroring or counterpointing the viewer's act of looking and the attempt to comprehend, installations such as *Viewer* (1996), present 'real time' recordings that press further toward the time and space of the gallery. Here, then:

Slightly larger than life-size colour images of seventeen day labourers, facing out from a neutral background, are projected on to a wall, about forty-five feet long, by five video projectors attached to the ceiling. . . . The men stand almost motionless, their movement limited to involuntary stirring – an incidental shuffling from foot to foot, slight movements of the hands, and almost imperceptible changes in facial expression. There is no interaction among them, each man standing quite alone and gazing out from the plane of projection toward the viewer.   [Quasha and Stein 1997a: 10]

Running in a ten-minute continuous loop, *Viewer* is presented in such a way as to suppress its framing as recording and reproduction. Thus, in an extension of Hill's earlier stripping back of the monitor's casing to align the monitor with the mediated body, the projection of *Viewer* emphasizes its image's congruence with the surface of the gallery wall, and so its articulation of the real spaces of the gallery *in* projection. In these recordings, originally composed separately and then composited together, Hill recalled, 'I wanted to avoid any notion of documentation' (Hill in Sans 1999: 72). From this position, *Viewer* recalls and amplifies Hill's direction of this real-time recording, in which, hired for an hour, each person 'was given the instruction to maintain eye contact with me – and the camera, which I was directly behind and in line with – for twenty to thirty minutes. The idea was not to stare *per se* but rather about two strangers making contact – viewing one another – being in a state of apprehending' (Hill in Sans 1999: 72). In such video work, Hill remarks:

the play with sculpture is very present, but even more so is the play on the word 'projection'. These are literally video projections and at the same time they are projecting out a certain look, perhaps a desire – any number of emotions. And we 'project' our view back to the projection and amongst ourselves in a space that continually inflects these words in many directions.   [Hill in Sans 1999: 73]

The emphasis on exchange and process, in which this work approaches and shapes the viewer's experience, directly reflects the musical basis of Hill's work. Following his encounter with the music of Terry Riley and Phillip Glass from 1969, Hill's engagement with 'minimalist' and 'serial' composition directed his attention to one of its early sources in the artist and composer La Monte Young's musical experimentations. Like the earlier and contemporaneous experiments of John Cage, on whose practices and sensibility Young's work drew, La Monte Young's formally radical work, which was in part associated with the Fluxus movement, had a wide influence beyond the immediate realm of musical composition and performance. Thus, writing with implicit reference to *Sums and Differences*, Giuliana Stella suggests that:

The first appearance of musical instruments in Hill's work is clearly a reference to the experience of La Monte Young. The instrument is the sound.

> The sound is the instrument. Sound and instrument are an image of time.
> Time and instrument are an image of sound.   [Stella 2005: 24]

Exemplified in aspects of his Fluxus compositions, including *Composition # 7* (1960), which designated F and B sharp 'to be held for a long time', and the invitation of *Composition # 10* (1960) to 'draw a straight line and follow it', La Monte Young's evolving compositional practice came to realize an extreme precision and extension of sustained frequencies. In his electronic music, in particular, Young pursued a 'very precisely articulated situation' comprising 'the most clear and sparse sounds' (Young in Nyman 1999: 142), developing from *Trio for Strings* (1958), whose opening C sharp extends for four and a half minutes, to *The Tortoise, his Dreams and Journeys* (1964–), which initiated an open-ended work intended to unfold in a discipline of performance occurring potentially, for Young, each day throughout his lifetime. Hill's response to Young extended, first, toward a synthesis and even implicit synaesthesia in his work that served to disturb the position and status of the image. Consistently with this, Hill has remarked that '*Sums and Differences* really works in term of sound and image actually becoming one another . . . In that tape, audio and video can't be separated. There's simultaneity of seeing and hearing' (Hill in Furlong 2000: 168). Importantly, too, this notion of a transformation over time is in accord with one of La Monte Young's fundamental propositions: that an extended time provides for the definition and synthesis of the elements of the work, such that in being before it the auditor might *inhabit* the time of the sound itself. In this regard, in particular, and where John Cage's musical concepts had also directly influenced earlier video practice through Nam June Paik's inauguration of video art from 1964, Hill emphasizes that 'Young was more of an influence than Cage,' noting that '[o]ne of them is the idea of being inside a sound. I think this comes across in my relation to physicality . . . the sense of being in the space with the images . . . The other idea that rings in my ears is that "tuning is a function of time"' (Hill in Lestocart 2000: 222).

'Tuning', in this context, directs attention to the *process* and *affect* of an extended temporal event, rather than toward a synthesis or unifying of elements. In *Viewer*, then, such a focus is reflected in Hill's attention to an exchange of 'projections' and the installation's realization as a developing experience of encounter and exchange through which an auditor negotiates the performance of dissonant and disjunctive times and spaces, and in which phenomena of presence are produced. It is a process amplified, too, in Hill's looping of the recording to produce a sense that *Viewer*'s subtle movements and activities are continuous and

without resolution and, correspondingly, that there is no specific beginning or end point to the auditor's engagement, even as *Viewer* mirrors
and so marks their looking in time. Implicitly extending the notion of
the 'co-performative' dynamic between word and image that George
Quasha and Charles Stein identify to encompass viewing itself, Hill thus
proposes that:

> Ultimately every word and every moment in a tape (or life for that matter)
> could be performative in and of itself in that sense. I think of La Monte
> Young's saying, 'tuning is a function of time'. Each event enters into an
> evolving relationship with the developing piece, spiralling around and
> folding so that at any moment you might 'begin' again from a different
> place.   [Hill in Quasha and Stein 2000: 257]

While such a construction and experience of time may pose
the question of the relationship between past (recorded) and present
times, so *Viewer* also emphasizes a traversing of virtual and real spaces.
Proposing that a sense of *spatial mobility* is a key effect of video, Hill
thus emphasizes the importance of 'the fractal nature of the medium
– its ability to disseminate an image as something that is not so much
an object but rather something that permeates space . . . and how does
one delimit this illumination' (Hill in Sarrazin 2000: 222). *Viewer*, then,
approaches this delimitation both in its diffusion of the image into the
'real' space of the gallery and its 'subject', which brings the act and experience of 'viewing' under question. Here the auditors of *Viewer* discover
their own act of apprehending mirrored back to them, replayed in the
real time of their watching. As a result, and in its implicit occupation
and mirroring of the present time and space of looking, *Viewer* provokes
a sense of a collocation of acts of viewing, which the auditor at once
stands before yet, *in viewing*, acts out and inhabits. In their documentation of *Viewer*, George Quasha and Charles Stein capture precisely this
sense of displacement, spatial mobility and exchange, recalling that:

> When we came into the room what we happened upon was *the view*. A
> room with a view, *inside*. The view is people looking *out* from where they
> are, in to where we are, here, in the middle of the space. It seems, perplex-
> ingly, that the view itself is viewing – viewing us . . . In an environment that
> is saturated with viewing, at a certain point it's as though the space itself
> views – a topological displacement of agency   [Quasha and Stein 2001: 18]

In these circumstances, Quasha and Stein suggest, the 'performance' of *Viewer* lies in the visitor's awareness and activation of the *space
before* the projection, for '[t]he real "event" is the performative space

itself – a site' (Quasha and Stein 2001: 24). Indeed, it is the emerging awareness of *Viewer*'s operation as a nexus of differential times and spaces, and so of its performative shaping of a process and experience *in time*, that reveals and amplifies the sense of these images' *being before*, their movement, in replay, in and toward a 'presence' to the viewer as an agent of the work. Furthermore, in *Viewer*, this operation is extended by the action and gesture that underpin the design of the work: in the viewing subject's effort to apprehend the other; and in the possibility of *change over time*, amplified in the *particularities* of viewings; in the sense of a social and personal *mobility of view*. Quasha and Stein's narrative account of the encounter continues:

> In *Viewer* the projection of the seventeen figures is very sharply focused (from an optimal distance, which is not close up to the wall). And as one engages this concrete focus, there is a personal charge relative to each of the men as one views it discretely; this is a human focus, a kind of individuation of attention. Then there is the *interactive focus*, by which we mean the phenomenon of focusing on the image of this *other* person in such a way that we ourselves seem to *get focused* . . . This in turn produces a *field focus*, activating the whole of the viewing space, so that the shared sense enlarges

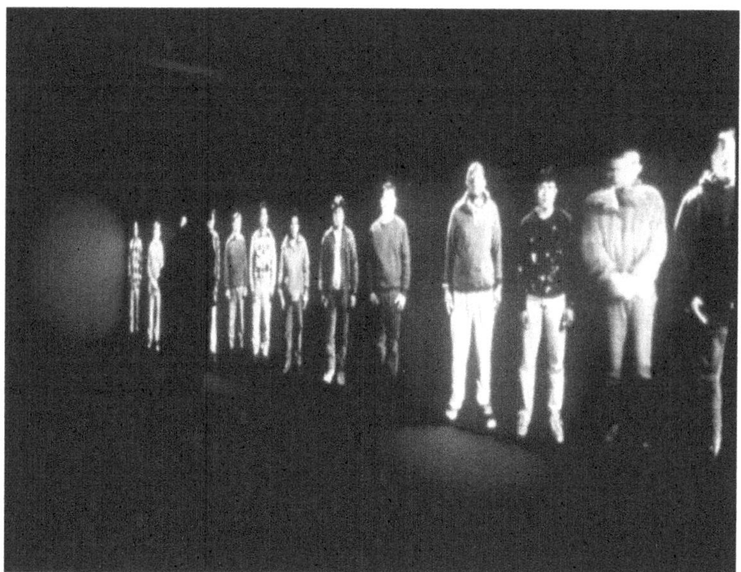

Figure 3.5 Gary Hill, *Viewer* (1996). Installation view. Five-channel video installation. Five video projectors, five-channel synchronizer, five DVD players and five DVDs. Edition of two and one artist's proof

and the other figures come alive in new ways.   [Quasha and Stein 2001: 22, original emphasis]

NICK KAYE What place do considerations of presence have for you within your work?

GARY HILL As much as I might sit around and ponder ideas – maybe using some new technology, method, or material, usually what gets me going is something closer to home, something very near by, perhaps even inconsequential. I might be just holding something in my hand in a strange way, be staring at something and forget what I'm doing and get startled by a sound. The key seems to be being open to what is happening and to take the gifts as they arise. It could even be a single word because I like the way it looks – just getting dumbstruck sometimes is all it takes. Whatever concept I might begin with, it's always tempered with the visceral which seems to have its fingers in presence.

[London, July 2007]

Importantly, too, this operation of *Viewer* across past (represented), present ('real') and future (anticipated) actions also reflects Hill's earlier reflections on the definition and experience of site. Thus, in relation to the single-channel work *Site Recite (a prologue)* (1989), Hill directed attention towards a definition of site as a crossing of tenses and thus in relation to events in time and change, so echoing Hershman's articulation of the experience of site as layered or subject to multiple times or tenses. Where, Hill proposed in his subsequent essay 'Site Re:cite' (1991), 'Site' is '[t]he place where something was, is or is to be located,' *Site Recite* implicitly puns between the enactment and occupation of site in multiple tenses and an act of 'recitation', which recalls, repeats and announces: '*Recite*, from Latin *recitare*, to read out, cite again: *re-*, back, again + *citare*, to set in motion, summon' (Hill 2000a: 301). *Viewer* operates in precisely such a play across sites and actions: in the visitor's recitation of the attempt by Hill's subjects to apprehend; and in the recollection, realization and projection of the gallery as the site for looking. It is *Viewer*'s operation across such differential times and spaces that foregrounds a performative shaping of experience; of a 'being there' defined in the enfolding of the viewer's action over time in the operation of the work, in *tuning*; in their 'completing' of the work, as their act of viewing maps the time of the image.

Significantly, too, this is an experience that corresponds to Hill's understanding of the underlying topology of video itself and its affect on experiences of presence. Contesting video's etymological root of 'seeing from a distance', Hill argues that '[v]ideo's intrinsic principle is feedback. So it's not linear time but a movement that is bound up with thinking – a topology of time that is accessible' (Hill 2000b: 290). Here, Hill sees video's operation as rooted in the experiences of doubling and reflexivity, experiences that inform his process of making work, which, he has noted, 'occurs in a cybernetic or feedback environment with cameras, monitors and signal flow; it's me and this media' (Hill in Lestocart 2000: 234). Indeed, the roots of this approach to the image may be identified with Hill's first experiences of video and his earliest experimentations with mediation, performance and visual feedback.

GARY HILL The first experience I had with video was in Woodstock, New York. Woodstock Community Video, formerly People's Video Theatre, had recently moved up from the city. On a whim I checked it out and the director, Ken Marsh, gave me a quick demonstration of a Sony Portapak. He left me with the system and a monitor to try out, and within about an hour I was asking him if he had another system so I could play back my image on one and record myself live interacting with the 'self' that I had just recorded. Now, this doesn't seem like a big deal, but somehow when you experience a kind of *Doppelganger* of yourself, it disturbs the mind in a peculiar way and one's thoughts are subtly shifted – a different sense of self is being registered. You are sort of in two places at once – in conversation with your 'other' in some way. This is really what video is about, pure and simple. Coincidently I'm rereading – which is an understatement, because it's all about rereading – the Maurice Blanchot book *The One who was Standing Apart from Me*. It's extraordinary in the sense that you get completely lost in the multiple voices of the protagonist – his other and the other of other – all of which could be the same identity or not. Is Blanchot making writing feedback of some kind? It gives me the chills – it's scary in a funny way. It's unfamiliar writing – it creates a very different kind of space – the kind I'm very much committed to. This is where my sense of time is far removed from what passes by while sitting in a movie theatre. This other ground is where I like to think I work from, that I 'throw' from like a potter working the wheel.

NICK KAYE Which seems to raise the question of where you are –

GARY HILL As long as it remains a question it's interesting. Presence, for instance – is it really possible to be present? It seems like the only way one could be completely present is if you were unaware of the self. As soon as we are aware of space, time, or being via thinking, speaking, or moving from point A to point B, so to speak, any idea of hyper-presence vanishes. Or perhaps it's always already happening all at once, in which case presence is moot. There's a beautiful short story by Spencer Holst I once used in the performance piece *Splayed Mind Out* that is surely close to a moment of presence if there ever was one. It reads: 'Up in heaven the curtains fluttered, the curtains fluttered, and the Mona Lisa entered at one end of a small hall, which was hung with many veils. Up in heaven the curtains fluttered, fluttered, fluttered, and the Buddha entered the hall at the other end. They smiled.'

[London, July 2007]

Such a 'topology of time', defined in relation to video feedback, reflects on structures of experience that surpass or delimit the video image, an effect produced in video's asymmetrical mirroring of the spaces and actions it mediates and reproduces. Indeed, even in the simplest live mediation, for example in a 'real time' visual feedback to a protagonist performing to camera, the video monitor's 'mirroring' of actions performed to camera will diverge radically from a mirror's tendency to unify action, reflection and image. The artist Dan Graham, whose series of early and influential video feedback installations created in 1974 incorporated systems in which viewers encountered their own image in feedback, thus points out that:

> a video image on a monitor does not shift in perspective with a viewer's shift in position . . . A video monitor's projected image of a spectator observing it, depends on the spectator's relation with the camera, but not his relation to the monitor.   [Graham 1979: 67]

In this process, the experience of *being before* 'live' video feedback produces a disjunctive relationship between time and image. In this 'mirroring' function, the 'performer' sees their image dislocated by the relationship of camera to monitor, yet the *time* of this image, its *affect*, its *feedback*, presses into the present tense of action, so enfolding the protagonist performing to camera. In turn, Hill's early experiments complicated this 'mirroring' of the self – and interrogation of self-presence – in a layering in mediation, recording and playback, so further dislocating the real-time or recorded image from his experience before it. It is in this context that Hill's work may be seen as overtly epistemological from its outset: as posing the question of what can be *known* through the image, of how the experience *of* the image, or of *being before* the image, might exceed or call into question its absences or erasures.

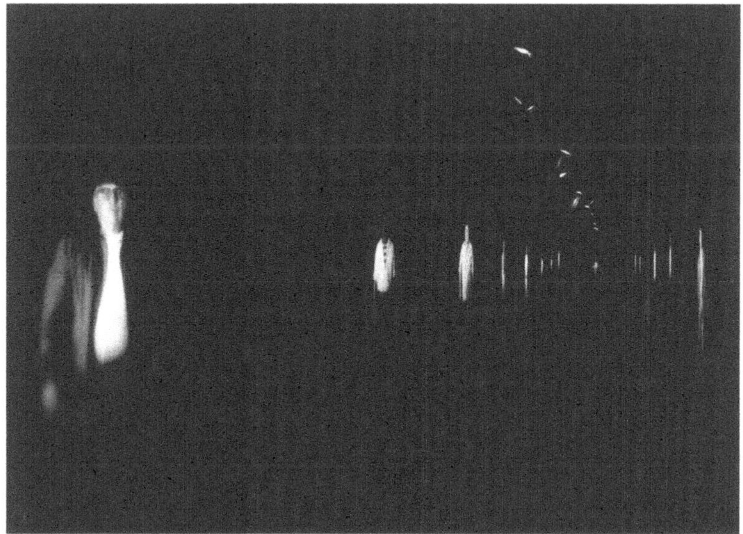

Figure 3.6 Gary Hill, *Tall Ships* (1992). Sixteen-channel video installation, silent. Sixteen modified 4 in. black-and-white video monitors (cathode ray tubes removed from chassis) with projection lenses, sixteen adjustable metal brackets, pressure-sensitive switch mats, black or dark grey carpet, computer with sixteen RS-232 control ports and controlling software written in DOS, sixteen laserdisc players and sixteen laser discs (black-and-white; silent). Dimensions of corridor: 10 ft high × 10 ft wide × 90 ft long (3 m × 3 m× 27 m). Edition of two and one artist's proof

In the projective installations, then, Hill stages conditions for 'feedback', seeking to enfold the viewer in their performative engagement with the medium's 'doubled' spaces and times; implicating them in the articulation of this unfolding 'presence' – this delimiting of the image – in strongly phenomenological confrontations and encounters with the 'absences' and displacements in which the image functions. It is an extension beyond the space and import of the image evident in Hill's very first projective works. Thus, for *Tall Ships* (1992), which, with *HanD HearD* (1995–96), Hill associates with this enfolding of the viewer and approach to projection and presence, the projected image is further delimited through a gesture towards direct interaction. Noting that this piece 'has to do with making something that is already immaterial lose its identity even further; watch it sprawl over things and dissipate into space', such that '[l]ight, image, and representation become a singular ontological presence that confronts the viewer' (Hill 2000b: 297), these images provide the only form of light within the installation, provoking an intense focus on the possibility of encounter. *Tall Ships* thus begins in a completely dark corridor space, within which projected images of individuals are may appear every 1.5 m, alternating on either side of the corridor walls.

These projections, Hill notes:

> are of (perhaps) typical people of various ethnic origin, age and gender. The images are high-contrast and somewhat blurred due to the nature of the projection system and the acute angle of projection . . . There is no border of light defining the frame of the image; it is the figure itself that gives off the light and is seen directly on the wall. The existence of these figures is ephemeral, fleeting and silent, yet a determined presence illuminates the space . . . The figures, standing or seated and ranging from one to two feet high, first appear in the distance at about eye level. As viewers walk through the space, hidden electronic switches are tripped and the people/ projections approach the viewer until they reach approximately life size. They remain in the foreground, slightly wavering, until the viewer(s) leave the immediate area.   [Hill 2002: 161]

Comprising of sixteen images, each independently interactive, *Tall Ships* produces a constantly varying set of approaches, confrontations and withdrawals. Here, interaction, and the promise of a meeting or encounter, acts as a delimiting of the illuminated image – a stepping outside or beyond 'the medium'. Yet, even as this installation hinges on this promise and possibility, the charge of these various approaches is left unresolved as the figures wait and waver, only to retreat from the promise of contact or exchange. Quasha and Stein recall that this work produces 'a particular state of psychological engagement in which we are going to meet – but don't. This is a state of apparent incompletion. I reach out but there is no one there to touch. I'm left with a projecting energy and no resting place' (Quasha and Stein 1997b: 22). In this way *Tall Ships* amplifies the viewer's role as receiver of an act yet to be completed, positioning them as in mediation between the reception of a past (represented) action and its future completion, but through a gesture which cannot be fulfilled or expended. For Hill, presence, here, is evidently linked to the action and speech that is to come, as he notes, 'I think that the silence in *Tall Ships* is more active – it feels present, in a way' (Hill in Quasha and Stein 1997b: 50).

In contrast, the stillness of *HanD HearD* invites an anticipation of the future act or event, to provoke the viewer's awareness of their occupation of a space and time *before* and *projection toward*. Consisting of five wall-size colour video projections, in this installation:

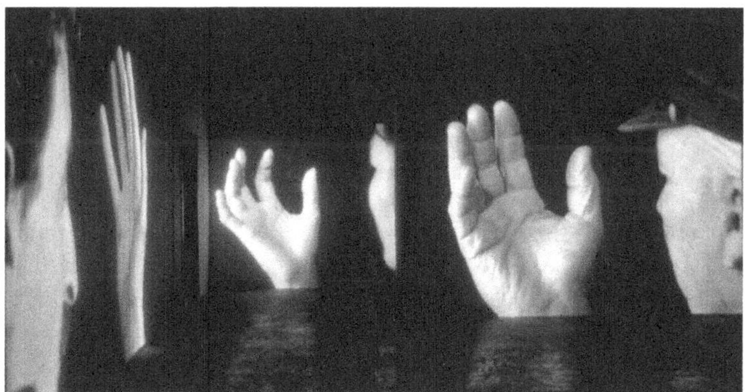

Figure 3.7 Gary Hill, *HanD HearD* (1995–96). Five-channel video installation, silent. Five video projectors, five DVD players and five DVDs (colour; silent). Dimensions variable; projections approx. 9 ft high × 12 ft wide (2.7 m × 3.7 m) each. Edition of two and one artist's proof

> All projections are of a fixed camera angle somewhere between a profile and over-the-shoulder view showing a person in a heightened state of reflexivity gazing at one of their hands. The attention can be felt throughout the room. The hand is held up out of its identity as primary tool/extension of the body. At times it looks to be like an autonomous living totem … At other times it feels like another's hand held up for inspection. The heads and hands loom over the viewer like statues of some kind. Every once in a while a figure's head turns as if to acknowledge the viewer. 'Nothing' is happening but something seems as if it's getting ready to happen. One wants to look at one's own hand or at least imagine doing so.   [Hill 2002: 195]

Indeed, in this series of projective works as a whole, the mediation of actions across tenses and times in silence forms another extension of Hill's interest in the emergence and variability of meaning and in whose anticipation presence is emergent. In his approach to language, Hill has noted, 'I want to suspend the either/or relation of sense and nonsense; see what happens inside the experience of language, as meaning is taking root or uprooted' (Hill 2000b: 291). Thus the silence of the projective installations is offered as an active state, a pause, a moment *in anticipation* of speech and sense, and which *Tall Ships* and *HanD HearD* specifically amplify. It is a moment, too, analogous to that which performance theorists such as Jon Erickson have associated with the theatrical realization of presence. Erickson proposes that:

> Presence has an inverse relationship to language. Presence seems to be most evident in silence, since it resists the disembodying proclivities of

> discourse. One is holding back the articulate meaning that the audience is
> expecting. Presence of the body is stronger when linguistic de-sublimation
> is absent; more precisely, not absent, but not yet manifested.   [Erickson
> 1998: 63]

In Hill's work, this silence and anticipation of future action amplifies the
sense of these works' temporal and spatial 'mobility': their performativity, their operation across past, present and future tenses and actions.
Here, too, lies these works' invitation to the auditor to project their
action forward, to invest in the future completion and emergent 'presence' of the work, to invest in the 'tuning' in time in which these works'
'presence' is presaged and performed.

This notion of the emergent experience of presence discovered in an
encounter with the work's functioning in time draws also, in Hill's work,
on Martin Heidegger's notion of 'neighboring nearness' (Heidegger
1971: 103), a link towards which Hill himself has directed attention,
noting that '"tuning is a function in time" . . . resonates with Heidegger's
notion of living in time or being face to face' (Hill in Lestocart 2000:
222). Set out in Heidegger's series of lectures *The Nature of Language*,
published in 1959, these concepts describe an emergence of presence in
an investment in and nearness to 'otherness'; a relationship mirrored in
these installations' provocation of the auditor's awareness of their position *before* an image whose articulation of time and space they come to
inhabit. Indeed, in this regard, Hill has suggested that *Tall Ships* trans-
poses the experience of feedback toward an engagement and encounter
with 'the other'. In his contemporaneous documentation of *Tall Ships*,
Hill thus noted that:

> I'm finding myself once again engaging the possibilities of feedback inher-
> ent in electronic media, however, more directly having to do with people.
> There is a profound difference here that has to do with a kind of presence
> which enfolds a real time mediation of viewer, viewed, signifier, signified
> that are continually shifting positions.   [Hill in Quasha and Stein 1997b:
> 51]

The relationship of otherness, Heidegger proposes, arises in 'neighborhood', meaning 'dwelling in nearness' (Heidegger 1971: 93), an
encounter defined, implicitly, in a co-performance of identification,
association and difference. Heidegger notes that:

> Neighborhood, then, is a relation resulting from the fact that the one settles
> face to face with the other. Accordingly, the phrase of the neighborhood
> of poetry and thinking means that the two dwell face to face with each

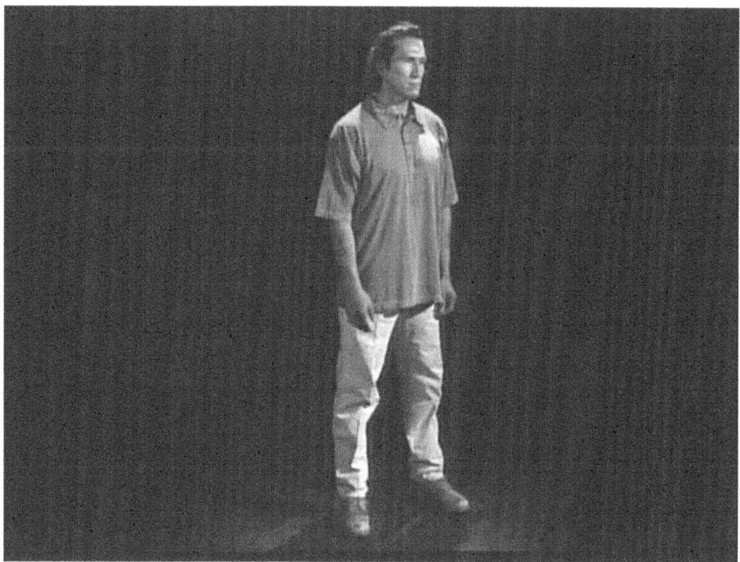

Figure 3.8 Gary Hill, *Standing Apart* (1996). Details. Two-channel video installation. Two video projectors, two laser-disc players and discs, and two-channel synchronizer. Edition of two and one artist's proof

> other, that the one has settled facing the other, has drawn into the other's nearness. [Heidegger 1971: 82]

Here, too, Heidegger arrives at a description of 'being' and 'being present' inflected through notions of emergence and relation, and in which 'presence' to and of the other is articulated as process: as an act of persistence. He proposes that:

> [t]he word 'being' now no longer means what something is. We hear 'being' as a verb, as in 'being present' and 'being absent'. 'To be' means to perdure and persist. But this says more than just 'last and abide'. 'It is in being' means 'it persists in its presence', and in its persistence concerns and moves us. [Heidegger 1971: 95]

In Hill's final works in this series of projective installations, an articulation of this emergence of presence in the persistence of the action and an affinity to Heidegger's 'neighboring nearness' (Heidegger 1971: 93) of self to other is brought strongly to the fore. *Standing Apart* (1996) thus approached a further division of the image. Challenging the ability of the viewer to stand apart from 'its' projection, *Standing*

Apart, and its companion installation *Facing Faces* (1996), enmesh the viewer into their time structures while amplifying the doubling, division and absences of the sign. Here, then, Hill presents the viewer with an incongruent mirroring and multiplication of their own looking, as, in approaching *Standing Apart*, the visitor finds themselves standing at the apex of a triangle defined by asymmetrical but seemingly identical projected images, while, for *Facing Faces*, the visitor encounters a doubled portrait of the same figure on monitors installed, similarly, at head height. *Standing Apart*, Hill notes:

> involves two separate (slightly larger than life) colour images of the same man projected on to two separate walls that meet at the corner . . . the effect is that one image seems to gaze out directly at the viewer while, at the same time, the second figure is looking at the first figure. About every two minutes the images switch positions: the second figure now gazes straight out at the viewer, while the first figure gazes at the second. [Gary Hill Studio 2002]

Although mirroring the viewer's viewing, *Standing Apart* introduces a disunity and multiplication into the experience of seeing and being seen. First, the installation articulates the complexity of 'recording', as the 'real time' recording of the figure is played back in the 'real time' of the viewer's looking. In this respect, *Standing Apart* plays on and amplifies a paradox evident in each of the projective installations. Thus, Hill points out, the very meeting with such recordings renders the present time complex, as the encounter 'happens in "the present" but the present has now gained a complexity that quite literally includes the replayed past' (Hill in Quasha and Stein 2000: 258). Here, too, the viewer's awareness of *acting out*, in the 'present tense', 'other' times is further amplified in the projected figures' relationship to each other, as the viewer's act and time of looking is re-enacted in their simultaneous and alternating attention. Here, 'presence' is articulated in the persistence, in the viewer's 'performance', of an action explicitly past; and so in the viewer's 'real time' re-enactment of the time to which this divided image refers. It is an act, too, in which the viewer discovers themselves 'face to face', in 'neighboring nearness' with this image, whose action they come, over time, to inhabit, experience and shadow even in its absolute 'difference'. In these various respects, *Standing Apart* also exemplifies, again, Hill's affinity to Blanchot. Considering the limits of the sign and the image, Blanchot proposes 'the prohibition of the sign as a mode of presence' (Blanchot 1999c: 485). It is precisely such an approach to the sign that is evident in Hill's projective installations.

Indeed, this work begins by amplifying the absences in which its signs and images function; yet, over time, Hill's tactics prohibit the resolution of 'the work' into this loss, into that which is simply marked as past or absent. Instead, in the encounter with these images' operation in time, the 'presence' of the viewer as agent and subject of the work – and of the absent body they find themselves before – is performed in their 'face to face' encounter; in 'neighbouring nearness' between the times and spaces of recording, replay, and enactment; and in their emergent and uncanny sense of acting out a *being before* the image they encounter. Here, the experience of presence is emergent in the investment in the signs of the other and in the modulation of one's own experience of 'presence' in this dynamic relationship: 'presence' is thus realized in process and persists in uncertainty, in relation, and so in a questioning or disturbance of one's own ground. It is in this context that Hill can be seen as approaching video's performativity as an engine of dissonance; as a medium that engages with the relationship between self and other by at once provoking and disturbing phenomena of presence. Of *Viewer*, Quasha and Stein note:

> No one's fooled when a video projector casts the image of a person upon the wall – and yet it has its own reality, its own *intensity of view*. What shows up in this hypersensualized space is how these quite simple and ordinary people, whose living and breathing images are projected on the wall, are in fact quite powerful presences – unavoidably engaging and almost eerily present presences. Yet they are merely projections. [Quasha and Stein 1997a: 19, original emphasis]

Presence and doubling

Integral to Hill's engagement with practices and experiences of presence is the notion of the artwork as a non-identical mirror, rooted in and reflecting processes of feedback. It is an aspect of Hill's work brought to the fore in these projective installations' capacity to simultaneously mirror and enfold their auditor's *being before*, at the root of which is an experience of 'neighbouring nearness', a sense in which the viewer invests in and defines their own 'presence' in relation to the 'otherness' of the projected image; its place simultaneously *in* and *before* their experience. In this way, too, Hill's work frequently begins and ends in the experience and encounter with the body, as he notes that:

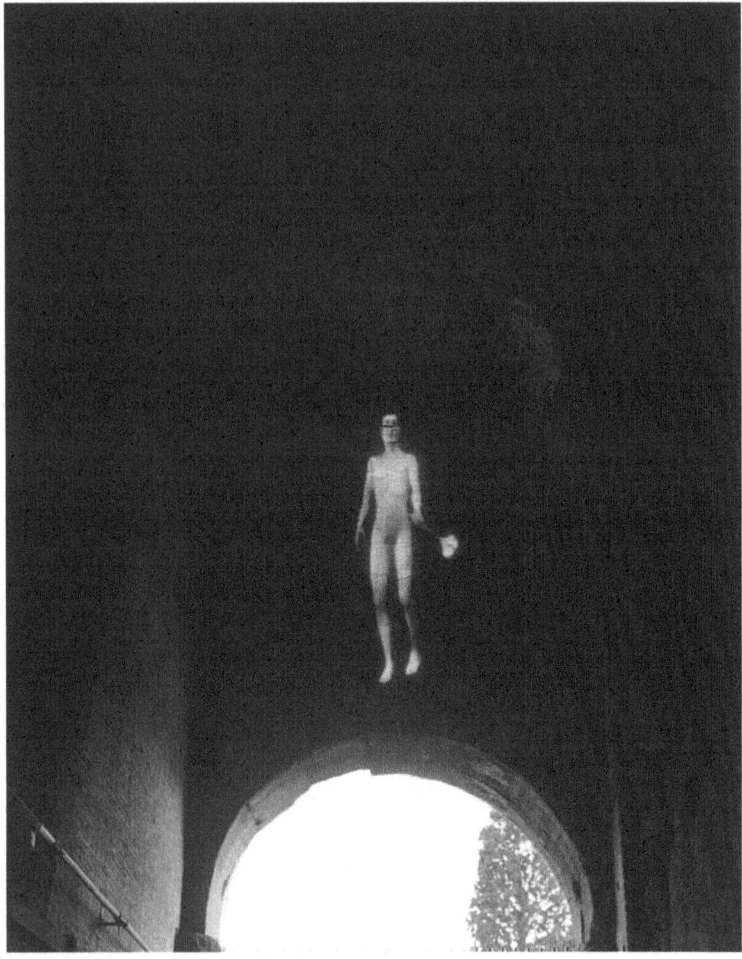

Figure 3.9 Gary Hill, *Resounding Arches/Archi risonanti* (2005). Site-specific installation with multiple projections and sound, for the Coliseum and Temple of Venus and Rome, Rome, Italy

The body for me is a kind of built in referent. It's important to realize that most of the time I work with my own body. It is close at hand, intimate and at different times annoyingly and pleasurably real. When you turn the camera and ideas back on to yourself it's a way of not working with the subjective visuals of images because although you see your own body displayed you feel it being seen. It is always mediated by the skin that separates you from the image.   [Hill in Sarrazin 2000: 223]

This notion of a phenomenological mirroring or doubling and its link to the trace and presence of the body is invested, too, in Hill's more recent approaches to site. Thus the figures enacting Hill's large scale site-specific installation *Resounding Arches/Archi risonanti* (2005) whose title itself plays on mirroring, doubling and difference, each announce their appearance in the arches of the Coliseum in Rome in their 'playing' of a single note that comes to pervade and resonate around this ancient site's spaces. As the note unfurls, so these androgynous simulated images, rendered from motion capture of Hill's 'original' enactment, step forward, unfurling instruments from and around their bodies, playing the sound, heralding an arrival. In this action Hill suggests, 'the figures declare their presence through a projection of sound as an extension of their being. They are bringing forth what is primary; what is their "firstness"' (Hill in Coen 2005: 148). Intertwining Hill's concerns for emergence, the unfolding of sound, time and action, and a traversal of past, present and future tenses, *Resounding Arches/Archi risonanti* aims, Giuliana Stella suggests, to 'simultaneously engender a present and visceral connection to history and future as if they ebb and flow from the same place' (Stella 2005: 12). In this context, for the visitor, the occurrence of this work is announced and shaped by the unfurling of the sound that pervades the ruin, and secondarily by the chance encounter with the unfurling of the image of the figure in one of many alcoves. It is a disturbance of the site in a sound resonant with the memory of a spectacle-to-come, while the figures' emergence in daylight is ephemeral, dispersed and elusive. Hill suggests that in this place

> if a viewer barely perceives one of the figures, with the multiple sound sources it's possible to begin to imagine these beings in a state of becoming . . . I'm trying to create a sense that something is coming – an event is approaching. Kind of getting the space prepared for activation.   [Hill in Coen 2005: 148]

Here, in the event, sound ghosts the ruined space, marking the dispersal of this work's visual elements while pervading the visitor's experience of the site in a shaping of sound 'so thick and sculptural that one will have the feeling of being inside the sound, while 'the projected figures become just points of departure for the "viewer"' (Hill in Coen 2005: 144). In this respect, this event exemplifies Hill's deployment of the image as a means of provoking the viewer's sense of the work as a 'point of departure,' as a prompt to experiences that exceed its appearance and import. In this work, specifically, then, this heralding of the site serves to 'engage a "live" audience with a mediated or absent reality' (Hill in Quasha and Stein 2001: 21), invoking an emergent sense of 'presence' that plays between anticipation and memory. Here, too *Resounding Arches/Archi risonanti* foregrounds the 'feedback,' out of which its form emerges and in which its import might exceed the image. In the creation of his work, Hill has emphasized:

> One is not engaged in setting up a scenario to represent something through an image. The outcome, the output, is more a blueprint *after the fact* of what occurred in the feedback situation . . . the whole thing has to do with keeping you in an agitated state or looking and being in a certain place and becoming engaged with what it means . . . An excited feedback situation.   [Hill in Quasha and Stein 2000: 266, original emphasis]

In Hill's work, phenomena of 'presence' are approached in the performance of dissonant relationships between times and places, in emergent experiences and actions, and in persistence; 'presence', in this work, is not a state, but invested in action emergent in time. Here, too, Hill's forms and tactics stand in contrast to Hershman's articulation of a network of traces. Yet in both Hershman and Hill's work, articulations of presence are produced in counter-intuitive means and in uncanny returns; in processes incorporating movement and transition. In Hill's work, too, presence operates in another form of doubling, in process, in the *dynamic* of 'being before' rather than in the occupation of the unique place or suppression of mobility, deferral or movement. In this sense, in both artists' work, it is in the slips and moves integral to difference, division and otherness, and in the dynamics of proximity and distance, that presence is emergent. In this context, too, Hill's work implicitly provides a position from which to examine the production of phenomena of presence in technologies that emphatically emphasize the *distance* intrinsic in mediation. In this work, exemplified in the artist Paul Sermon's use of telepresence, an emphasis on process gives way to a fragmentation and multiplication of place and position produced in 'real time' mediations of actions and interactions between distinct and defined locations. Here, too, however, the displacements and dynamics of mediated exchanges and approaches become themselves engines for phenomena of presence.

4

distance Paul Sermon

Paul Sermon is an interactive media artist known internationally for his experimental works utilising telepresence. Technically, Sermon's installations combine teleconferencing facilities (cameras, video mixers and projectors) with chroma-keying technologies to enable remote participants to be framed within the same screen image and interact with each other. Within these environments, potential participants soon become 'actors', engaging in conscious behaviours that explore their proximity and even intimacy with other remote participants, so engendering a sense of co-presence in a condition of physical distance; a sense of 'telepresence', or presence at a distance. This chapter combines an analysis of Sermon's principal works – *Telematic Dreaming* (1992), *Telematic Vision* (1993) and *The Tables Turned* (1997) – with a detailed examination of the implications of *Headroom* (2006), a site-specific telepresence installation developed as part of a Taiwan Visiting Arts Fellowship funded by a joint initiative between Visiting Arts, the Council for Cultural Affairs Taiwan, British Council Taiwan and Arts Council England. Explored here in dialogue with extracts from Sermon's correspondence from Taipei, in which he recorded the processes of the making of this artwork, the design and functioning of *Headroom* articulates and exemplifies the overlapping and multiplication of the subject-participant's spaces and positions through which, in these performative telepresence works, distance and difference become instrumental in the construction and amplification of experiences of presence.

Defining telepresence

When, as Marvin Minsky suggests, tele-operation systems are used in 'remote object-manipulation applications' we talk of telepresence (Minsky in Campanella 2000: 27). Some scholars, however, simply refer to telepresence as a 'technology for a person to be present *in some form in a distant place*' (Wilson 2002: 526, original emphasis). This suggests that telephone, video-conferencing and e-mail could represent forms of telepresence. Other definitions of telepresence imply the ability to perform a distant action, through, for instance, robotics. Stephen Wilson notes how telesurgery or tele-exploration of other planets are examples of this strand of telepresence and stresses that it is not only the ability to perceive an environment but the 'ability to act' within it that distinguishes it from other forms of telecommunication (Wilson 2002: 527). In fact, some scholars see the fundamental purpose of a telepresence system as the extension of an operator's sensory-motor facilities and problem-solving abilities to a remote environment. This leads to understandings of telepresence 'as a human/machine system' in which a participant or operator receives 'sufficient information about the tele-operator and the task environment, displayed in a sufficiently natural way, that the operator feels physically present at the remote site' (Rosenberg in Wilson 2002: 527).

The impulse toward the integration of these features and experiences into artworks is evident in the earliest forms of installation and performance incorporating electronic telecommunications technologies. One of the earliest of such experiments with telecommunication was Allan Kaprow's *Hello* (1969), a 'multi-site happening' that extended Kaprow's earlier 'happenings for performers only' that were frequently distributed across multiple sites and extended in time. *Hello* thus 'used the facilities of WGBH-TV in Boston to link four locations in the Boston area: a hospital, an educational videotape library, the Boston airport and MIT' (Salz 2001: 73). Another such departure took place in 1977 when the artist Douglas Davis created a live telecast, which was transmitted via satellite to over thirty countries. This concluded with Davis' *The Last Nine Minutes* (1977) in which the artist 'tried to break through the TV screen and reach the other performers' (Popper 1993: 137). The same year Kit Galloway and Sherrie Rabinowitz of Mobile Image produced the *Satellite Arts Project* (1977) in which several groups of dancers interacted with each other from different and distant sites creating 'a performance space with no geographic boundaries' (Galloway and Rabinowitz in Salz 2001: 73). Only three years later, the artists realized the project *Hole in Space* (1980), which was enabled by a satellite link between New York and Los Angeles. Here a number of video cameras and displays were installed in a department store in Los Angeles and the Lincoln Center in New York 'so that the public could communicate by image and voice'. As there had been no advance publicity – and on the occasion of the work no signs or instructions for the understanding or making of the piece available at either site – *Hole in Space* was 'simply discovered by passers-by who were suddenly confronted by images on the screen. The crowds drawn into this "hole" in space/time were able to communicate with the opposite group in the other city with less inhibition, because neither group could see itself' (Popper 1993: 136–7).

Subsequent engagements with telecommunications and telepresence produced works and events on a global scale, including Robert Adrian X's *Die Welt in 24 Stunden* (*The World in 24 Hours*, 1982) in which artists from sixteen different cities communicated with each other and exchanged art on the net (Baumgärtel 2001a: 156) and Nam June Paik's mid-1980s series of performances using a television satellite, including *Good Morning Mr. Orwell* (1984), which simultaneously connected New York, Paris and New Delhi and saw the participation of artists including Laurie Anderson, Allen Ginsberg, Joseph Beuys and John Cage. Paik's *Bye Bye Kipling* (1987) connected New York, Seoul and Tokyo and included Lou Reed, Keith Haring and Philip Glass, among other artists, while *Wrap Around the World* (1988), organized with the Olympic Games in Korea, featured David Bowie and Merce Cunningham (Baumgärtel 2001b: 37–8). All these experiments shared the attempt to connect distant participants and incorporated the production of new types of spaces that at once included and superseded the localities from which participants were broadcasting. More recently, Ken Goldberg's *The Telegarden* (1995) used telecommunication technologies to create a portable garden, located at the Ars Electronica Centre at Linz, which incorporated an industrial robotic arm controlled by the web that allowed remote participants to plant seeds and water the plants created in the garden. Extending this, telepresence work by Ed Bennet and Eduardo Kac in the series *Ornitorrinco* (1989–96) brought together aspects of robotics, telecommunications and interactivity (Kac 2002) to produce multiple spaces and perspectives occupied simultaneously by its participants. *Ornitorinco in Eden* (1994) thus not only connected the distant locations of Seattle, Chicago and Lexington but allowed participants to share the robotic body of 'Ornitorrinco,' which became 'a substitute-body shared and "inhabited" by the participating public' (Bureaud 2000: 8). Similar experimentation between human, animal and non-human participants was at the heart of Kac's *Rara Avis* (1996) in which a telerobotic bird machine was enclosed in a gallery aviary with real birds. Here, visitors to the work could assume the perspective of the bird machine by using the internet or data glasses and observe themselves, or the other real birds in the aviary, from the birds' point of view (Stocker 2000: 82). Remote participants could also use their own microphones to trigger the birds' vocal apparatus, hence affecting the other birds in the aviary such that '[n]etwork ecology and local ecology mutually affected one another' (Kac 2000: 187). As *The Telegarden* and *Rara Avis* suggest, these forms of telecommunication and telepresence arts not only connected distant locations but also allowed direct interaction between them, thus creating a new hybrid ecology constituted by both physical and virtual locations.

As these developments suggest, and as Minsky points out, with regard to presence telepresence induces a 'feeling that you are actually "there" at the remote site of operation' (Minsky 1980: 120). This is distinct from conventional understandings of the functioning of presence within immersive virtual reality environments, such as CAVE, which, for the participant, is directed toward 'feeling like you are present in the environment generated by the computer' (Minsky 1980: 120). Thus whereas through virtual reality presence is achieved *within* a computer simulation, in telepresence artists and scientists have striven to achieve not only 'the illusion of presence at a remote location' (Sheridan 1992a: 120 ff.) but to facilitate actions that will demonstrate the affect that one's presence has had in this location. In this mechanism, as Oliver Grau suggests, telepresence produces, for the participant, an experience of presence in at least three locations at once: '(*a*) in the spatio-temporal location determined by the user's body; (*b*) by means of *teleperception* in the simulated, virtual image space (the point to which attempts in art history have led so far to obtain Virtual Reality), and (*c*) by means of *teleaction* in the place where for example a robot is situated, directed by one's own movement and providing orientation through its sensors' (Grau 2000: 239). Implicit in this definition of telepresence is not only an occupation of multiple sites but also the ability to perceive a telepresent site and act within it. Lev Manovich thus notes that whereas virtual reality provides the subject 'with the illusion of being present in a simulated world' and allows 'the subject to actively change this world', telepresence 'allows the subject to control not just the simulation but reality itself' in that '[t]elepresence provides the ability to manipulate remotely physical reality in real time through its image' (Manovich 2001: 166–7). It follows that not only does telepresence involve the capacity to perceive oneself at a distance and act at a distance, but the subject perceives this act as occurring in 'real time'. It is in fact this spatio-temporal paradox, marked by the experience of 'being' in different spaces *at once*, and the concomitant experience of presence in an amplification of distance and spatial expansion, that constitutes a fundamental feature of this phenomenon. But this is not the only paradoxical aspect of this form of telecommunication. Manovich correctly identifies the level of the image or representation (Manovich 2001: 165) as the site within which this identification operates but then, surprisingly, defines telepresence as a form of 'anti-presence' (Manovich 2001: 167). Likewise, Kac defines telepresence as a 'union of telematics and remote physical action' (Kac 2000: 181) that allows the creation of artworks in which 'immediate perceptual encounters are expanded by a heightened awareness of what is absent, remote' (Kac 2000: 182). This suggests that telepresence not only, as Grau indicates, operates in at least three localities – the site(s) in which the participants(s) are located; the simulated or virtual space; and the place in which the participants' actions come to an effect – but also that these localities operate not only in *addition to* but simultaneously *in negation of* one another, in a spatial dynamic that positions a form of absence as integral to this performance and experience of presence.

Practising telepresence

Paul Sermon has worked with teleconferencing and telematics, and experimented with user-generated narrative, since the mid-1990s. In *Telematic Vision* (1993) two sofas positioned in two different locations were integrated virtually through ISDN telephone links, which transmitted live chroma-key-edited video images through which participants could interact telematically in the virtual space created on the monitor by moving in their own respective environments. Visitors to the work found themselves sitting on a sofa watching a television that was showing them on the screen. In fact, participants could see themselves as another would see them, so that according to Sermon they were able to create 'their own television program by becoming the voyeurs of their own spectacle' (Sermon 2003). Once a participant from the other remote location also sat on their own sofa, the two images were merged and

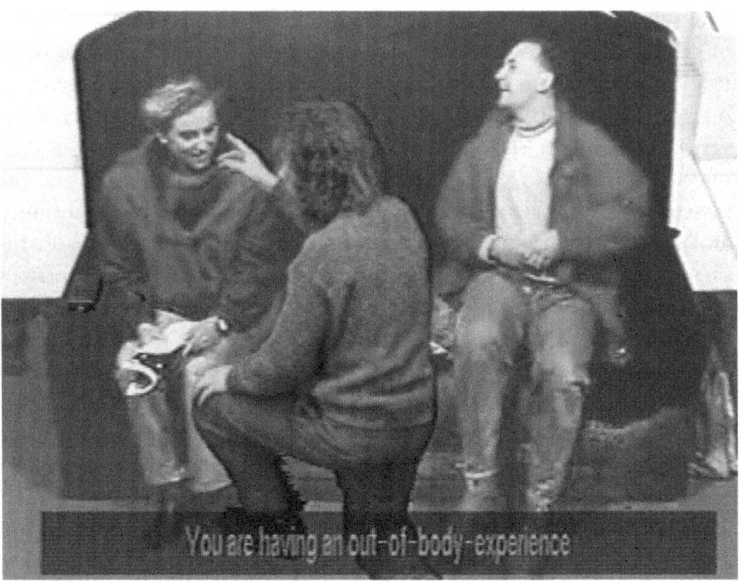

Figure 4.1 Paul Sermon, *Telematic Vision* (1993)

they could see themselves sitting alongside remote participants located elsewhere. Once they were connected on the television set, they could also begin to explore the possibilities of interaction offered by this joint 'telematic vision'.

Similar dynamics were explored in Sermon's later piece *The Tables Turned* (1997), which consisted of a table and a number of chairs set in two different locations. The drawers of each table contained fragments of texts and objects. One or more participants sitting at one table could interact with remote participants sitting at the other table and attempt to create a coherent narrative by putting together the fragments, rec-omposing the last verse of William Wordsworth's ballad 'The Tables Turned' (1798) after which the piece is named (Schwarz and Shaw 1996: 146). Participants could also interact with one another by hiding parts of their own bodies through a glove or mask and see how they could super-impose themselves upon the remote participants. In *The Tables Turned*, Sermon suggests, participants

start to explore the space and understand they are now in complete physical control of a telepresent body that can interact with the other person. The more intimate and sophisticated the interaction becomes, the further the user enters into the telematic space. The division between the remote

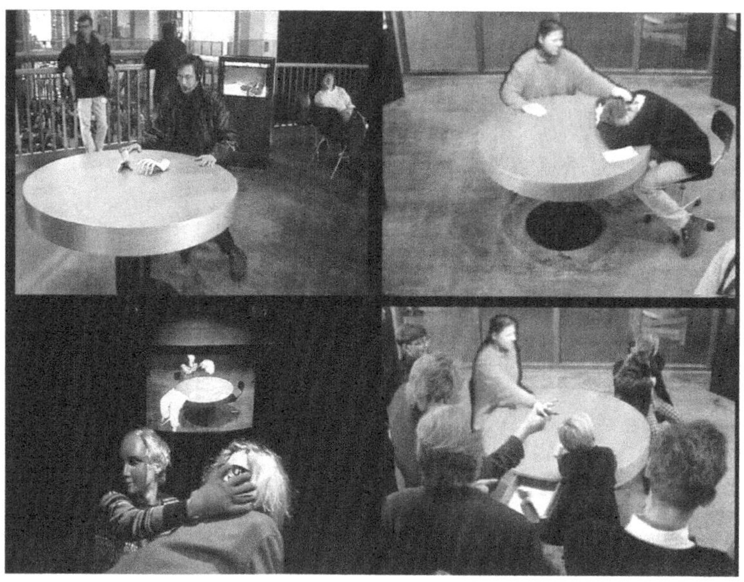

Figure 4.2 Paul Sermon, *The Tables Turned* (1997)

> telepresent body and actual physical body disappears, leaving only one
> body that exists in and between both locations.   [Sermon 2003]

As Manovich notes, one of the distinctive features of telepresence
is that participants experience the paradox of acting in multiple sites
in real time. Paul Virilio proposes that when individuals communicate
in 'real time' through such interactive systems 'the event does not take
place, or rather, it takes place twice. The topic aspect gives way to the tel-
etopic aspect, the unity of time and place is split between the transmission and reception of the signals, both here and there simultaneously'
(Virilio in V2 1997: 339, original emphases). This suggests, in Virilio's
words, that '[t]he *real* and the *represented* are being switched optically
in such a way that the body of the observer is the only thing still present
in his here and now and becomes the last mainstay of someone who is
otherwise immersed in a virtual environment' (Virilio in V2 1997: 339,
original emphases).

In an earlier piece, *Telematic Dreaming* (1992), Sermon had utilized
two beds set in different locations, and taken experimentation with
telepresence further by adding a performed dimension to the piece. On
one bed, in a space inaccessible to the audience, was the artist himself;
on the other bed was the participant. Through a camera, the bed on

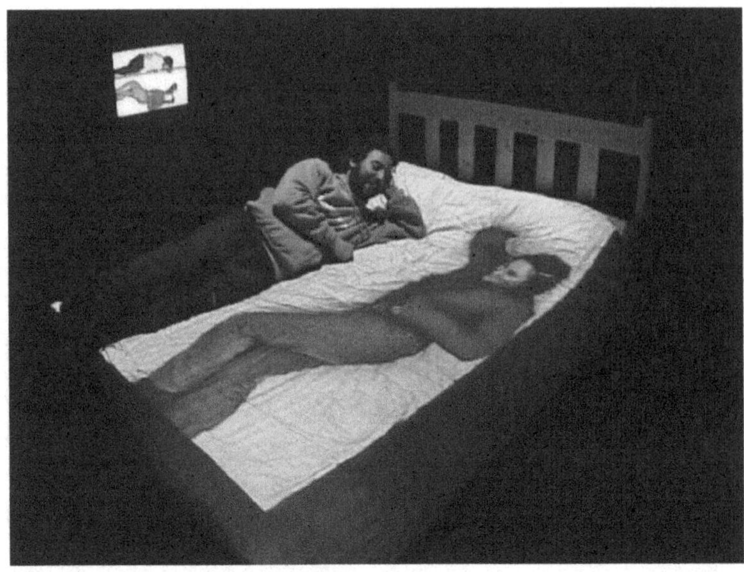

Figure 4.3 Paul Sermon, *Telematic Dreaming* (1992)

which the artist lay was projected on to the bed in the exhibition space such that 'a visitor can lie or sit with "the artist" on this bed and both can react to each other and make contact, at a distance' (Mulder and Post 2000: 75). Susan Kozel describes her response to seeing the piece as follows: '[b]y observing monitors around his bed, he [Sermon] was able to respond to the movements of the person. The effect was astonishing: it was one of contact improvization between an image and a person, between ghost and matter' (Kozel 1994a: 36). Kozel notes that the 'intimacy between the two divergent bodies was compelling' and that the participants often attempted to interact with Sermon by reaching for his hands and that, 'paradoxically, even though he appeared as a projected image he was still able to intimidate' (Kozel 1994a: 36). As pointed out by Sermon, this piece 'deliberately plays with the ambiguous connotations of a bed as a telepresent projection surface' (Sermon in Wilson 2002: 520). Indeed, it is precisely the context of the bed, and the fact that something was 'enacted' on it, that rendered this experiment socially charged. Interestingly then, entering the piece implied a degree of social negotiation. Sermon describes this experience as follows:

> once the viewer takes on the role of the performer they lose contact with the
> audience and discover that the actual performance is taking place within
> the telematic space, and not on the bed or sofa . . . Bringing your self back

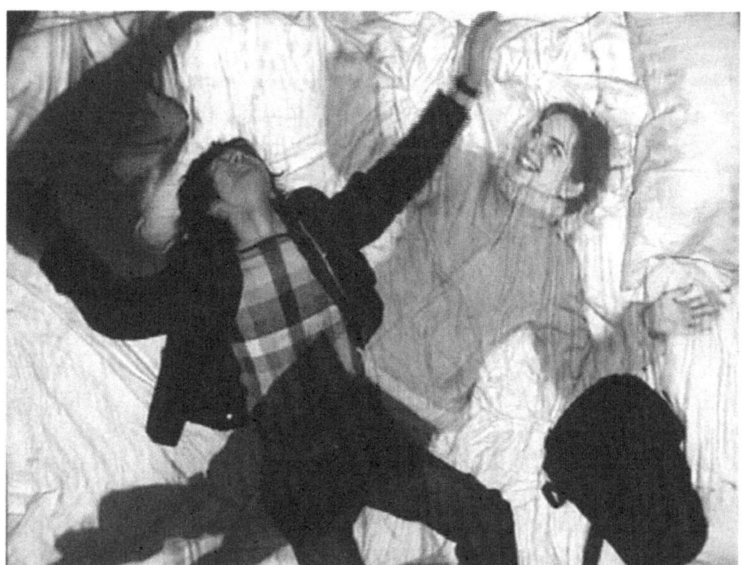

Figure 4.4 Paul Sermon, *Telematic Dreaming* (1992). Detail

to your actual body is as hard as getting your self on to the bed or sofa in the first place, and being able to communicate in the actual space and the telematic space simultaneously is almost impossible. [Sermon in Wilson 2002: 520]

What emerges here is the proposition that the more absorbing or engaging the telematic action, the less likely it is that a participant is able to perceive of themselves as located in both the physical and a virtual world. In *Telematic Dreaming* this experience is further intensified by its performative dimension, which generates audiences that may be located elsewhere. Kozel describes her engagement with the piece as follows:

[t]he bed became my performance space. Our movement occurred in real time, but in a space which was entirely created by technology. I was alone on my bed, moving my arm and legs in physical space as if in some sort of hypnotic ritual dance, yet in virtual space I carried on intense physical improvisation with other unknown bodies. [Kozel 1994b: 12]

Although Kozel claims that her experience was one of 'extending' her body, rather than 'losing or substituting it', she notes that she quickly withdrew from the telematic space when faced with the threatening behaviour of one member of the audience who had a knife and made her feel uncomfortable (Kozel 1994b: 13), or another who elbowed her in the stomach, in response to which she felt physically shaken (Kozel 1994b: 31), or, even more brutally, when two members of the audience assaulted her virtual image, an incident so horrific that Kozel seemingly detached herself from her telepresent persona in what she describes as 'an involuntary act of self-preservation – a primordial reaction in a sophisticated technological context' (Kozel 1994b: 13).

Works such as these suggest that, in order to experience telepresence, participants must displace their 'here and now', or sense of 'present tense' experience, toward the remote location to which they intend to convey an action or, as in the case of Sermon's work, carry out this action. With regard to experiences of presence, these displacements effect a traversal of spaces such that the participant's sense of 'being there' becomes mobile – subject to a spatial displacement in the 'present tense' of action. Phenomena of presence arise here, then, in the flow of action across distinct and simultaneous spaces; in the dynamics between a temporal continuity and the spatial divisions in which this continuity is produced and articulated. As Sermon's work suggests, such experiences of displacement and augmentation *in action* are more or less difficult to achieve through telepresence systems and are contingent not only on a given technology's ability to facilitate 'tele-action' but also on the social encounters performed through it. It follows from this that the phenomena of presence achieved in these spatial traversals will occur gradually and also change and be modulated over time. In this regard, the phenomena produced in telepresence are consistent both with Hill's modulation of the experience of presence where 'tuning is a function of time' and with the tactics by which Hershman engages the visitors to her site-based works in acts of location and participation – in actions that *locate* the visitors in the perceived sites of the work. In Sermon's telepresence installations, however, it is the sense of a 'present tense' action traversing perceived spatial distances and differences from which the experience of presence emerges. It is this process, in turn, that Sermon's site-specific telepresence installation, *Headroom* (2006), both further advanced and elaborated.

In and out of spaces: *Headroom* (2006)

PAUL SERMON I arrived in Taiwan on Tuesday and I'm starting to settle into the studio at Taipei Artists' Village (TAV). I will be here

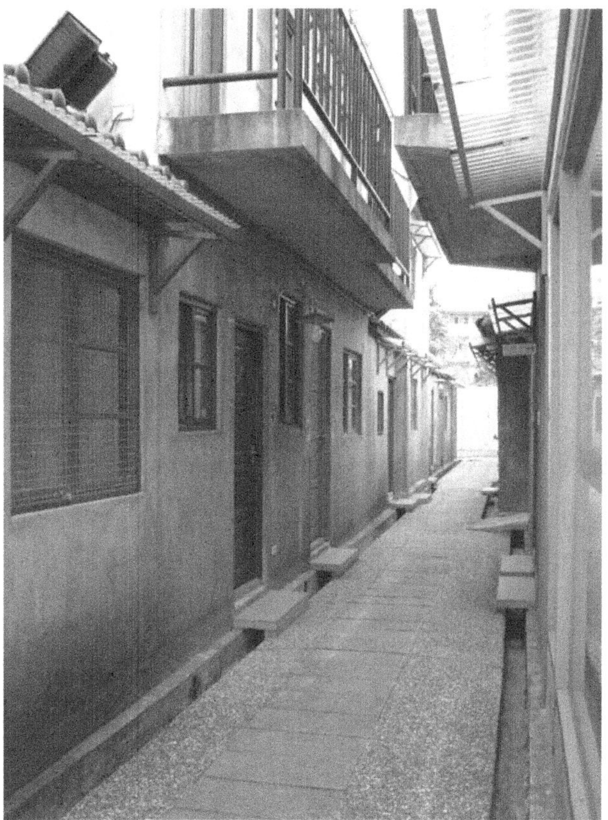

Figure 4.5 Streets in Tapei

until May 6th with the intention of producing a new installation for exhibition at the end of the residency. I have not really anticipated anything as yet and have arrived here with a 'blank canvas' so to say. I am starting to plan and divide up my time, which will begin with some traveling, venue visits and meetings. The TAV team have already been very helpful and I had an initial meeting with the Director Ms Yaohua Su, and have explained that I would prefer to work and exhibit in a site-specific context rather than a classical white box gallery space, as I feel this would bring about a greater conceptual response and reaction to the environment I am working in. This afternoon I am going to visit a housing complex built by Chinese soldiers in 1949 after the retreat of the Japanese occupation. The houses were built without any particular architectural or town planning and sprung up in an ad-hoc organic model. There is now a preservation order on the buildings and a group of Taiwanese artists and curators are involved in this. It is still not 100% sure if the space is available, but it sounds extremely interesting – I will know more very soon.

[E-mail, 2 March 2006]

Headroom (2006) was a site-specific telematic work. It was site-specific because, as can be seen in the extracts from the artist's diary written at the time of the inception of the piece in Taipei, it carefully placed the telepresence installation within a matrix of architectonic and cultural references that expanded the work beyond its immediate architectural and geographic parameters. It was telematic in that it combined two physically separate but almost identical room installations within the same video image via video-conferencing technologies.

PAUL SERMON I visited another site yesterday, located to east of the city in the shadow of the 101 tower and Taipei's world trade centre. Similarly to the last, this is a Taiwan War Veterans housing complex built around 1949, but this site has been renovated and converted

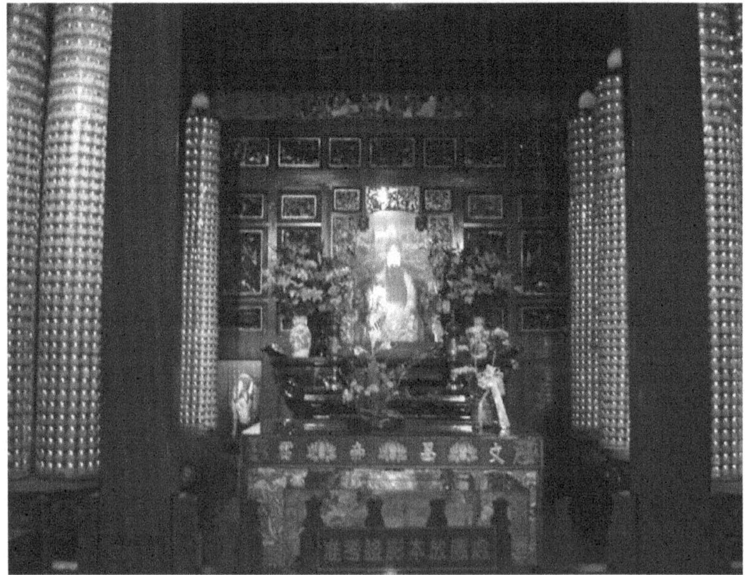

Figure 4.6 A shrine whose colour scheme informed the design of one of the rooms for *Headroom* (2006)

into a museum and exhibition space. It sits on some of the most commercially sought after spaces in the city, but because of its historical importance to the liberation of Taiwan it is a listed building. The back-to-back terraced streets have been knocked through to create entire buildings – three large exhibition halls – which retain the original appearance of the houses on the outside.

The spaces that interested me most were the small facade rooms created by the larger space conversion. These have been separated from the gallery space by interior glass walls and are only accessible from the external outside doors. These two facade rooms are identical in size and could potentially be used to house a connected telepresent installation. It is interesting that the audience in the gallery can observe the participants in the space through the glass, but the people in the facade rooms can not see the other user in the facade room next door. Both rooms are only about 2 meters by 3.5 metres and 2 metres high. The original houses were longer, but no wider and they often halved the height of the rooms to create separate sleeping and living areas. This was also explained in an attached permanent museum exhibit in one of the gallery spaces. This split level of the space interests me, rather like the outside of space that contrasts with the looming 101 tower in the background in stark contrast to the little houses huddled around the base. This can be said for much of life in Taipei and I am interested in the archaeology and history of the space and its interior, the very basic living conditions (bear in mind this is a museum reproduction) that still reflect the way people live today. I am also interested in the places and ways people escape the everyday through the temples/shrines and KTV bars that are also found in many homes.

[E-mail, 7 March 2006]

The sites visited by the artist revealed a stark contrast between inside and outside, private and public, local and global. This dialectical tension constituted an integral mechanism of the piece, which was based on a series of doubles. In fact, *Headroom* consisted of two rooms. Each room was divided in two halves, lower and upper, from which a telepresent space was accessible. Both rooms could be seen from the spectating area located outside the two rooms, which, however, was still located inside the building. The two rooms, which could only be accessed from the outside, had false ceilings, which were lowered to a level of approximately 1.5 m. The cavity space above each room forced visitors to bend down when entering the spaces. The rooms were located within one another. As a consequence, in order to penetrate the telematic space, participants

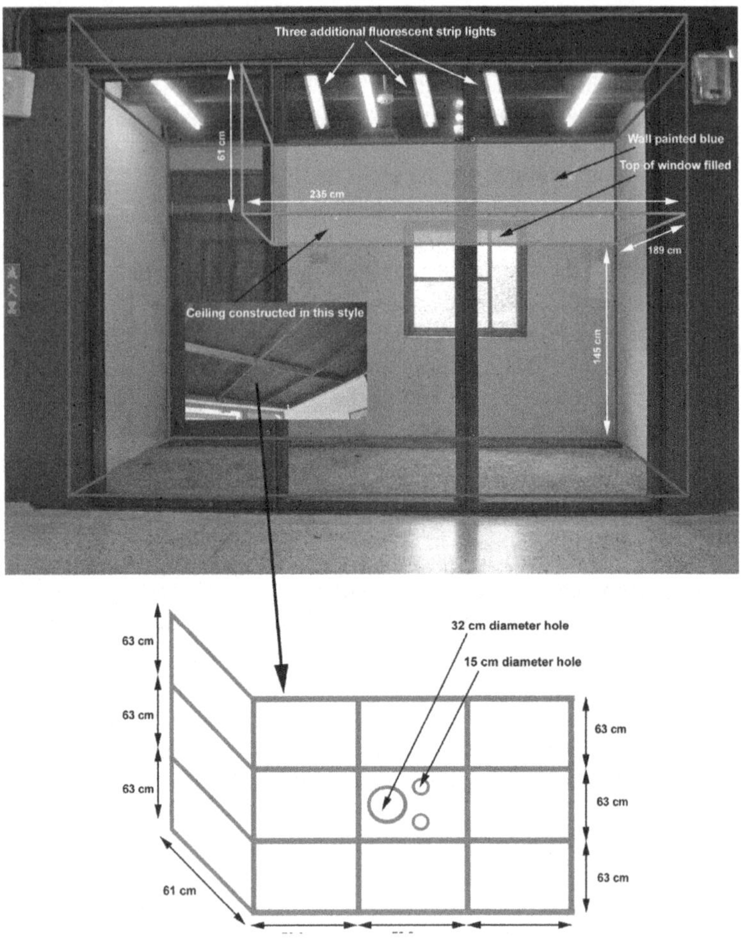

Figure 4.7 Paul Sermon, *Headroom* (2006), the blue room

had to enter each of the two rooms, separately. From each of these rooms participants could then access the two 'headrooms'. And from each of the headrooms they could enter the telematic space where they could interact with other participants. Each space was narrower than the preceding space and led to a closer encounter with a different world.

PAUL SERMON The venue and location (the two rooms with glass walls) have been confirmed. I now have about two weeks to prepare the installation and finish developing the concept. The technical description I have prepared is as follows:

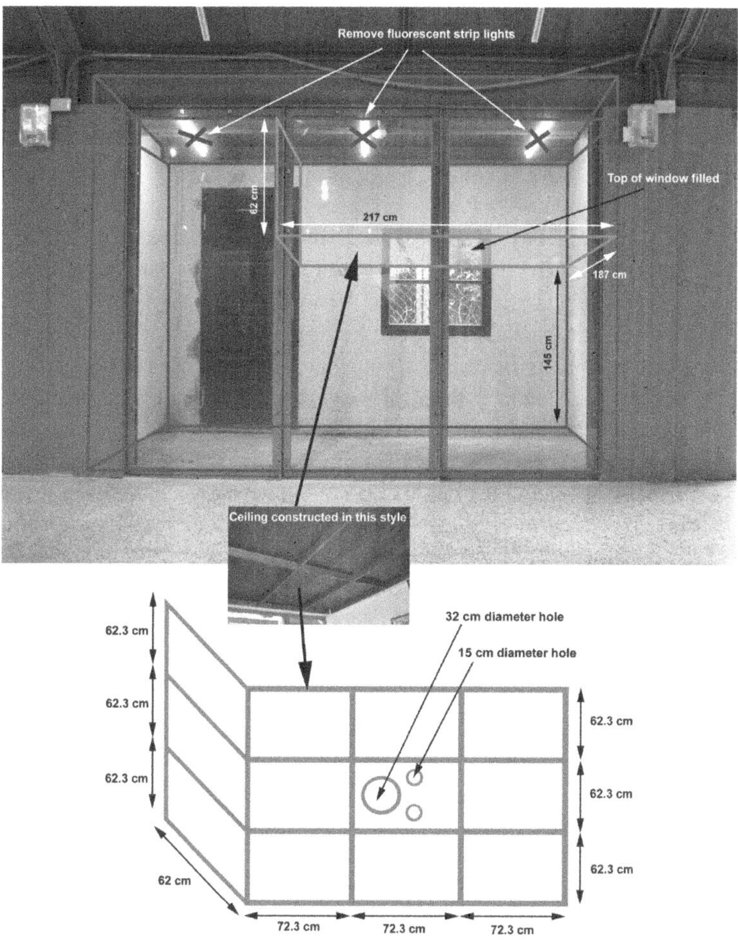

Figure 4.8 Paul Sermon, *Headroom* (2006), the red room

'HEADROOM (working title). This project functions by combining two identical room installations within the same video image via simple videoconference techniques. The two rooms have false ceilings lowered to a level of approximately 1.5 meters. This leaves a cavity space above each room of approximately 1.2 meters high and will also force the gallery visitors to bend down when entering the spaces. However, there will be one location in each room where the viewer will be able to stand up straight and put their head and hands through a hole in the false ceiling and into the cavity space. Although each room will share identical dimensions, each will have a different appearance. One of the rooms will contain drab, used furniture in the lower part with a very lived-in appearance; the cavity space above it will be very dark, with the exception of a video projected image and some small lighting effects. The other room, by contrast, will not contain any furniture in the lower section and will be very bright in the cavity above, including green or blue-lit walls. A video camera in each space will record a live image of the head and arms of each participant and feed it directly to a video chroma-key mixer. One of these head shot images will be recorded against a green or blue background, which will be extracted by the video mixer and replaced by the other live head shot – placing the two heads opposite each other within the same live video image. I am working on the conceptual idea further, but the space below will resemble a very small Taiwanese bed-sit space that will be ambiguous and could also be thought to be an actual temporary shelter for a homeless person – of which there are some in the area. The space above is an escape to an alternative world of intimate proximity with another (telepresent) person. I am working on this space but it will also be an ambiguous mixture of content drawn from my visits to Taipei's temples, shrines, KTV clubs and television, whilst simultaneously being an analogy of an intimate internet encounter.'

[E-mail, 15 March 2006]

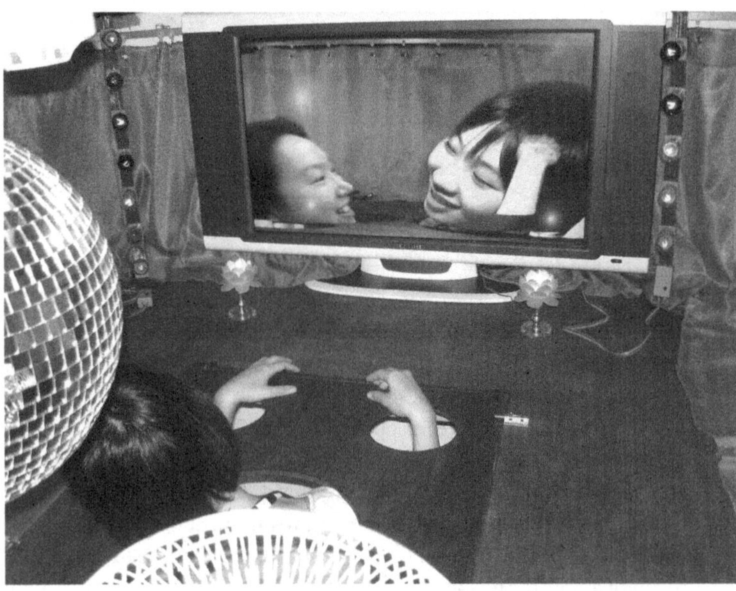

Figure 4.9 Paul Sermon, *Headroom* (2006), the red room head space

The sites brought together in *Headroom* operate in dialectical tension to one another. Two parallel processes occur, one of augmentation or inclusion and one of removal or exclusion. The participant is removed from the concrete location in which they stand and replaced in the headroom, then, further, they are removed from the headroom and relocated within the telematic space. However, participants never entirely leave the spaces from which they have been removed. Thus, while *in* the concrete location, they are also in the headroom and in the telematic space. Moreover, each space is articulated in a set of references: the homeless shelter, the white gallery room, the bar, and the internet. The bedroom recalls the local shelters, while the bed itself – for those who are familiar with Sermon's work – recalls the earlier *Telematic Dreaming*. Here, then, participants are located not only between rooms but also between the intercultural and intermedial references these various spaces create.

The complex dynamics around presence and absence set into motion by this interplay of intimacy, distance and displacement are similar, though not identical, to those of Robert Smithson's series of antinomies named 'Sites/Non-sites' (Smithson 1996: 152–3). Described as 'dialectical propositions that constantly disrupt the premises of traditional sculpture' (Hobbs 1981: 14), Smithson's series of 'Non-sites' of 1968 presented materials that had been collected from designated outdoor sites, deposited in bins constructed after a simple, clean minimalist aesthetic, and set in a gallery beside information characterizing the geographical or geological location from which their materials had been removed. In such configurations, Smithson's 'Non-sites' consisted of two principal components: the absence of the Site or designated location from which the materials incorporated into the 'Non-site' were taken; and the 'Non-site', located in the gallery, which implicitly deferred attention to the Site. As a consequence, in encountering the 'Non-site' and 'its' materials, Smithson suggested, 'what you are really confronted with . . . is the absence of the site . . . a very ponderous, weighty absence' (Lippard and Smithson 1996: 193). In certain works, including *A Nonsite, Franklin New Jersey* (1968), Smithson amplified this paradox by incorporating the suggestion that 'Tours to sites are possible' yet, in a contemporaneous interview, emphasized that the 'Non-site' 'is a map that will take you somewhere, but when you get there you won't really know where you are' (Smithson in Béar and Sharp 1996: 249). Indeed, at the 'Site' of these works, a viewer may encounter materials similar to those re-presented in Smithson's 'Non-site', but would not be able to recognize the actual extraction in which the 'Non-site' is formed. In this dialectic, Smithson concludes, 'the location is held

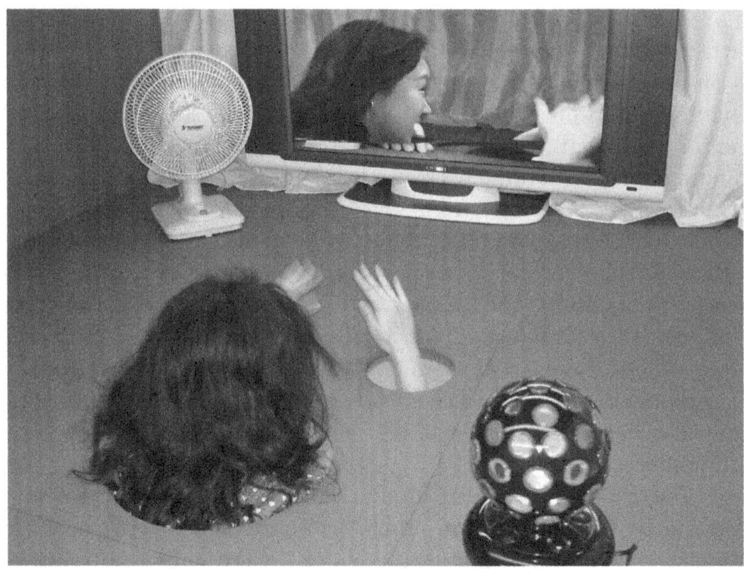

Figure 4.10 Paul Sermon, *Headroom* (2006), the blue room head space

in *suspense*. The nonsite itself tends to cancel out the site. Although it's in the physical world, it's not there,' so resulting in a situation in which '[i]n a sense, the nonsite is in the centre of the system, and the site itself is the fringe or the edge' (Smithson in Béar and Sharp 1996: 249).

Analogously, in *Headroom*, the telepresence site is the centre of the work not only because it brings together the two headrooms, which are located in two physically separate rooms, but because this is where the action or drama takes place. Thus, the 'site itself' points both toward the sites, whether actual or imaginary, from where its materials are taken (for example, the homeless centre) *and* the site through which these become another (the representations in which telepresence takes place). These sites, which at once include and exclude each other, then make it possible for the participant to reposition themselves in an uncanny (*unheimlich*) world in which inside is always also outside, in which the familiar becomes unfamiliar, the private is turned into public, and vice versa.

PAUL SERMON There is a juxtaposition between the location of the space and its surroundings, between the experiences and sights of the city, between the way people live, as in Treasure Hill, and the way people escape through the abundance of neon lights, temples

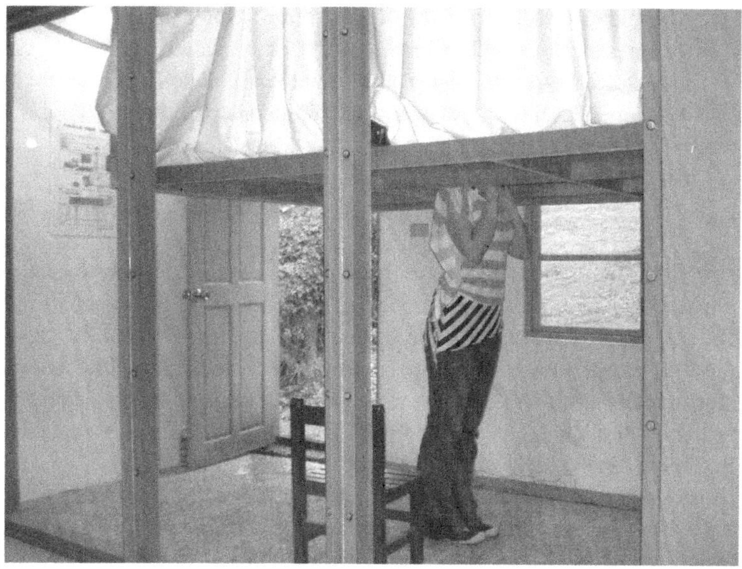

Figure 4.11 Paul Sermon, *Headroom* (2006), the blue room, lower section

and KTV clubs, serving as an analogy between the solitude in the bedroom space below and the divine telepresent aspirations in the Internet space above. This is in part a reference to Roy Ascott's essay, 'Is There Love in the Telematic Embrace?' (1990), where he attempted to attribute to electronic art the potential to embody love. Ascott addressed a common concern amongst critics of electronic art at the time: the fear that technology would overwhelm and dehumanize the arts, a last bastion of humanist values. If it could be shown that telematic art had the potential to embody love, then it would not be a paradox for art to be electronic and simultaneously serve humanist principles.

In an unusual way this exemplifies it too. The reasoning behind the (above) headroom space is as follows. The temples and shrines here are designed and constructed to emanate divine wisdom from the Buddha to the worshipper through an elaborate symmetrical display of surrounding lights and decorations that frame the Buddha, as a portal or gateway (and I mean this in a telematic sense too) to love and happiness. Also reminiscent of Nam June Paik's early Buddha TV installations. This is a reflection of the self in the telepresent space simultaneously as the viewer, as the performer and as the controller of this private and intimate meeting/encounter.

> The television 'screen' is transformed into a stage or a portal to the 'telepresent site' which we can only talk of in relation to the observer and controller/performer of the visual cause and effects that takes place in this shared space, and simultaneously in the minds of the participants as solitary viewers – the experience of being 'here and there' in the telepresent exchange.
>
> [E-mail, 21 March 2006]

In these respects *Headroom* may also be read in relation to earlier constructions of time and space in video and media installations. Indeed, early video installations, such as Nam June Paik's *TV Clock* (1963), comprising twenty-four manipulated black-and-white television screens, each reduced to a single still line of light that in sequence marked the passage of twelve hours (twice), had sought to explicitly juxtapose 'real' (clock), narrative and subjective temporalities. *TV Clock* thus operates in a temporal accumulation of 'clock time' and 'day time' with the viewer's choice and negotiation of *their own time*. Indeed, Paik's influential articulation of a *plurality* of times in his video works, while specifically drawing on the experimental musical practices of the composer John Cage, also more broadly reflected post-Einsteinian models in science and philosophy in their articulation of relational terms and durations that are both particular and unpredictable (Kaye 2007a: 58–64). More specifically, the tendencies of early video art, and the musical practices to which it related, to produce time structures that juxtaposed, layered or embraced different measures of time shared Einstein's rejection of 'absolute time', which, Stephen Kerns reminds us, was grounded in the realization that 'time only existed when a measurement was being made, and those measurements varied according to the relative motion of the two objects involved' (Kern 1983: 19). In relation to this, in activating *Headroom*, a multiplication of spaces occurs, each defined by its own distinct set of spatio-temporal dynamics and in which no one space is able to act as a unifying paradigm. Indeed, in the absence of any overarching or fixed position, there are only unpredictable and relative means to encounter this work *in its differences*. In this way, each room is perceived through another room. The units of time and space are split at the level of both the physical space and the telematic space, and participants are always already in different places: that is, present to themselves in the lower room, the headroom *and* the telematic space. Furthermore, while *Headroom* produces an amplified sense for participants of their presence in the telematic space, from 'outside,' and so for other visitors to the gallery space, it is the presence of the lower body that can be seen. Thus, in *Headroom*, not only the experience, but also

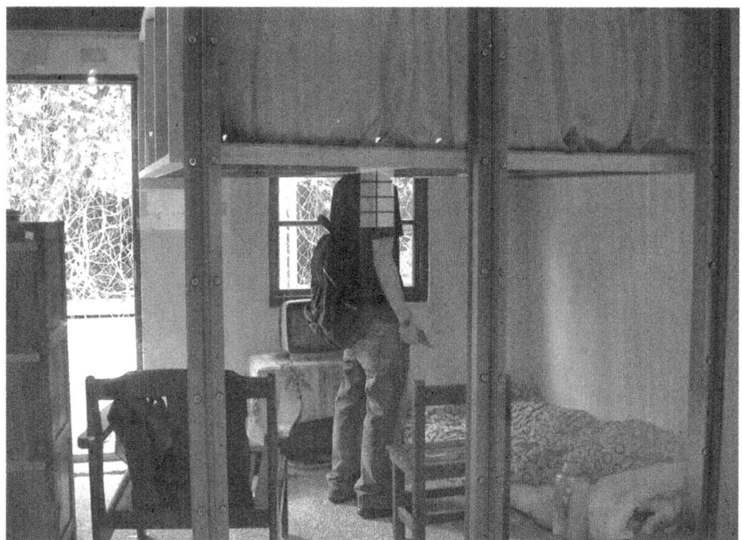

Figure 4.12 Paul Sermon, *Headroom* (2006), the red room, lower section

the spectacle of telepresence is seen in its spatial fragmentation, while the participants' sense of acting in 'real time' is precisely a function of *Headroom*'s displacement toward subjective experiences rather than the articulation of any overarching temporal structure. Each participant to *Headroom* thus acts in multiple spaces in their 'own' time.

PAUL SERMON Only two-thirds of each space will have a lower ceiling level so it will be possible to open and close the doors to the spaces. This will also create a small space where it is possible for the audience to stand and read a statement about the work on the wall before having to bend down to enter the space, I am not intending to limit the amount of people in each space, but it will only be possible for one person at a time to stand up and put their head through the hole in each room. The room above will be decorated entirely in red drapes and curtains. In the other head space the one wall will be painted blue, rather than green, in order to complete the chroma-key compositing process.

[E-mail, 26 March 2006]

Supporting this, there were marked differences between the two rooms. The red room looked, from a distance, like a very theatrical, illusionary space. The blue room, by contrast, appeared to be more functional. The red room was the reconstructed bedroom, thus presenting itself as a theatrical set, a space for drama (action) and spectacle (viewing). The blue room, on the other hand, was more like a gallery space, and constituted a space for reflection. Whereas in the red room there was much to see in the lower part of the room, in the blue room the viewer was able to learn about the installation itself. Combined, the two rooms drew attention toward the different modes of engagement constructed by this particular work, which constituted both a site-specific installation and an interactive telematic experience.

PAUL SERMON The entire head space will not be visible to anyone else except the people inside it so it will be very intriguing to see how the visitors inside the main gallery space interpret and read the movements of the headless body behind the glass wall, and also how these headless bodies behave as they are conscious of being both private (above) and public (below) at the same time. As with much of my work it will only be possible to measure the level of immersiveness and interaction within the piece when we first see how the visiting public start to enter the space.

[E-mail, 28 March 2006]

In *Headroom* it is in the breaking down of oppositions – of inside/ outside, local/global, private/public – and the subsequent experience of their 'own time' of action by its participants – that these participants' sense of their own presence as well as that of their co-performers is amplified. In this aspect, too, *Headroom* extends a disruption of oppositions in which video art/installation and site-specific work have frequently operated. Video art has often played on the 'intimacy' of television viewing, and so the placing and playing of a 'private' realm in a 'public' (gallery) space (Kaye 2007a: 98–123). Site-specific art and performance have frequently operated in a challenging of the limits of work and site, so disrupting the boundaries between 'inside' and 'outside', centre and periphery, as in Smithson's 'Site/Non-sites', cited above. In *Headroom*, where co-performers act out these seemingly dichotomous states, the title itself emphasizes the intimate nature of this overlaying of spaces – the aspect of fantasy, vision or dream – while the public nature of the installation sanctions or appears to give permission or consent to this closeness. In this context, co-performers discover themselves 'coming closer' in a paradoxical distribution and fragmentation of presence – an intimacy produced by a process of distancing and of facing oneself as other, a move and investment which underlies phenomena of self-presence. Here, then, visitors discover themselves occupying and

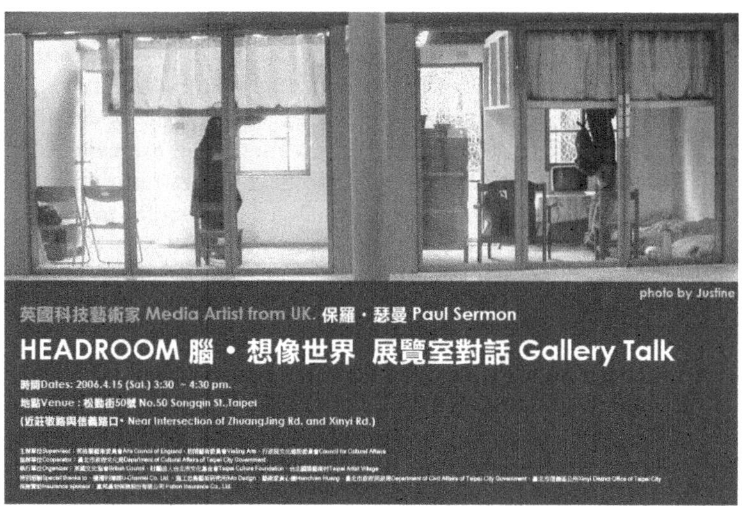

Figure 4.13 Poster for Paul Sermon, *Headroom* (2006), showing both rooms next to each other

acting out their co-performers' private space, while seeing their own 'private' space now performed by their telepresent partner. The spatial rules of public interaction are therefore breached, producing a particular and shocking closeness, and a dialectic between the explicit sense of being here (in the bedroom, for example) and being there (acting out the space of the other), whilst seeing and responding to their co-performers' mirroring of their space, time and action.

PAUL SERMON The two rooms have a very different appearance and function, and I decided to depict this by placing alternative description/information panels on the walls in each room. In the blue (control/technical) room I had a video flow diagram showing how the installation functions and in the red room I used a conceptual statement that outlined the thinking behind the installation and the contrast between the makeshift bedroom below and the intimate headroom above. In many ways the red room represents the primary installation space, whereas the blue room functions as the leading performers control room, always appearing in the dominant foreground position. In the image below the person on the left is in the foreground blue room and the person on the right is in the installation red room background. These images are all taken from initial moments when the participants puts their heads into the space,

sometimes friends, couples or strangers encounter on another. The reactions and subsequent interactions are often in complete contrast to the initial response when entering the solitary bedroom space below. It is important to consider and imagine the body standing in this space when looking at this selection of expressions and emotions in the video stills. I think these images really speak for themselves when we consider the dialectic between the two spaces. I was visiting the gallery yesterday and was asked by a visitor if I am currently sleeping in the bedroom space below during my stay in Taipei. I found this a really interesting observation and was very pleased someone genuinely thought this. I wanted the installation to appear as if somebody really was living here and had actually created this alternative headroom space to escape from the lonely world below. And that this bizarre installation was not created by an artist at all, but was actually something 'ready made' I simply came across.
[E-mail, 17 April 2006]

In these various ways *Headroom* sets in motion a multiplication of the gaps and differences between spaces and times in which telepresence systems function and which, in turn, these systems provoke and engage phenomena of presence. Thus in this installation spatial divisions and differing times are amplified and made explicit – while no one space or position is offered as a unifying paradigm. Observed from 'outside', then, *Headroom* visualizes how, in their immersion into telepresence, its participants may perceive themselves at a distance but remain visibly anchored to the space and time of an external onlooker. Experienced from 'within,' and like other telepresence works, *Headroom* is immersive in so far as it removes the participant from their immediate physical context. Thus, within the 'headspace', participants act in response to the screening of their own present-tense action and response to others. Yet, in effecting this transition from external observer to participant and object of attention, *Headroom* also threatens a fragmentation of this process of immersion itself, even as each visitor is displaced and then displaced again from the 'actual' space in which they are situated and framed. Spatially, this experience suggests processes of 'retention' and 'protention,' as the participant at once engages with a spatial augmentation (the participant is present in more than one location) and a subtraction (the participant feels immersed and so withdrawn from one space and relocated to another). It is a traversal of spatial boundaries also amplified by the uncomfortable closeness of the participant's interaction with their co-performer – their explicit intrusion into personal space. It is in this spatial flow and dynamic too that *Headroom* engages with the expression of the presence of self and other. Here, *Headroom* frames the experience of the self *in action* as that which, in multiple form, appears 'before' or 'in front of' itself, and is caught in the act of it making itself: of acting and reacting in the 'present tense' of other spaces. It is in this rhythm and dynamic, too, that these participants experience phenomena of presence: that they experience themselves 'acting at a distance' even as this distance is brought back, returning to them in the very closeness of the image in which their 'being here' is temporarily and uncannily displaced.

5

simulation CAVE

This chapter analyses presence in a particular type of virtual reality environment called CAVE. Described by its creator Dan Sandin as a 'virtual reality theater' for its capacity to offer simulated experiences to groups, CAVE constitutes a model virtual reality environment within which to research the experience and performativity of presence in responses to simulations. In computer science, experiments in CAVE have provided means of researching participants' capacity to 'feel present' within a simulated environment in interaction with avatars, or agents – three-dimensional representations of human beings – and to test these responses in the context of specific technologies as well as ideas relating to perception, psychology, social and group interaction, among others. This mode of presence research through CAVE has implicitly positioned the 'spectator' as 'participant' or 'performer' within the simulated environment they negotiate and interact with. In turn, this emphasis suggests possible relationships between the design and outcomes of experimental practices in science and the pragmatics and effects of contemporary media-based installations and other artworks that engage with the viewer's experience of mediated bodies, environments and actions. This chapter, then, considers current research on presence in virtual environments and explores the processes and outcomes of two experiments at University College London in 2007–8 and 2008–9 devised in the context of the Performing Presence project to explore responses to the introduction of a sense of doubling, framing or layering in performances mediated through motion capture into virtual reality environments. In this context, this chapter focuses on exchanges between discourses and practices in the arts, performance and visual art theory and experimental practices in CAVE, a nexus in which ideas and practices of presence can be defined, 'tested' and challenged. Here, in particular, the relationship between real and virtual spaces and bodies within CAVE simulations and the participant's traversal of spaces toward an immersive experience speaks to engagements with presence in relation to site, mediation and simulation also evident in the artworks and performances considered in this volume.

Experiencing CAVE

In order to approach the significance of CAVE to an understanding of presence in performance and media theory and practice, it is important, first of all, to consider the emergence and impact of this technology within science-based discourses around virtual reality, presence and 'immersion'.

The term 'virtual reality' was first coined by Jaron Lanier 'in 1986. Referring 'to technologies or environments that provide realistic cues to some or all the senses, sufficient to engender in the participant a willing suspension of disbelief' (Tice and Laurel 1992: 280), virtual reality can be delivered in three ways: firstly in an 'immersive' or 'inclusive' way (through goggles, gloves or data suits). In this case 'the participant feels as if he or she is inside the graphic, or virtual world'. Secondly, it can be delivered through a 'desktop VR', which involves viewing the 3-D world though a window or a screen. The third way of delivering virtual reality is through what has been described as 'third-person VR', in which 'you view and steer an image of yourself interacting in the virtual world' (Tice and Laurel 1992: 281). All three delivery systems refer to three-dimensional visual worlds in which a viewer can interact with the environment and the avatars or agents this may contain as if 'he or she were inside the image' (Robins 1996: 44). As early as in the 1960s, head-mounted displays were used to create simulations that were able to change as the user moved through them. As suggested by Lanier, the main difficulty was to 'create that basic relationship between your head and the outside world in order for virtual reality to simulate presence in a virtual space' (Lanier 1992: 272). Head-mounted displays, however lightweight, constituted the main medium through which the experience of immersive virtual reality environments was possible. In head-mounted displays, a video screen is placed in front of each of the user's eyes, thus filling their field of vision with a moving image so that '[e]ach eye is presented with a slightly different image, to create a three-dimensional illusion. When you move your head, the scene around you changes, just like in the physical world' (Lanier 1992: 272). Another commonly used tool is the dataglove, which, quite literally, 'puts your hand inside the virtual space' (Lanier 1992: 273) so that the user can touch and pick up virtual objects as if they were 'real'.

A key feature of both the head-mounted display and the dataglove is that they *augment* the user's capacity to perceive the world around them. Similarly, desktop virtual reality and third-person virtual reality, taking place through different types of interfaces, also have this 'prosthetic' quality that allows the subject to lead a *double* existence, both within the material world and inside the simulation. It is this doubling, too, that leads Katherine Hayles to conclude that, with regard to ontology, the technologies of virtual reality render any discourse that positions presence and absence in a dichotomous relationship as 'irrelevant' (Hayles 1996a: 261) and that in virtual reality body motions affect what happens in the simulation such that 'one both is and is not present in the body and in the simulation' (Hayles 1996b: 14).

In the context of this notion of a 'doubling' in experiences of presence in response to simulation, it is also crucial to distinguish between different theoretical models framing the relationship between virtual worlds and the 'real'. In the early 1990s, Tom Caudell coined the term 'augmented reality' to indicate that we should focus not so much on models of virtuality in itself as on the idea of an augmentation of the 'real' (Caudell and Mizell 1992), although the concept of approaching virtuality as a superimposition of computer graphics and the actual world had originally been proposed by Ivan Sutherland and his team at the Universities of Harvard and Utah in the 1960s (Sutherland 1968). Subsequent to Caudell's identification of the possibility of an 'augmented reality', the term 'mixed reality' was coined to indicate a field spanning from augmented reality to augmented virtuality and in which real and virtual world objects are presented together on a single display (Milgram and Kishino 1994) or, according to subsequent viewpoint elaborated by Steve Benford and the Mixed Reality Laboratory at the University of Nottingham, are 'adjacent to one another and then stitched together by creating a "window" between them' (Benford *et al.* 1998: 205).

Where Milgram and Kishino's continuum is constructed in implicit opposition and so potential juxtaposition between 'virtual' and

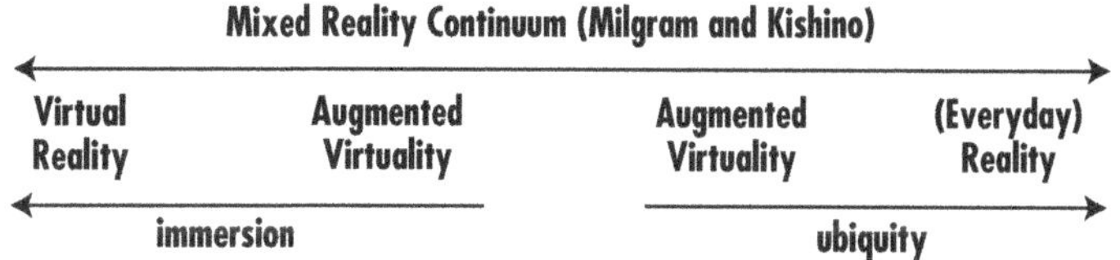

Figure 5.1 Milgram and Kishino's Mixed Reality Continuum

'everyday' reality, Benford's re-reading of this relationship emphasizes the operation of mixed reality as hybrid (Benford and Giannachi 2011). It is this hybridity, expressed in a doubling and layering of positions and spaces in the design of the two exercises created for CAVE, that underpins the hypotheses driving the scenarios considered here and the exchanges between performance practice and experimental design in which they were shaped. Indeed, while such exchanges and layering of the 'real' and the 'virtual' may be implicit in the range of work considered by this volume, these distinctions are central in the subsequent analysis of pervasive presence in Blast Theory's *Day of the Figurines* presented in Chapter 8, which the company created in collaboration with the Mixed Reality Laboratory.

The CAVE is one of the best-known virtual reality environments, a facility originally developed by Tom DiFanti and Dan Sandin of the Electronic Visualization Laboratory at the University of Illinois in Chicago. The CAVE was premiered at the ACM SIGGRAPH 92 conference where it was presented as 'a virtual reality *theater*' (Sandin in Janko *et al.* 1996: 85, emphasis added). Indeed, the term CAVE stands for CAVE Automatic Virtual Environment, a title inspired by Plato's exploration of perception, illusion and reality through the metaphor of the cave in *The Republic*. Sandin described the environment as a:

> multi-person, room-sized, high-resolution, 3-D video and audio environment. Graphics are rear projected in stereo on to three walls and the floor, and viewed with stereo glasses. As a viewer wearing a location sensor moves within its display boundaries, the correct perspective and stereo projections of the environment are updated, and the image moves with and surrounds the viewer.   [Sandin in Janko *et al.* 1996: 84]

CAVE is a surround screen and sound system that creates the sensation of immersion through the projection of 3-D computer graphics into a, roughly, 10 ft × 10 ft × 10 ft cube composed of display screens that surround the viewer. Through head and hand tracking systems the correct stereo perspective is produced. CAVE users do not need to wear helmets but merely a pair of lightweight polarized glasses, and are free to move about the physical environment of the CAVE as they please. The glasses allow the user to see the polarized 3-D images, which are projected on all the surfaces of the environment and continuously updated by the computer to facilitate the user moving simultaneously through the physical space of the CAVE facility and the virtual reality environment the system and specific application create. These graphics are projected to the left and then the right eye alternately at the speed of ninety-six images per second. Here, the viewer can become part of a story and experience the virtual world from their own mobile perspective. Furthermore, a lead visitor can guide a group through a position-sensing device while an interactive wand, a kind of 3-D mouse, allows them to control the direction and movement. In this respect, CAVEs are unique in that they allow multiple users to experience a given immersive virtual environment simultaneously. Cynthia Goodman records that:

> [t]he participant to the CAVE experiences an unprecedented sensation of immersion in a room-sized environment while navigating a wand which transports him or her from one part of a scene as well as from one of the many visually compelling, fanciful worlds which have been created for this system to another.   [Goodman 1998: 257–8]

Michael Heim notes that whereas the head-mounted display mode of virtual reality produces 'tunnel VR or perception-oriented immersion', the projection or CAVE mode of virtual reality produces 'spiral VR or aperceptive immersion' and that 'the VR that tunnels us down a narrow corridor of perceptions differs subtly but profoundly from the virtual reality that spirals us into higher layers of self-perception' (Heim 1995: 71). Yet, for Heim, this experience of immersion does not imply a simple resolution, in the user's experience, of the difference between an occupation of 'virtual' and 'everyday' reality. Thus, Heim notes, the CAVE immersion 'does not constrict but rather enhances the user's body' (Heim 1995: 72), so much so that we 'remain aware of ourselves alongside computer-generated entities' (Heim 1995: 73). Other literature in new media, such as Hayles, cited above, but also Söke Dinkla, share this view, and note that CAVE is in fact based on the very 'strategy of dislocating the subject, who experiences the sensation of being in two places at the same time' (Dinkla 2002: 29). In this sense, the experience of immersion in CAVE may function in experiences of dislocation, spatial hybridity, doubling or layering.

Companies such as General Motors and Volkswagen, which employ the environment to study car design and to test virtual prototypes, most commonly use CAVE commercially. Medical researchers who wish to explore the human body through VR applications as well as NASA scientists, who have employed the CAVE in the space programme, also use the technology. Since its inception, CAVE have also been used in art programmes such as Hisham Bizri and Maria Roussos's *Mythologies* (1998), which is based on the Cretan myth of the Minotaur; the Apocalypse of St John, Dante's *Inferno* (1307); Albrecht Dürer's woodcuts after the Apocalypse (1498) and Jorge Luis Borges's *Library of Babel* (1941). Other well known CAVE environments are Josephine Anstey and Dave Pape's *The Thing Growing* (1998) which has been described as a 'virtual Frankenstein experiment' (Ansty and Pape 1998: 226) and Franz Fischnaller and Yesenia Maharaj Singh's *Multi Mega Book* (1997), which allows a participant to turn the pages of a gigantic virtual book, move into the various worlds within and travel through an idealized Renaissance city, view a recreation of Leonardo's *Last Supper* or use Johann Gutenberg's printing press and visit the ideal digital city of the future. Most CAVEs draw on photo-realism, but some are successfully adopting other styles. A well known example of this is the cartoon-like *Crayoland* (1995), built by David Pape at the Electronic Visualization Laboratory at the University of Illinois, which allows the viewer to travel through a child-drawn landscape complete with forest, flowers and even buzzing bees and randomly flying butterflies. *Crayoland*, consisting of the drawings of flat, two-dimensional objects which are encountered in a three-dimensional world, proved that the most effective environments were not necessarily the ones displaying the highest degree of realism, and that the construction and perception of presence were more dependent on behavioural or performative features than photo-realism.

Presence in virtual reality

To the extent that CAVE takes its effect in an experience of the body as 'double', as Hayles suggests, or in the production and traversal of hybrid or multiple positions, or, as Dinkla proposes, in 'the sensation of being in two places at the same time' (Dinkla 2002: 29) the experience of 'presence' produced through these technologies may be seen as broadly congruent to the earlier analyses in this volume. However, such propositions are by no means uncontentious and need to be set against the use of the term 'presence' in computer science as well as readings of recent and current literature on the functioning of CAVE and, in particular, the character of immersion within such environments.

In the context of the literature and experimental science defining the functioning of virtual environments, including CAVE, 'presence' is a contraction of 'telepresence', which has been described as the 'defining experience of VR' (Steuer 1992). In this specific context the functioning of 'presence' in virtual environments conventionally indicates the degree to which participants feel that they are somewhere other than where they 'physically' are while experiencing a computer-generated simulation (Sheridan 1992a, b; Barfield and Weghorst 1993; Slater and Usoh 1994; Barfield *et al.* 1995). It follows that the concept of 'presence' in virtual reality is not so much concerned with 'aura' or awareness of 'self' or 'other', or being *as such*, but rather with 'the *illusion of being here or there*'. This, for Frank Biocca, indicates that 'the fundamental issue at the root of the problem of presence is the perception of reality, usually under the domain of epistemology, not reality itself, usually discussed under the banner of ontology' (Biocca 2001: 550, original emphasis). It follows that although the literature defining virtual reality deploys the term 'presence', in so far as it indicates 'telepresence' this use reflects a position and set of concerns different from a broader concept of 'presence'. Thus, where 'presence' may indicate 'the sensation of being in an environment', or 'being there', in the sense that 'presence can be thought of as the experience of one's physical environment' (Steuer 1992: 75), telepresence refers to 'the experience of being in an environment thanks to a means of communication' (Steuer 1992: 76). In CAVE, however, the experience of 'telepresence' is itself distinctive. Whereas in conventional telepresence systems participants relocate their being and ability to act 'here' to a distant 'there', and will usually be aware of the process of mediation that this entails, in virtual reality a participant's 'here' is displaced to another 'here', and, it is argued, if 'presence' is experienced, then this may be to the degree that the participant may no longer be aware that this relocation has occurred as the result of a process of mediation (or communication).

Significantly, too, while presence in these contexts may be linked to immersion, 'presence' and 'immersion' do not necessarily coincide. Thus Mel Slater and Sylvia Wilbur categorize immersion in a virtual environment as a quantifiable aspect of a display technology, primarily determined by the extent to which displays are 'inclusive' (in the sense that stimuli from the real world are excluded from the user), 'extensive', 'surrounding' (for example, the panoramic quality of displays) and 'vivid' (for example, the resolution of the displays). Whereas 'immersion' here indicates the features of the technology employed to immerse the participant, presence indicates 'a state of consciousness, the (psychological) sense of being in the virtual environment' (Slater 1997:

604 f.). In this sense presence is a subjective perception (Lombard and Ditton 1997). It has been shown that the higher the level of immersion the higher the level of presence, and 'the more that a system delivers displays (in all sensory modalities) and tracking that preserves fidelity in relation to their equivalent real-world sensory modalities, the more that it is "immersive"' (Slater 2003). In other words, the more a system is able to immerse the participant into a display that somehow mirrors the modalities of a physical or 'real' environment the more it is likely that 'presence' will be experienced.

For Slater, the experience of presence in CAVE is, in fact, 'a human reaction to immersion' which means that, given the same level of immersion, participants may still experience presence in different ways. Consistently with this, 'presence', he argues, 'only really makes sense when there are two competing systems – one typically the real world, and the other the technology delivering a given immersive system' (Slater 2003). Within the functioning of a VR environment such as CAVE, then, presence is 'a perceptual mechanism for selection between alternative hypotheses: "I am in this place" and "I am in that place" ("I am confused")' (Slater 2002: 435). To further elaborate his position, Slater uses the example of a participant who is standing in CAVE, or a CAVE-like system, 'wearing a head-mounted display, feeling the cables, temperature, and the physical signals of that real place' but is *feeling* present in a 'room with a dangerous precipice' so that, although they know that they are safe, in CAVE their 'visual perception overrides this knowledge and the bodily system reacts as if they were in the pit room: heart rate rises, locomotion is carefully judged, and the subject reports symptoms of anxiety' (Slater 2002: 436). It is on this basis, too, that the experimental investigation of presence in immersive projective environments has deployed 'breaks in presence' both as a deliberate control in the investigation of these experiences and as a hypothesis to support this proposition. During the time in which participants are located in an immersive virtual environment, Slater proposes, they are likely to perceive two streams of sensory data: 'the first from the real world in which the experience is taking place, and the second from the virtual world displayed by the virtual reality system' (Slater *et al.* 2003). A 'break in presence' thus occurs when 'the participant stops responding to the virtual stream and instead responds to the real sensory stream' (Slater *et al.* 2003). Breaks in presence may also occur due to 'uncanny valley' a phenomenon that refers to 'a sense of unease and discomfort' experienced by some participants when engaging with realistic virtual humans. According to one study, the increase in similarity between humans and avatars can 'bring about a very strong drop in believability and comfort'. Whereas some scholarship suggests that this effect is due to inability to categorize something as dead or alive (Tomlinson 2000), others argue that, unlike a break in presence, 'uncanny valley is not 'a switch but a superimposition of two hypotheses' (Brenton *et al.* 2005). It is interesting that eye movement is known to play an important role in this matter, so that 'when the eyes communicate a different (or ambiguous) intent to an ensuing unpredictable behaviour, there is a mismatch which may promote uncanniness' (Brenton *et al.* 2005). Both breaks in presence and uncanny valley are interesting phenomena to analyse within a performative context in that they disclose the mechanisms of the process generating the conditions by which presence may be experienced.

Similar issues and questions over presence also pertain to other immersive technologies. Thus, while there are substantial differences between immersive projection technologies (IPT) (including CAVE) and immersive virtual environments (IVE) (which may use head-mounted displays) (Steed and Parker 2005: 511), analogous processes and research over immersion and response continue to define these developing technologies. Anthony Steed and Chris Parker emphasize that 'IPT systems attempt to exclude the real world, so that the virtual environment is perceived as a continuous and consistent environment' which 'surrounds or appears to surround the user' (Steed and Parker 2005: 511), who is also constrained by the physical environment of the CAVE. In contrast, immersive virtual environment systems track the body of the user and utilize this information 'as an aid to interaction in the system'. On a head-mounted display this tracking information is often 'given a geometric form, and is rendered as an agent. Thus as the user looks around the environment and their own body, the agent is updated to reflect the actual body movements made' (Steed and Parker 2005: 512). In other words, in immersive virtual environments the system changes around the participant such that they are left feeling the world is changing with them, if not according *to* them, and so much so that arguably the virtual world becomes a prosthetic of the participants themselves.

The experience of presence in virtual reality has also been described as being a function of focus (Fontaine 1992), selective attention (Triesman 1963), vividness of an experience and the level of interaction (Sheridan 1992a, b; Steuer 1992) or involvement (Witmer and Singer 1998). Factors that have been described as influencing immersion, and which in turn may affect presence, include 'isolation from the physical environment, perception of self-inclusion in the VE, natural modes of interaction and control, and perception of self-movement' (Witmer and

Singer 1998: 227). According to some scholarship there is evidence of a 'spatial fidelity' model of presence that indicates that this sense of presence may be dependent on the degree to which spatial, auditory, and haptic transformations of objects in a virtual environment correspond to transformations of objects in the real world (Barfield and Hendrix, 1995; Barfield *et al.* 1997). In other words, mapping dislocations, ambiguities and coincidences between the virtual and physical environments the participant occupies may influence their sense of their own presence within the virtual.

Yet while these analyses of presence focus, in particular, on the relationship between 'competing systems', there is also evidence that presence within CAVE may be produced in response to mediations generated by artefacts, both physical and conceptual, 'between actors and between them and objects both near and remote' (Mantovani and Riva 1999: 541). This proposition, which suggests that virtual reality environments are 'spaces in which experience is always mediated by physical and intellectual tools', constitutes 'the first step towards a sociocultural conception of environments and of presence that is no longer dualistic but relational and interactive' (Mantovani and Riva 1999: 541). What is particularly interesting here, and is also suggested in the operation of Paul Sermon's work *Headroom* (2006), is that virtual reality environments in which presence is experienced behave like 'networks in which people and things construct themselves mutually' (Mantovani and Riva 1999: 541). Such networks suggest that a sense of 'presence' on behalf of the participant may also be a response to behaviours and relationships that actively negotiate between ostensibly competing systems and spaces – and so arise within an ecology in which the actor, or participant, defines their active place. Indeed, and as Sermon's work suggests, it is evident that 'the quality of presence and telepresence does not depend so much on the faithfulness of the reproduction of physical aspects of external reality . . . as on the capacity to produce a context in which social actors may communicate and cooperate' (Mantovani and Riva 1999: 542). Not only is the presence response therefore 'always mediated by both physical and conceptual tools that belong to a given culture' but also, Giuseppe Mantovani and Giuseppe Riva suggest, 'the criterion for presence does not consist of reproducing the conditions of physical presence but in constructing environments in which actors may function in an ecologically valid way' (Mantovani and Riva 1999: 547).

This notion of the importance of the network of actions, communications and contexts to the production of experiences of presence in CAVE also points to the potential complexities that surround the experience of virtual reality for naïve participants, who are conventionally the subjects of these investigations and experimental practices. Indeed, most participants to experimental scenarios in CAVE are relatively inexperienced when it comes to decoding what they encounter. Thus, faced with a virtual human, they are unlikely to know whether they are facing an 'avatar', that is, a virtual human driven by a remote human counterpart, or an 'agent', meaning a virtual human driven by artificial intelligence or pre-scripted behaviour (Garau *et al.* 2005: 105). In fact, participants' reports of their experiences in CAVE are frequently as much the product of their imagination and projection than of a given application itself, suggesting that individual readings of circumstance and social and personal interaction are also significant influences on responses to these immersive experiences. Consistently with this, Matthew Lombard and Theresa Ditton suggest that to perceive a virtual other as a social entity there must be a level of interactivity (1997) whilst Biocca claims that social presence occurs when users feel they are in the proximity of intelligence (1997). Evidently, too, it may be possible to simulate both 'interactivity' and 'intelligence' within pre-scripted scenarios: in the former by employing a number of variable scenarios that may be cued by an operator; in the latter through non-verbal gestures and attitudes in the virtual agent's animation that imply awareness of the participant and their behaviour. There is also evidence that 'virtual human behaviours can have an impact on people's social responses' (Garau *et al.* 2005: 105). In an exercise created at University College London in 2005 under the hypothesis that 'the greater the responsiveness of the agents the higher the likelihood that participants would have had an experience of being with people', agents were encountered in CAVE in a library/reading room. This scenario presented four degrees of agent responsiveness: (1) static (agents were frozen in a reading move); (2) moving (agents were animated and behaved as if in a reading room, fidgeting, turning pages, looking around); (3) responsive (same as moving but also engaging in gaze behaviour and changing posture when approached by participant); (4) talking (as in responsive but also speaking to participants) (Garau *et al.* 2005: 106–7). This experiment was investigating participants' responses on a number of indicators, including 'co-presence', meaning 'the extent to which the participants had the sense of being with other people' (Garau *et al.* 2005: 109). The findings suggested that users who experienced the responsive agents had a higher sense of personal contact with them and 'responded to these agents as if they were people rather than aspects of a computer interface' (Garau *et al.* 2005: 111). Experiments such as this may lead us to conclude that the more avatar-like the agents were the more interaction and intelligence they displayed, and the more exchanges, interactions and connections may be articulated between the participants' world and the virtual world in CAVE the more likely that participants will experience 'presence' given the same processes and factors of immersion.

Considered as an 'ecology' in which active participants enact and negotiate their place, the environment and experience produced in CAVE would seem to exemplify the performance and performativity of presence, whereby the experience of 'presence' is a function of the visitor's active place and definition of a network they also enact. Such a performativity may also suggest that these experiences of 'presence' operate in the participant's active negotiation of 'competing' signals, whereby their experience is in part a function of particular kinds of active participation, which may also account for differing responses and degrees of 'presence' experienced by individuals in technically immersive environments. Furthermore, Mantovani and Riva's proposition that presence is aligned with behaviour in which 'people and things construct themselves mutually' (Mantovani and Riva 1999: 541) suggests that perceived and enacted relationships between self and other may also be implied by such a performance of presence. In these contexts and perspectives, the particular experience of 'telepresence' defining CAVE may also be congruent with phenomenological analyses of the performance of self and other as a root of phenomena of presence.

Performing CAVE

It is in this debate and these broader contexts that the experimental scenarios considered here, and developed under the Performing Presence project, emphasize relationships and disjunctions between 'virtual' and 'everyday' reality in CAVE in order to create experiences of ambiguity and hybridity between 'real' and 'virtual' realms and acts. In presenting overtly 'mixed reality' scenarios within an immersive environment, these experiments also looked toward the creation of ecologies or networks of differing positions and worlds the participant may choose to negotiate, with the purpose of exploring whether or not such processes might amplify the participant's sense of their own presence to these environments and agents. Both scenarios implied 'interactivity' between virtual and human 'characters' in the scenario and between these characters and the participation, so implicitly setting the participant between positions. Elements of scenario 2 were designed as interactive, with virtual reality animations cued by participant interruptions or questions, should they occur. The detailed design for these scenarios drew specifically on the practices of artists, performers and practitioners invited within the broader Performing Presence project to workshop their engagements with performer, viewer and audience 'presence', as well the emergent analyses presented in this volume. This approach is broadly consistent, too, with the notion that the relationship of the 'real' to the 'virtual' is one of implication and contamination, rather than of mutual exclusivity or alternative and opposed modes of experience or states. Consistently with this, and with regard to the functioning and experience of the 'presence' of other and self, this approach also implies that the signs of embodied, 'real' acts and disembodied, 'simulated' acts are connected at a level of the experience of and encounter with signs of presence.

Such a position also follows earlier philosophical and semiotic considerations of simulation that have been influential on art, perform-ance and literature. Thus Jean Baudrillard, considering the hyperreal in *Simulations* (1983), in an analysis preceding the enactment of presence within VR environments, reminds us that, in approaching simula-tion and the hyperreal, one should note that 'the real is not only that which can be reproduced, but *that which is always already reproduced*' (Baudrillard 1993: 73, original emphasis). Here, Baudrillard draws attention to relationships between simulation and 'the real' under the functioning and order of the sign, whose operation he implicitly assumes to always already eclipse an encounter with a transcendental 'real': with the 'authentic' or the 'original'. In this context, Baudrillard goes on to observe the consequences of the advent of 'the age of simula-tion' through the circulation of signs in the mass media, which would effect 'a liquidation of all referentials'. In this event, with regard to 'the real', he concludes, simulation is 'no longer a question of imitation, nor of reduplication ... It is rather a question of substituting signs of the real for the real itself' (Baudrillard 1983: 4). Significantly, in Baudrillard's elaboration and critique of the simulacra it is 'the real' that is at stake in simulation, in its amplification of the sign's 'operation to deter every real process by its operational double' (Baudrillard 1983: 4). In this reading, simulation simultaneously enacts and differs from 'the real', at once invoking, reproducing and eclipsing its signs and effects as its 'operational double'. Indeed, simulation functions in the *effects* of the real at the very moment that it calls the experience of the real into ques-tion. Such a notion of simulation's reproduction and contamination of the signs and experiences of 'the real' may also suggest that the 'pres-ence response' in CAVE may be amplified in the connections and con-taminations between the signs of virtual and everyday 'reality', where simulation's dependence on perceptions and 'experiences' of 'the real' is foregrounded. Under this dynamic, experiences of presence in immersive environments such as CAVE may be produced in relationships of *doubling* between simulation and the real and in experiences of 'seamfulness' provoked by the operation of immersive virtual reality applications within the physical and material circumstances and constraints in which their supporting technologies function.

It is under these contexts and assumptions that the Performing Presence project experiments were designed, using motion capture to create extended and 'mixed reality' scenarios for the CAVE environment. The word 'experiment' is used here to indicate that the team worked from hypotheses intended to be tested against qualitative data arising from participant responses to scenarios, including questionnaires, semi-structured interviews and 'presence graphs', in which participants reflect upon and map graphically the extent to which they consider themselves to have responded to virtual events and agents 'as if' they were real. The hypothesis for the first scenario was that a participant's sense of a virtual agent's presence – by which we mean their response to the agent as if it were 'real' – may be enhanced by an explicit and perceptible 'doubling' or 'layering' of the signs of their activity. Drawing, in particular, on work by Bill Gaver, Jacob Beaver and Steve Benford (Gaver *et al.* 2003) which argued that ambiguity can be a useful resource for the design of human computer interactions, we decided to create ambivalent mappings between actual and virtual localities, as well as between intelligent ('real') and pre-scripted ('virtual') agents that would play with the participants' sense of presence within a given CAVE scenario. In particular, the scenario sought to explore how operating performatively at the level of context and creating ambiguity of interaction, especially at the level of non-verbal communication, could be key in generating the conditions by which presence is experienced in CAVE. Important here, too, is the approach to the experience of disjunctive relationships and transitions between the 'virtual space' occupied and acted within by the virtual agent and the coterminous 'real space' occupied by a human actor, who also interacted with both the virtual agent and participant. In the first scenario, specifically, the 'human performer' mirrored and emphasized the participant's occupation of the 'real space' of the CAVE facility, in contrast to the agent's functioning within the virtual architecture generated by the application. Here, the participant finds themselves interacting variously with the virtual agent and their human counterpart, and so engaging by turn in 'virtual' and 'real' spaces of performance. The hypothesis for the second scenario, developed iteratively on the basis of findings from the first, was that interaction between participants and virtual characters would enhance the participants' sense of their own presence in the virtual environment and that this experience may be further amplified and modulated in overt articulations of relationships between different orders of space and spatial experiences in which the CAVE functions, including areas and activities inside and outside the immediate CAVE facility.

The design for the first scenario was also informed by observation of a series of workshop exercises conducted by Tim Etchells, artistic director of the British performance and media company Forced Entertainment at the University of Exeter in 2006 as part of a series of explorations of questions and concepts of presence in live performance hosted under the broad umbrella of the Performing Presence project. Thus, in addressing 'Presence and Absence Intertwined', Etchells explored a dialectic between the implicit refusal of activity over an extended time and a stepping into – and through – a threshold toward 'performance'. To this end, Etchells worked with a group of performers, positioning them behind a series of tables facing an audience. Performers were invited to either look at the audience or at each other, without using any form of verbal communication, and in their own time and according to their individual initiative stand and then return to being seated. In the event, the initial form of the exercise commenced with a thirty-minute period of sitting and so a mirroring of audience looking, broken, finally, by a single performer standing, in an action that, in watching, appeared to mark a step into a new register of 'being before' the audience, which was then responded to by fellow performers in a subsequent stepping forward from and withdrawing to a base line of attention and relationship.

TIM ETCHELLS We [Forced Entertainment] tend to think about a
kind of base line, about the performers being present, in a certain
way, more or less as themselves, or as a kind of slightly exaggerated
or extended version of themselves. And from there, there is a kind
of process of a stepping into either task, or character, or role – or
into some kind of enactment anyway. Certainly, the performers are
present, let's say, 'as themselves', doing the job, and then, kind of, in
a layer above that you will see them enacting or stepping up into
something that's slightly more artificial or staged, if you like, or that
maybe is not exaggerated.

Perhaps we could think of presence as something that happens
when one attempts to do something, and whilst attempting to do that
thing you become visible, visible in not quite succeeding in doing
it, visible through the cracks or the gaps. As humans we're always

present or perceived through something – through a particular aperture or through a particular grid or through a particular frame. I'm talking about social structures, frames of behaviour, social space and expectation. In fact, it's these layers or frames or constrictions that make you visible – that make you there. . . . in the real world we are already all performing too much, there are already too many frames, codes, limits and needs that we are performing in relation to and appearing through.

Presence is something that, on the one hand, perhaps as subjects we deploy certain signs in order to appear, but actually presence is so much about reception. It's about reading. And reading is a complicated act. One of the things we do as readers of signs and situations – and of all things – is that we respond to absences – and we fill absence. . . . Blankness is a huge magnet. People really, really rush into that, they fight it as well too of course, because at first they can get nervous in art or cinema or performance if they're 'not being told anything'.

Fundamentally this is about frames, which are apparently quite restrictive, but which can be extraordinarily productive in terms of letting people appear. The constriction can become a kind of gift inside which people operate as agents, but also can be read with an extraordinary level of profundity.

[Exeter, February 2006]

In addition to Etchells' proposition, the development of the scenario drew on the work of practitioners who utilize techniques of estrangement between their character and themselves as a performer (or actor) with the aim of refocusing the audience and addressing and strengthening the audience's perception of their presence on stage. Here, too, performative strategies of 'doubling' played a particularly important role, first with reference to Fiona Templeton's Performing Presence workshop of the same year, which addressed presence and 'audience participation', focusing on the mutual mirroring, repetition and reframing of activity by two groups of audience participants. Also of particular importance to the scenario was the positioning of the viewer and participant between doubled physical and a simulated environments, as in Lynn Hershman's *Life to the Second Power* discussed in Chapter 2; the articulation of the coterminous virtual and material spaces of video installation, evident in work by Tony Oursler considered in Chapter 6; and the doubling of players' presence between a board and a virtual community for a mixed reality performance, as in Blast Theory's *Day of the Figurines*, discussed in Chapter 8. In preparation, rehearsal and execution, the scenario also implicitly drew on The Builders Association's juxtaposition and overlaying of the 'live' and 'mediated' performances of Kyle DeCamp and the video child in *Super Vision* (2005), analysed in Chapter 7.

FIONA TEMPLETON I often think that to some extent presence is necessarily communicative – which is why I say it is contingent on attention. Not just communicative in the sense that it communicates, but communicative like a communicative disease in that it can't help but communicate. This is not to say that it could be undiscovered or ignored, but that is its nature. One reason that interests me is that, for example, in the book *You – the City* (Templeton 1990) I talk about 'a meaning'. But it isn't something that you can necessarily have, a discrete unit of meaning. The performances that were going on next door in the workshop today were much more about discrete experiences. But you can have experiences that are, sort of, promiscuous, in the sense that what they come into touch with changes them – or they are open to them. And, for me, meaning really works like that. I mean, there are sort of disguises of discrete meaning, but most meaning really opens up in that way. I think that presence operates in that way, like meaning does. When I say 'promiscuous' I mean it will change. It's sort of alive, obviously. That's one way of thinking about it: not that it's discrete, but that it's communicative.

[Exeter, May 2006]

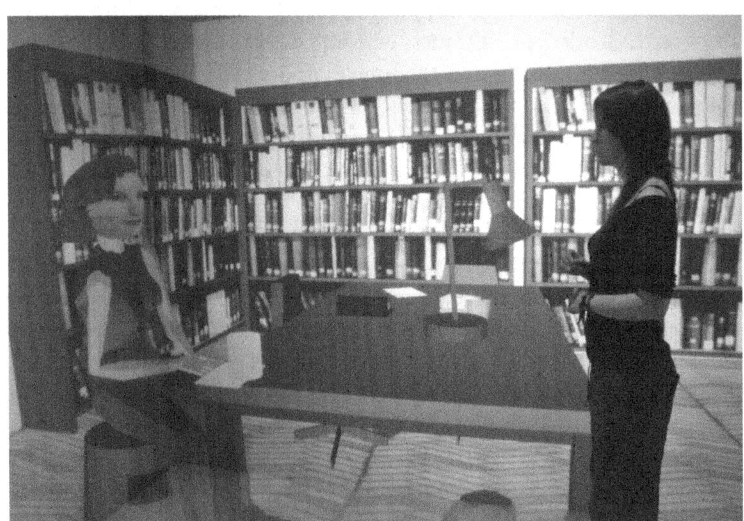

Figure 5.2 Performing Presence, CAVE Scenario 1. The human character observing the virtual agent's performance before intervening

The first experiment set the participant as witness within the CAVE environment to an exchange between a virtual agent and a human 'character' focused on the nature of the virtual character's performance, and in which, finally, they are actively implicated. After being introduced to the CAVE facility and adopting the shutter glasses, each participant was allowed a period of time to become familiar with the environment and, if they chose, to test a physical navigation of the virtual space. The scenario proper was initiated by the entry of the virtual agent from the participant's left, apparently from an adjacent room, and a subsequent entry by the human performer from the CAVE laboratory, who then crossed the participant's sight of the agent to face their virtual counterpart across a virtual table. As the scenario unfolded, the participant was presented with the human character's repeated interruption of the virtual agent's behaviour, apparently to admonish 'her' over the quality of her appearance and behaviour and to announce and emphasize the differences between the virtual agent and human performer. The virtual character, which was described by participants as 'cartoonish', with a 'really nervous disposition', 'attempting to act human' and 'a little bit sulky', was built by using motion capture from the performer who interpreted the human character, so generating an uncanny resemblance between the movements of the virtual and human characters. While at the beginning of the scenario the participant was positioned as a spectator, towards the end they were invited to state their own view of the virtual character's performance. Left alone with the agent, the virtual character addressed them directly: 'Tell me, did I perform well?' to which the majority of participants replied either positively or negatively.

Set in a library room, the scenario progressed through five sections. In the first, the virtual character acted out a simple and straightforward sequence of actions without comment over a two-minute period, watched by the participant and the human character. These were loosely based on Etchells' exercise: thus, after a period of relative stillness and silence, the agent stood and stepped 'into' performance. In the second, this sequence was repeated and the human character forcefully interrupted the agent's activity, to which the agent in turn responded. The human character stated that the virtual character's behaviour was 'unsatisfactory': their movements were not smooth enough; timing and rhythm were imperfect; speech response was predictable and it was not correctly synchronized. Under the human character's direction, and punctuated by the agent's responses and comments, the virtual agent's actions were then broken down into units, and rehearsed and repeated. In this sequence, and through the human character's comments and actions, a contrast was created between the imperative to 'act' (that the

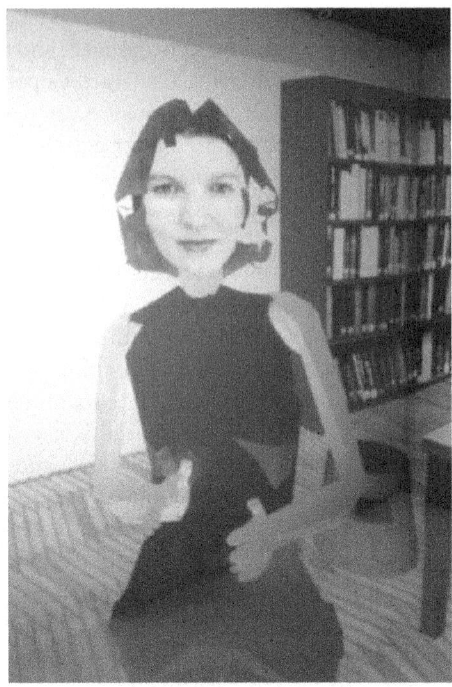

Figure 5.3 Performing Presence, CAVE Scenario 1. Female agent approaches
the participant

virtual character should perform of prescribed 'human' actions) and
the refusal to 'act' (through behaviours that the human character suggests conflict with, depart from, interrupt or disrupt this 'performance',
including hesitations, technical matters of motion capture, and other
matters observed and responded to in the rehearsal of the scenario).
Throughout this sequence, differences between the human performer
and virtual agent in their modes and qualities of action and behaviour
were highlighted in their dialogue, while the inadequacy of the agent's
functioning as an animated representation of a human character and in
relation to the material conditions of their environment was stressed.

In the third section, seemingly dissatisfied with this process and
the 'criticism' offered by the human character, the agent finally refuses
to continue, so prompting the human character to demonstrate aspects
of the sequence the virtual character was attempting to complete.
Subsequently, the virtual character turns to the participant and suggests that they will now demonstrate their 'avatarness'. In this context,
the virtual character engages further with the participant, repeating the

original sequence 'successfully'. At its culmination, the agent approaches the participant and moves close to them. A virtual sheet of paper passes from the agent to the human character and, by means of a trick, as a real piece of paper from the human character to the participant. On giving the paper to the participant, the human performer leaves the CAVE. In this final sequence, the agent addresses the participant directly, asking them how effective their performance had been.

The sequence was intended to invite the perception on behalf of the participant of distinct layers of action and performance while emphasizing differences, exchanges and thresholds between the actions of the virtual agent and human performer, in order that signs and signals of presence might be mirrored, 'doubled' or 'layered'. Section 1 allowed the participant to encounter the virtual character before the introduction of a distinction between modes of 'performance' to establish a control condition. Section 2 elaborated the theatrical conceit that the virtual character was attempting to 'perform' in the manner of their human partner in the scenario, distinguishing, through the human character's various responses and the virtual character's reactions, 'good' (human-like) performance and 'bad' (agent-like) behaviours. Sections 3 and 4 further developed this opposition, first through the virtual character's 'refusal' to 'act' but also through the human character's demonstration of 'acting human' and, in response, the virtual character's demonstration of disruptive 'agent' behaviour. The broad mirroring of behaviours between the virtual and human characters – they, at different times, both refused to continue with the sequence in an effort to demonstrate their 'difference' – served to heighten the distinctions and dialogue on which the scenario rested. Section 5 re-presented the virtual character's 'performance' in the context of the 'layering' or 'doubling' of performance modes established in sections 2–4. Here, it may seem, the virtual character has 'knowingly' 'presented the pretence' in self-reflexive behaviour and performance. The agent's direct address to the participant was intended, in turn, to elicit self-consciousness on behalf of the participant, as they now find themselves in the position of the human character they had been watching – a position underscored by the exit of the human performer immediately before. It was postulated that this instance would generate a peak in the experience of presence, followed by a 'break in presence', or BIP, marking the moment at which the scenario ends, a proposition supported by the majority of the presence graphs produced by the participants.

The outcomes of the first scenario, which incorporated presence graphs, semi-structured interviews and questionnaires of eighteen participants to provide a qualitative assessment of responses, showed that

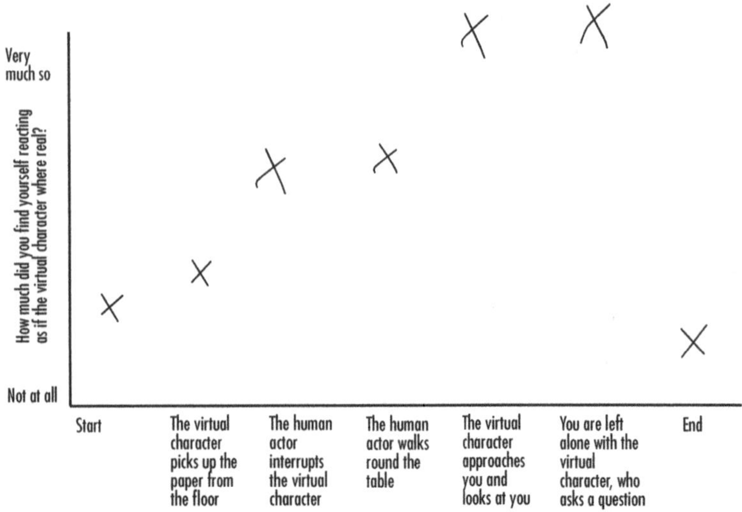

Figure 5.4 Performing Presence: CAVE Scenario 1. Presence graph by a participant showing the differing levels by which they experienced presence in the piece and indicating clearly that the moment of interaction with the agent generated a peak in presence followed by a break in presence at the end of the scenario

the presence of the virtual agent was 'most forceful' during or after the interaction with the human character, suggesting that the articulation of the co-presence of virtual and real agents to the participant heightened their experience and that the presence of the 'real' performer served to amplify the participant's engagement with the virtual environment and agent. This translated, for most participants, into an enhanced sense of their own presence in the virtual environment during moments of interaction between the real and virtual characters and produced a peak during the interaction between the agent and themselves, often resulting in a desire on behalf of the participant to join the exchange. So, for example, one participant felt that they ought to step in 'to stop an argument' while others 'expected an answer back' from the virtual character even though they were aware of being before a simulated individual with no intelligence. Participants also often ascribed human qualities to the agent by referring to their 'gender'. One participant stated their 'emotional responses to *her* were as if *she* were human' (added emphasis). Another implicitly noted the difference between their emotional response and understanding: 'initially I wanted to say 'Hi' to *her* as *she* entered the room . . . I knew that *it* was not real, but when *she* sat down and started doing something on the table, I wanted to say hi to *her*'

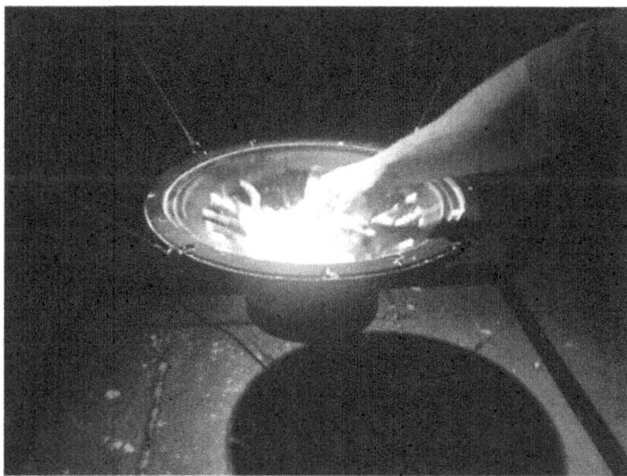

Figure 5.5 Yoshimasa Kato and Yuichi Ito, *White Lives on Speaker* (2007).
Potato starch bubbling in response to sound generated by Gabriella
Giannachi's brain waves. The arm in the image belongs to a bystander who
touched the potato starch during the interaction

(added emphasis). By contrast, another player's denial of empathy suggested a similar conflict between understanding and experience: 'I didn't find any empathy for her – well, except for the last bit where she asked me "Did I do that right?" I somehow felt the impulse to say yes.' Other participants assumed that the virtual character had been responsive: 'I was curious to see if I approached her . . . if there was a reaction to that. I think there was – because I think she stepped back, and I don't think that was accidental.' Finally, one participant revealed, 'when *she* approached me the first time I felt *she* was really invading my space, actually. Which was, I suppose it was kind of, in a way, a case for realism, but at the same time it was – it felt a bit unnatural, somebody coming that close to you. So I actually did step back, which is bizarre' (added emphasis). Consistently with this description, this participant's act of stepping back suggested a response 'as if' the agent was real, a strong indication of a peak in presence at this stage in the scenario.

Such responses could suggest that the articulation of 'real' and 'virtual' spaces through the coterminous presence of the performer and avatar served to heighten the participant's engagement in an active negotiation in this network of activities and between the various dynamics between 'real' and 'virtual' characters. Rather than simply alert the participant to the 'real' world of the CAVE facility and its 'conflict' with the virtual world it delivers, this play between virtual and real characters, events and acts suggests that in mirroring and articulating the participant's displacement across real and virtual environments a greater engagement and negotiation within this 'ecology' may be produced.

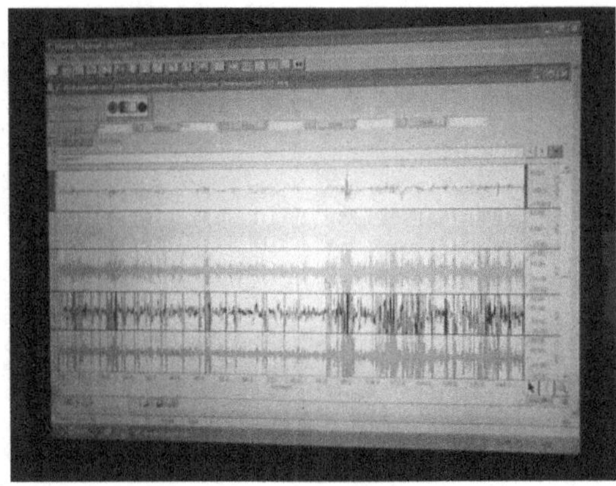

Figure 5.6 Yoshimasa Kato and Yuichi Ito, *White Lives on Speaker* (2007). Interface showing Gabriella Giannachi's brain activity during her interaction with the work

On the basis of the findings of the first scenario, a second scenario was developed to explore further the role of interaction in the generation of experiences of presence. This exercise also drew on an interactive work by Yoshimasa Kato and Yuichi Ito, *White Lives on Speaker* (2007). This work, which was shown at the ars electronica festival in 2007, consisted of an installation in which potato starch was dissolved with water and placed on a loudspeaker, which vibrated to the subsonic output from a computer that generated sound by measuring the participant's brain waves, particularly alpha and beta. Although the material looked fluid, it felt hard to the touch when stimulated, but returned to a fluid state when this stimulation subsided. By touching the sculpture, participants, who were wired into a computer, could touch configurations that had been 'generated' by their own brain waves. When Gabriella Giannachi experienced the piece, she was encouraged to touch the potato starch bubbles and it was noticed, at the end of her interaction, that her brain wave activity had substantially increased at the point of physical contact with the work. This implied that interactivity, particularly when combined with a sensory experience of 'feedback', may provoke a state of hyperactivity in the brain and, as Giannachi's experience of this particular work suggests, generating and heightening a sense of being *in* the work and *before* it, which can in turn be constructed as an experience of 'presence'.

The hypothesis for the second scenario was not only that interaction between participants and virtual characters would enhance the participants' sense of their own presence in the virtual environment, but that this interaction and response would be heightened by an explicit

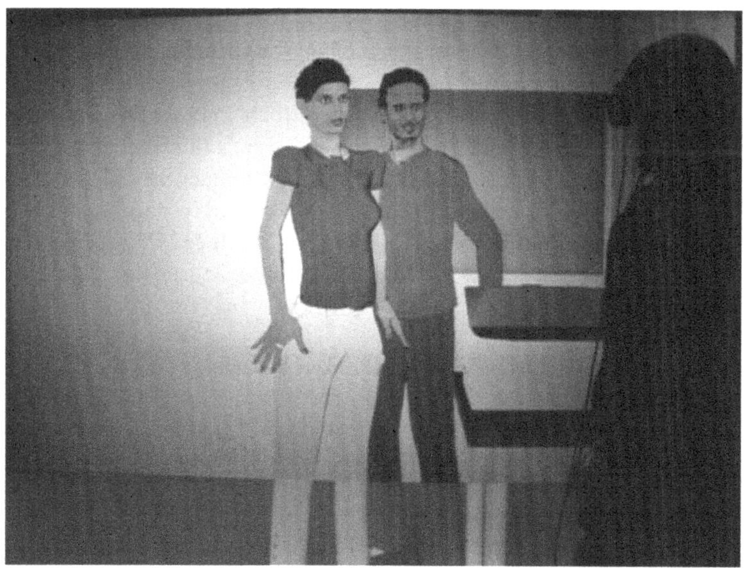

Figure 5.7 Performing Presence, CAVE Scenario 2. The agents introduce the 'experiment' to a participant. Video documentation still

articulation of relationships between the different spatial contexts and experiences in which the CAVE facility functions. The scenario was produced in a dual form: a scripted, rehearsed performance by trained actors, then motion captured; and a second version, in which the script, timings and physical actions of the actors' performance were reproduced and motion was captured without rehearsal by naive performers. In the context of this study, this dual process allowed a focus on the effect of the scenario structure and dramaturgical design for participants over performance style.

As a whole, the scenario exposed and stressed the participants' experience of a virtual space within the 'real' environment of the CAVE laboratory and the dynamics and different relationships between them. It also emphasized the broader context of the UCL virtual reality laboratory within which this CAVE is physically set, while reproducing aspects of an 'experiment' within the scenario itself. In turn, the dynamic of the scenario rested on the virtual agents' acknowledgement of activity beyond the virtual spaces 'they' occupied, and in this context their interaction with the 'real' manager of the virtual reality laboratory, Dr David Swapp, who was in fact conducting the experiment and cueing the virtual agents in the 'real time' of the participant's experience from consoles immediately outside the CAVE. In this way, Swapp was treated as an active agent and 'human character' in the virtual scenario: 'David', a point of reference and apparent source of antagonism for the virtual female agent and her male counterpart in their interactions with each other and the participant. Stressing, in this way, a fluidity between the inside and the outside of CAVE, the agents frequently called out to 'David', who replied and interacted with them, even responding to their complaint regarding equipment by stepping into the CAVE scenario to adjust the position of GSR (galvanic skin response) sensors placed on the participant's finger.

Extract from Section 1: the experiment has a false start

The AGENTS finally pay direct attention to the participant. The FEMALE AGENT moves closer to the participant and looks them up and down.
FEMALE AGENT:
Jesus! That's not on right – can't he ever get it right?
The MALE AGENT turns to face towards CAVE's (curtained) rear wall.
MALE AGENT (*calling out*):
David, you've messed up the GSR sensors again – can you come back and fix it?
DAVID re-enters to adjust the equipment. The AGENTS look in his direction.
FEMALE AGENT (*turning away*):
Every day there's some kind of cock-up.
FEMALE AGENT leaves.
MALE AGENT:
Yeah.
DAVID leaves the CAVE and closes the curtain behind him, inadvertently leaving a slight gap. The MALE AGENT approaches the participant.
[From Performing Presence, CAVE scenario 2, script]

From the participant's point of view, the virtual agents' activity was shaped around an experimental study based on the typical investigations that take place in CAVE. The scenario thus presented the participant with a fictitious psychological experiment about 'emotional intelligence'. Interaction between the participant and the virtual agents was afforded by direct questions from the virtual agents, typically but not exclusively within the context of the experiment. This strategy necessitated the preparation of a number of pre-authored responses by the virtual agents to whatever the team had predicted the participant might say to them, as well as stock responses for unexpected questions. Another design goal was that the interaction among the virtual agents, the participant and 'David' should be as 'natural' as possible within the confines of a limited range of possible responses both physical and

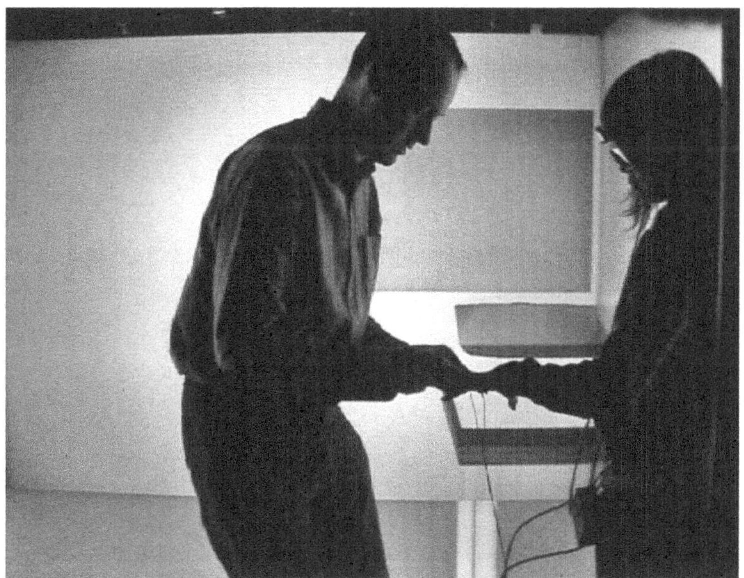

Figure 5.8 Performing Presence, CAVE Scenario 2. David Swapp re-enters the CAVE environment to adjust the participant's equipment. Video documentation still

verbal on the part of the virtual agents. This articulation of relationships between contexts and spaces also allowed a further heightening of a sense of the virtual agents' stepping in and out of 'performance'. Thus, in the course of the 'experiment' conducted by the agents with the participant, various interruptions – technical, emotional or 'physical', as the agents cough – require their tasks to be interrupted, delayed and restarted or performed again. Following the 'experiment', the virtual scene in the CAVE abruptly changes, and in a 'false ending' the agents overtly 'step out' of character to ask the participant direct questions about their experience: 'How did you feel about all that?'

Extract from Section 3: the agents conduct the 'experiment'

Female agent (*to Participant*):
[SF20] Thanks for coming. Now we can begin. We'd like you to complete a task about emotional intelligence: you know, empathy, sympathy, that kind of thing. I know David has explained this already – or he should have done. OK. On the wall we're going to bring up a picture of a well known celebrity. You will then see a series of questions that we would like you to respond to. There's no right or wrong to this: anything

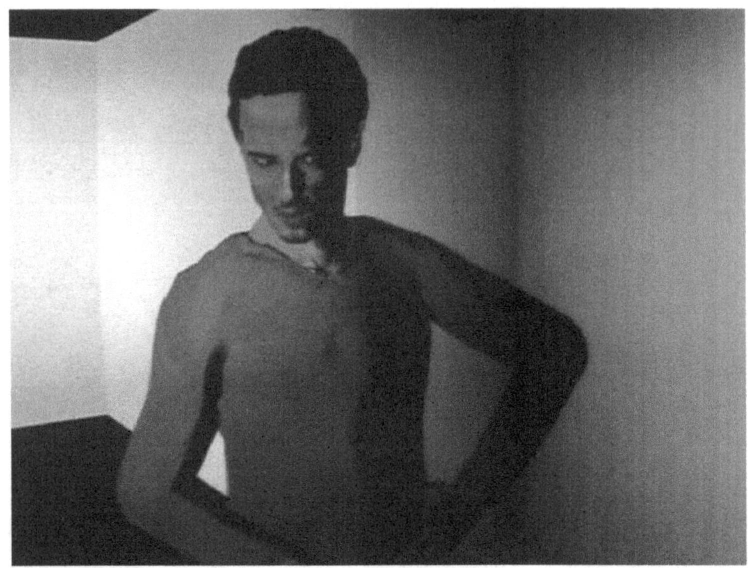

Figure 5.9 Performing Presence, CAVE Scenario 2. The male agent
approaches the participant. 'You did something with the glasses, right?' Video
documentation still

> you say will be really helpful. We'll practise – so this isn't the real thing.
> (*To David*) David, can we have the first practice picture? (*To partici-*
> *pant*) If you have any questions, just ask.
> A blurred image of someone unrecognizable is projected on to the wall.
> Female agent (*to David, agitated*):
> **[SF21]** David, has something gone wrong?
> David (*from outside CAVE*):
> No, it's fine here.
> Male and Female agents look at the participant. Female agent looks
> at the ground, then leaves. Male agent moves closer to the Participant.
> Male agent (*to Participant*):
> **[SF22]** We kept telling you not to touch anything, didn't we? You did
> something with the glasses, right? We're responsible for what happens
> in here, you know. Just don't make it any worse for me.
>   [From Performing Presence, CAVE scenario 2, script]

Within this structure, the scenario also presented a number of
exchanges and negotiations between the two virtual agents, revealing
tensions and mistrust between them, and between the virtual agents
and 'David', whose competence was continually questioned. The script
design thus aimed at positioning the participant, who was invited to

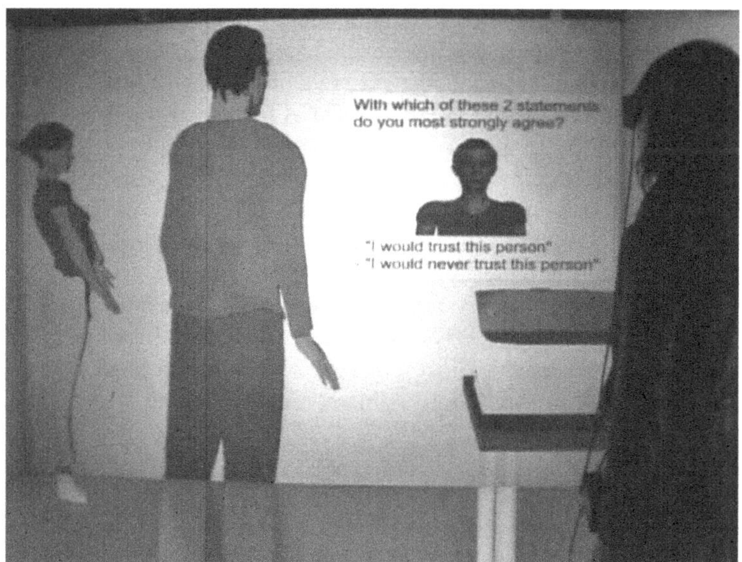

Figure 5.10 Performing Presence, CAVE Scenario 2. The agents conduct the 'experiment': participants are invited to comment on their feelings toward the female agent. Video documentation still

respond at various points to each virtual agent and to the experimenter, in the context of a dynamic and changing set of relationships between real and virtual agents, between the distinct 'characters' they appeared to express and between the spaces they occupied. During the course of the experiment, each of the agents also displayed a variety of attitudes toward the participant through indirect responses as well as direct address. Attitudes were also expressed, as in the first scenario, through continually changing proxemic relationships between the virtual agents and the agents and the participant. Yet, throughout this process, the agents' focus remained on stepping in and out of their performance of the experiment, a shifting that, in reference to 'David', repeatedly stressed a flow of action and exchanges between 'real' and 'virtual' environments, processes and roles.

The analysis of questionnaires and interviews arising out of the experiment showed that overall, of the forty individual participants experiencing scenario 2, many felt involved in the characters' interaction, and that their emotional and physical response to the virtual characters was as if they were 'real', even though most participants commented on the fact that the agents were not real. One participant claimed, 'When the man asks if I had fiddled the equipment I knew it wasn't real but I found myself behaving as if it were real.' Most participants felt to some degree intimidated by the female agent's directness, an aspect amplified in the actors' version of the scenario. A participant commented on feeling uncomfortable, because of a clash between realistic expression and behaviour and the possibility of interaction. When asked why they felt uncomfortable, the respondent replied, 'I think because her facial expression was actually quite neutral, but the look was directly into my eyes. . . . So she didn't really show any kind of believable emotion when she actually looked directly at me. . . . It was – it was the intensity of the look, actually, because it was really directly into my eyes, not just, like, next to my head, maybe.' Finally, this participant then pointed to one of the central outcomes of this experiment, remarking that:

> you know that they're not real, but I think like we're used to seeing computer-generated images perhaps, like a smaller screen, kind of, like, safely contained, and when they're the same size as you and they can speak to you and they can come, like, towards you, it's very uncomfortable, maybe because you're not used to seeing them quite in that way. . . . Maybe I was frightened that she was going to like try and touch me or something (*laughs*), even though I knew she couldn't . . . if she tried to do anything I think I might have . . . had to take the glasses off or something.

Another participant also remarked on the female agent's 'rudeness' and felt this somehow made her seem more 'real' while suggesting that the male agent was 'fake', he was 'acting':

> before I went in there was this girl, she seemed very rude and she was screaming, so I guess that made the experience more real . . . when I walked in she was still upset, she was upset with you [David Swapp] because there was something wrong, and so you had to come in and fix it. And then she comes in and she was still upset. . . . And that's when I thought, maybe she is somewhere here, she must be real, she seemed real. But when the guy came in from the toilet and I could hear the flush, that didn't seem real at all. So the male part didn't seem real at all. And then he came and he stood next to me and he was asking me if I did anything, but that seemed like it was fake, he was acting.

Mainly, participants felt that they were part of the experiment, though they did not always feel equally involved. One participant clearly stated that the interaction itself 'made it seem more real', and another commented on the fact that it was the agent's coughing and moving, and, most important, the directness of their gaze that made them react to the scenario. Interestingly, this participant also suggested that they felt part of the experiment because David was interacting with the agents: "cos you were treating them as interactional things, so it made me feel like . . . I was part of the whole interaction as well'. Another participant noted that David's interaction with the agents made them more 'believable' and, when asked to comment on the agent's behaviour, answered, 'Abusive. The woman was abusive towards you. Rude. I felt bad for you. I was thinking, Oh, she's really rude [laughs], that's not a way to treat a professor.' Some participants felt the agents were responsive, so much so that one participant read the agents' lack of response as significant, claiming: 'I smiled at them and they didn't respond. [Laughs.] So I thought, Okay, they're not going to be friendly, I shouldn't say anything.' Similar comments were made for the scenario using naive performers, with two participants emphasizing the effect of the agents' proximity: 'At some points the characters seemed to stand a little close and I stepped back, which is what I would do in real life.' Others commented on feeling uncomfortable when 'they stood too close. . . . there were times when both of the characters stood a little bit close, so I found myself stepping back because of the lack of personal space'. Participants again tended to feel as if they were part of an experience or 'real life experiment', in which context they often perceived strong differences between the male and female agents. For a significant number of participants, such responses were also heightened in those moments in which the scenario explicitly combined or juxtaposed 'virtual' and 'real' aspects, leading one participant to directly articulate a heightened presence response in a moment of overt hybridity between 'real' and 'virtual' spaces and contexts. Recounting her experience in interview with David Swapp immediately following the experiment, the participant notes that 'I went into the room and you set me up with the right equipment. And you were told it wasn't right, so you had to come back into the room. Which was quite interesting to me also, because it felt that the two worlds inside and outside the room were merging, which made it feel even more realistic.'

In its design, scenario 2 emphasized a multiplication of spaces and transitions between them: the space of the 'real' experiment in the lab; the overtly 'virtual space' of the agents' 'experiment'; the intrusion of David Swapp from the lab into the CAVE application; the agents' continual reference and referral to the space 'outside' and conversations with 'David' across the threshold of the virtual and real spaces; the agents' occupation of different virtual spaces as the scenario unfolds. In doing so, the design looked toward a continual 'stepping through' of thresholds and traversal of frames and spaces by both virtual and real 'participants', including the subject themselves. In turn, these multiplications and traversals may be seen as amplifying the doublings and overlayings of the virtual and real that form the underlying condition and structure of the participant's experience of CAVE applications. In this context, the 'merging' or 'blurring' spaces in which the experience of the 'virtual' approaches that of the 'real' suggests a performance of *this place* by participants, a transitory claim to 'being there' in their enactment of the 'mutual' construction of their own and others' positions in this collocation of spaces.

Such outcomes also suggest that for these participants the co-presence and interaction of 'virtual' and 'real' performers and their engagement with spaces and contexts beyond the virtual world generated by the CAVE application did not diminish – and may have amplified – their response to virtual agents' behaviours. It is an effect suggested, also, by the high level of active participation by subjects, who, almost exclusively, responded to the 'real' questions asked of them by the agents in conducting the 'virtual' experiment. In turn, a heightened experience of these participant's *own presence* was produced in moments and events that articulated the 'two worlds' in which the scenario functioned, or, more precisely, their positioning simultaneously *in* and *before* the 'virtual' and 'real' worlds that face each other in this scenario. Here, rather than negotiate between 'competing signals' to achieve a sense of presence in the experience of a continuous or unified realm that defines their place in a 'virtual' 'here' by excluding signals from the 'everyday', these participants responded strongly to the interrelationship of virtual and real locations, behaviours and actions. In these scenarios, then, and for these participants, the response to the virtual environment, agents and actions 'as if' they were real has been amplified *in* moments of hybridity and apparent spatial and contextual disjunction. Indeed, some participants identified a sense of movement between states and spaces, between 'virtual' and 'real' performers and performances – and so between the 'simulated' and the 'live'– as a specific axis in which their experience of 'presence' gained ground. 'Simulation', in these moments, returns to a movement in relation to 'the real', while the experience of 'presence' becomes processual and so related, in kind, to phenomena of presence produced in *tracing, emergence* and in the traversal of difference or distant spaces and positions.

Such conclusions echo and may clearly inform understandings of the operation of presence through performance and media art. Thus in their installations and media artworks Hershman and Hill both articulate a 'facing' of the mediated, represented and the 'real' – and collocations of these figures – in approaches to phenomena of presence.

Sermon, whose telepresence installations are in relation to technologies and experiences of virtual reality, emphasizes spatial fragmentation, difference and distance precisely in order that the *action* and engagement of the participant might realize 'their' experience of presence across this system and network. In the work of Tony Oursler, The Builders Association and Blast Theory, too, this analysis of the experience of CAVE is pertinent. Tony Oursler's video installations emphasize the *ghosting* of one order of space by another, to provoke a sense of the 'presence' of 'media entities' produced in the viewer's traversal of real and virtual spaces and investment in media forms. The Builders Association's multimedia theatre performances, in contrast, articulate *disjunctions* between orders of space and modes of performance to explore phenomena of presence produced in the 'interface between live and electronically mediated' (The Builders Association 2002) channels of address. Finally, Blast Theory and the Mixed Reality Laboratory produce experiences of 'pervasive presence' in modes of work that position the participant's actions simultaneously across multiple networks operating in differing configurations of space and real and 'dramatic' time. In each of these departures, the experience of presence arises in a multiplication or dislocation of place and space and through a mobility and exchange of place and position.

6

ghosting Tony Oursler

Tony Oursler's work spans single-channel video, video installation, projection, performance, music and DVD-ROM. Emerging in the late 1970s, his engagement with media has been closely tied to an interrogation of the affective nature of video, television and film. Latterly, Oursler's work has advanced these concerns by engaging with the performance and perception of presence in ways that articulate and test relationships between individual experience, identity and media forms. Indeed, since his exhibition of *The Waiting* in 1992, which incorporated multiple projective figures set in 'real' space, Oursler's work has emphasized the operation of the video image in the spaces and times of performance and encounter, approached in the location of projected and screened images on to three-dimensional objects, including dummies and mannequins, flowers, spheres and abstract sculptural forms. Overtly theatrical in their negotiation of place, presentation and projection, these works cast ostensibly 'acting' or 'interacting' recordings, including faces and figures, over fixed forms, objects or sites, and in doing so direct attention towards the liminal spaces and conditions between media, mediation and the internal states and belief systems in which identities are drawn. It in this nexus of spaces – and in the uncanny mirroring of the viewer in the animated forms and media they encounter – that Oursler also engages with the possibility of 'affect ' in its various meanings – in the sense of media's capacity 'to have an affect on the feelings . . . or on things', but also in correspondences between media forms and 'mental disposition . . . desire, passion' or even 'bodily disposition' (*OED*). Within the mechanisms of Oursler's work, it is as a function of these interstices and overlaps that phenomena of presence arise between these installations' constituent elements and the viewer's investment and action. It is in this enacted 'sense' of presence, too, that Oursler's work 'ghosts' its various forms, and in which it turns towards the interrogation of mutual dependences between identities and 'media structures'. Here, too, in prompting empathic and cathartic responses to the frequently conflicted, ambiguous and repetitive behaviours of a 'media entity' (Oursler in Rothschild 1999: 14), Oursler's works produce ambivalent and ironic challenges to the individual's consumption of, participation in and subjection to phenomena of presence explicitly produced in media signs, forms and systems.

Inhabited spaces

A meeting with *Bluerealisation with Head* (2007), one of seven such 'splatter paintings' (Cooke and Oursler 2008: 87) grouped in a single room under the title *Ooze* for the Lehmann Maupin Gallery, New York, February–March 2007, immediately confronts the visitor with the overt

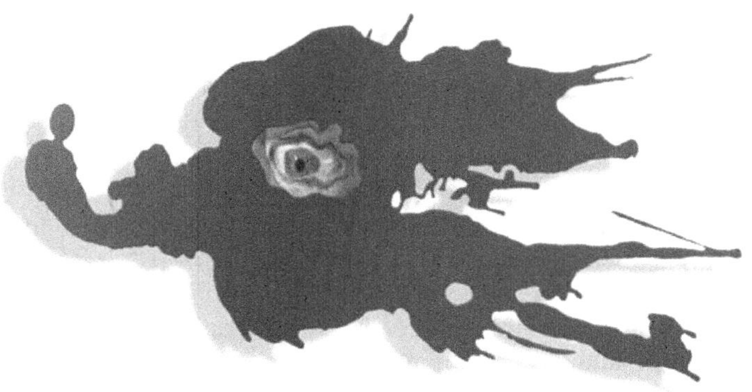

Figure 6.1 Tony Oursler, *Bluerealisation with Head* (2007). Aluminum, acrylic, LCD screen, DVD player. Dimensions 92 in. × 42 in. × 4½ in. (233.7 cm × 106.7 cm × 11.4 cm)

play across forms, spaces and times in which Oursler's work frequently captures the onlooker's attention. Formed in aluminium, and set slightly off the gallery wall to achieve an explicit depth in real space, each of these pieces presents a hand-painted surface which has been opened to reveal mediated body parts – an eye or eyes, a face, lips, fingers – morphed to reflect the abstract shapes in which they are captured. It is a form that plays on pictorial and painterly space, as well as sculpture, video and performance. Indeed, in re-siting the signs of video art within painting and offering references to the painted surface, as well as abstraction and the hand, *Ooze*, like a number of Oursler's series since 2003, recollects his early shift of medium from paint to video. Remarking in his essay, 'Sketches at Twilight' on the evolution of the single-channel tapes that formed a principal focus of his work from 1979 to 1992, Oursler notes that during his training at Cal Arts:

> [t]he possibility of entering a video space was radical and ultimately desirable for me . . . My experiments in painting ended up in front of a camera and I often painted while looking through a camera . . . Through the lens my pictures could be electrified with all the attributes of life: if they needed a hand or a mouth I would just cut a hole and stick the body part through it. . . . I was struck by the ability of the camera to alter the laws of physics; to transform matter, space and time, inanimate to animate: worlds unto themselves.   [Oursler 1997]

In an extension of his early conclusion that 'video contains the history of image making' (Oursler 1997), *Bluerealisation with Head* asserts a 'media space' that is liminal and transformative – and one defined in a contamination of the various worlds in which it is constituted. Formed, Oursler notes, from 'a blowup of a trace of a drip, or drop or drool – some kind of liquid spill' (Cooke and Oursler 2008: 87), each work in the *Ooze* series plays between the muteness and distance of abstract painting, the intimacy of the video or television screen and an animation of the body and its products. Carrying forward Oursler's sculptural address to the body through his projections on to dummies and objects that formed a principal departure in his work from 1992 and playing directly to the viewer's tendency to anthropomorphize three-dimensional, animated and time-based forms, the panels in *Ooze* operate as palimpsests of meaning and identity. With respect to this series Oursler notes:

> Colour is such a personal thing . . . yet colour carries a slippery cultural history of absurd codification. Depending on which subculture you read, red is for valentines, white for purity or semen, purple for mourning. In

these panels I wanted to play across the projected light of TV and the reflected colour fields, suggesting body fluids, blood splatter patterns and a history of painted space . . . In any one of these works there are pools of different mediums, perspectives and conflicting languages. This is an attempt to reconcile two worlds that can't coexist.   [Cooke and Oursler 2008: 87]

It is a crossing of worlds underpinned, too, by Oursler's overlaying of pictorial, physical and sculptural spaces, whereby, he notes, screened and projected images are 'trapped to resonate in sculptural form' such that 'the disembodied is recontextualised in the installation' (Oursler in Kelley 1999: 47). In *Ooze*, then, over time, the mediatized eye in *Bluerealisation with Head* mimics an exploration of the space before it: looking down, the eyelid closes, opens again. Eventually, the performer on video (Oursler himself) moves back, articulating a further virtual depth behind the picture plane. Moving in and out of shadow and focus, at times shaking his head rapidly, his mouth then comes to take the place of the eye; the 'panel' 'speaks texts very quietly', following Oursler's prescription that 'a painting should whisper if it has to say anything' (Oursler in Cooke 2008: 87). In intimate proximity to the viewer, the work introduces a further reference, seemingly science fiction: 'see outside range of your vehicle . . . see . . . yes, I cried'.

Simultaneously, on an adjacent wall, the lips of *Red 'Love Hurts' Laboratory* (2007) purse repeatedly and with some difficulty; it whispers. Like its partner pieces, *Red 'Love Hurts' Laboratory* operates in disjunctive relationships between spaces and practices. On moving closer to listen its construction becomes apparent: the hard surface, the brushstrokes, the screen, and distortion of the mouth; the skin of the performer blushed red with make-up. The whisper is difficult to make out: 'It happens.' Grouped together with *Pink-too-long Fluid* (2007), *(Usually) Black Anythingyou want* (2007) and its four other companion pieces, these works seem to take up each other's time. Fixed to the wall, they assert a belonging to the animated realm of the visitor: some of them appear to look and wait.

In their trespass into 'real space', Oursler's installation of screened and projected images exploits and amplifies the liminality of the video and television image, its definition and operation *across* rather than *in* locations and spaces. Indeed, a complex relationship to television in Oursler's work and its link to the staging and performance of 'presence' is evident, too, in his earliest video works. Oursler's first tapes explicitly interrogated television and its formats as a transformative and invasive medium, in work which employed deliberately impoverished materials and partial forms, a tactic prompting the artist Tony Conrad's later

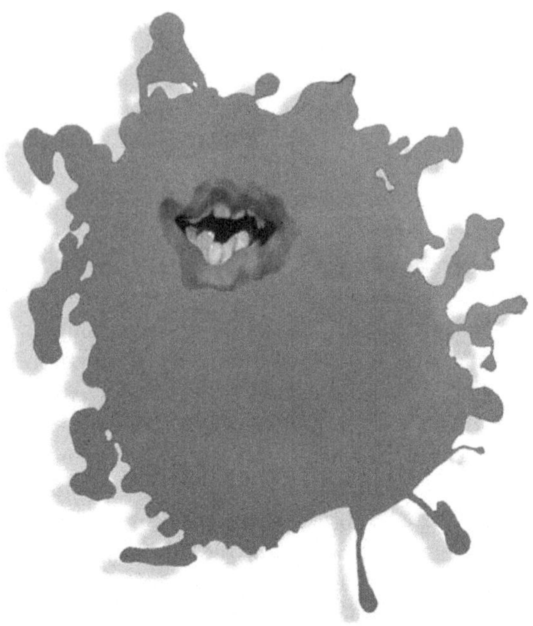

Figure 6.2 Tony Oursler, *Red 'Love Hurts' Laboratory* (2007). Aluminium, acrylic, LCD screen, DVD player. Dimensions 58 in. × 47 in. × 4½ in. (147.3 cm × 119.4 cm × 11.4 cm)

observation that Oursler's 'work is built on inaccuracy in representation' (Conrad in DeJong and Conrad 1995: 7) and which serves to draw the viewer towards an investment in its codes and forms. Here, too, the importance of performance and painting to Oursler's development of a 'video grammar' is evident in the recording of his overtly theatrical realization of improvised scenes within hand-made and painted sets. Foregrounding his function as performer, *Life of Phillis* (1977), Oursler's earliest extant tape, is comprised of a series of vignettes in which Oursler's hands are seen manipulating dolls, objects and materials in rudimentary set constructions in such a way that, he recalls, 'nothing was really hidden from the viewer' (Oursler in Kelley 1999: 40). Originally an installation in which episodes were played live to camera and reel-to-reel VCR at noon each day at Cal Arts, and later compiled into a 55-minute single-channel work, *Life of Phillis* plays through fragmentary, tabloid-inspired narratives that, Oursler recalled, 'revolve around a desperate, young, abused girl character, someone out of the pages of the *National Enquirer*' (Oursler in Kelley 1999: 42). In doing so, the piece exemplifies the 'personal/pop' sources of his early work, which he details as:

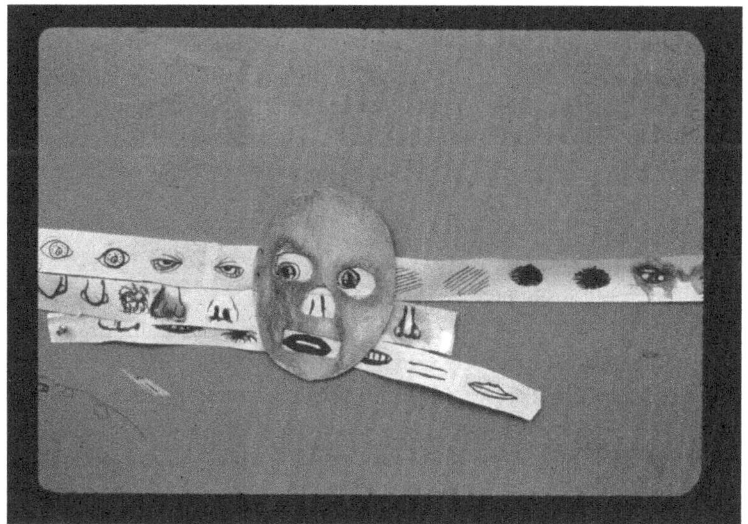

Figure 6.3 Tony Oursler, *Life of Phillis* (1977). Production still

a combo of supermarket tabloids and personal experience, mostly things that I picked up aurally from others. I was like a narrative antenna in the early work – studying and collecting urban legends, fables, folk tales. The only unifying factor in these tales is that they never really happened. They are always told second or third-hand: 'Listen to this: a friend of a friend had this happen'.   [Oursler in Kelley 1999: 71–2]

Filtered through 'the grainy, almost mystical space' produced by early mono video, in which, Oursler suggests, '[y]ou could almost see the machine turning reality into a shimmering approximation of itself' (Oursler in Kelley 1999: 39), these early single-channel tapes engage with video's construction of the meaning and reception of the mediated object. Like the subsequent *Diamond Head* (1979) and *Good Things and Bad* (1979), it is a tape that plays overtly on the viewer's reading of degraded objects and indexical signs as the protagonists and victims of extreme events and emotions, a process in which the theatrical character of Oursler's performance to camera, his reference to familiar formats and the visual allure and distancing of the screen, are instrumental. Here, Oursler suggests, 'I was playing with our desire to get lost in narrative space/time. We love a story so much that we will breathe life into it no matter how much it is degraded' (Oursler in Kelley 1999: 40). Indeed, in these early works the transformative effect of this video space – and the viewer's desire for its production of meaning – is exposed, leading him towards the conclusion that '[w]hat we call narration is, in fact, a psychic or mental predisposition of the reader or spectator more than it is a structure' (Oursler in Ardenne 2005: 43). Such tapes directly set the ground for Oursler's later relocation of the video image into three-dimensional space through their interrogation of electronic media as systems whose terms include (and so shape) the viewer's predispositions, and thus the performance of meaning, emotion and affect.

From 1980, Oursler extended these processes towards the camera's intense illumination and remediation of colour, manipulating the camera controls to amplify the shifts produced in contemporary analogue technology. Adapting graphic ideas from his painting to video, Oursler applied paint while looking through the lens, mixing colours to exploit the screen's illumination, and combining 'all sorts of styles and levels of symbolism' while playing 'with voice, sound, and music and narrative' (Oursler in Kelley 1999: 40). Here, too, he approached his single-channel tapes and subsequent installations as embedded into and referencing wider systems that embraced and defined the viewer's position, as, he suggests, 'I use a method of connecting systems: personal to public. That is why I'm intrigued [by] psycho-history' (Oursler in Janus 1999: 73). Indeed, these single-channel tapes and the early installations play overtly on equations between media technologies and psychological states and processes. Here, too, Oursler's work examines media in reference to historical and contemporary associations in popular culture between electronic media and the supernatural, 'spiritual' or 'other-worldliness' (including science fiction), as well as triggers and cues to emotional response and expectation. These dream-like works were thus 'designed to mirror a thought pattern or process', and so operate 'in opposition to a film grammar, which is . . . attempting to replace the eye' (Oursler in Janus 1999: 70–1). It is a grammar that serves also to challenge the containment and over-determination with regard to meaning and experience that Oursler has identified with conventional and commercial film practice. To this end, this work presents images in states of apparent incompletion or that are emergent through a layering of form and practices and as part of an address to the character of video as an *affective medium*: a medium that is implicitly *in exchange* with those it addresses, and in relation to which attitudes, behaviours and dispositions are formed. Oursler has thus noted that underpinning his practice is the proposition that 'if an image *exists*, then it has already destroyed the possibility of being constructed by the viewer. I'm like the guy who goes to church because he likes the smell of incense. I'm lost but I'm looking for the magic' (Oursler 2002: 165).

In this step, too, Oursler's 'grammar' coalesces explicitly around issues of presence, prompting questions such as 'What constitutes a media entity? Would a moving dot with a voice attached be accepted as a real actor? What makes something animate?' (Oursler in Rothschild 1999: 14). As a consequence, while including residual references to plot, storytelling, scene and character, this address embraces the viewer's complicity in animating the work; their participation and investment in its form and import. Thus Oursler noted that for *Grand Mal* (1981), one of the most influential of his single-channel works, 'I thought of the viewer as the character. He or she is actually participating in a state of mind. That was the goal; to collaborate with the viewer, give them enough room to dream, to read into the signs yet to follow a loose path' (Oursler in Kelley 1999: 44).

It is a transposition of the image towards three-dimensional space, too, that further calls into question its 'proper place' and formation, its 'containment' within the narrative trajectories it may invoke and the visual and time-based work of which it forms a part. Indeed, for the philosopher Samuel Weber it is precisely the 'uncanny confusion' over the 'proper' place of the mediated image that accounts for 'the specificity of the televisual medium' (Weber 1996: 109). Writing in *Mass Mediaurus: Form, Technics, Media* (1996) Weber identifies the functioning of the television and video image with the effect of an uncanny temporal and spatial *closeness*, in an analysis that further links the functioning of the mediated image to questions of presence. Rather than simply offer the capacity to see objects and events at a distance, Weber argues, the televisual image asserts a *presentness* of vision to its object, expressed in a *continuity of view* (the camera's reproduction of vision) that it sets before those who watch. In this operation, Weber proposes, television 'transports vision as such and sets it immediately before the viewer. It entails not merely a heightening of the naturally limited powers of sight with respect to certain distant objects: it involves a transmission or transposition of vision itself' (Weber 1996: 116). As a consequence, Weber suggests, integral to the experience of broadcast television, and reproduced in video's recorded image, is a doubling or layering of vision, for 'What we see, above and beyond the content of the images, is someone or something seeing. But that someone or something remains at an irreducible distance from the television viewer' (Weber 1996: 122). Here, while television and video's mediations bring absent objects into view, so their pressing of 'vision' towards the viewer produces a simultaneous closeness in experience and perception, such that, in these images, '[f]ar and near' become 'no longer mutually exclusive but rather converge and overlap' (Weber 1996: 125). In this context, Weber

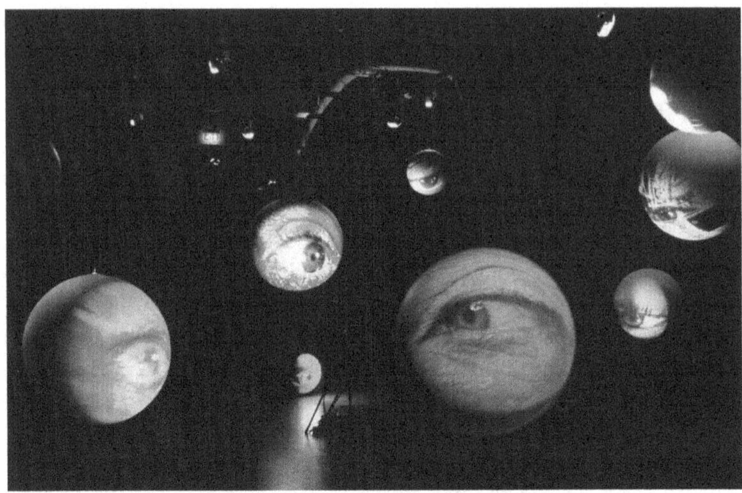

Figure 6.4 Tony Oursler, *Eyes* (1996)

understands the common use of the phrase 'to watch' television (as opposed to 'see' or 'seeing') as a perceptual response demanded by this layering of vision and its production of images that seem 'neither fully there nor entirely here' (Weber 1996: 20). 'To "watch",' Weber argues, 'is to look for something that is not immediately apparent. It implies effort, a tension and a separation' (Weber 1996: 119). It is a separation that extends to the time of watching too, as, Weber concludes, the 'irreducible distance' produced in this layering of vision 'splits the "sameness" of the instant of perception' (Weber 1996: 122). Television, then, doubles and mimics the viewer's viewing, introducing an awareness of and distance from 'seeing' in perception itself; it is a medium that 'presents' vision, but also transforms it.

In this context, the frequent emphasis in Oursler's installations on the eye and the gesture of these 'disembodied' images' return of the gaze articulates multiple dimensions of this media's relationship with the viewer. 'Trapped' as they are in the 'real' spaces of their installation, these forms animate and amplify television's 'uncanny confusion' of its image's 'proper place'. Here, too, the media entity's 'surveilling' of the spaces before it plays on the demand on the viewer 'to watch', asserting a look that *looks back* in a parodic and figurative articulation of the mediated image's construction of 'someone or something seeing', and with this the image's claim to intimacy, its entry into 'the home', into 'private' space. It is an equation between camera and eye, too, that furthers the implicit investigation in this work into the media

as an anthropomorphic mirror that disturbs the position of its auditors, opening the possibility that it may displace its viewers rather than
simply reproduce them. Oursler thus notes that:

> Eyes are always talked about as being the mirror of the soul, and I expected
> them to be expressive. But when you tape just the eye, disembodied from
> other facial features, it is totally blank. It looks cold and reptilian. Seen
> alone, the eye comes across as a light-measuring organ devoid of emotion,
> like a camera.　　[Oursler in Rothschild: 24]

Although quite distinct in form, the works in *Ooze* are similarly
designed in alertness to the time and attention of the viewer and towards
a testing of response. Indeed, the *Ooze* series shares a referential complexity with Oursler's earlier de-compositions of narrative structure. For
Ooze, in a room adjacent to the installations at the Lehmann Maupin
Gallery, seven corresponding works on paper, comprising clusters of
images, drawings and notes, allude to outlines, contexts, forms and
processes that underpin various aspects of these animated presences.
Relating these works, in part, to the major site-specific piece, *Blue
Invasion*, created in collaboration with Constance DeJong to take place
throughout Hyde Park North, Sydney, Australia, in January 2007, this
aspect of the exhibition links these individual installations to Oursler's
published writing on colour, as well as referencing ghosts, extraterres-
trial contact, the electromagnetic spectrum, meteors, colour-blindness
tests, and the aurora borealis, while also presenting overtly intertextual
connections with his other works and writing. Indeed, the use of colour
in these installations is implicitly linked to the *TimeStream* project
(Oursler 2001), Oursler's publicly available and extensive media archaeology exploring popular responses to new media and its psychological
and folkloric consequences and counterparts. Here, and as with many of
Oursler's installations since the mid-1990s that are infused with references to the history and practices of media, the works in *Ooze* offer allusions to the layers of meanings within which media structures operate.
In this context, and suggesting that '[t]echnology embodies Science and
Fiction, literally' (Oursler 2002: 161), Oursler has aligned his address to
popular, psychological, and hysterical responses to media with perceptions of presence or, more precisely, with a sense that: 'Technologies
attach themselves to the interface between our conscious and unconscious states, so, in a sense, they *are* alive. Or at least, they seem to be
. . . The anthropomorphizing of media,' he concludes, 'is very natural'
(Oursler in Neri 2001: 61, original emphasis).

Being before itself

Oursler's introduction of projections on to the figure of the dummy from 1992 explicitly directed this grammar towards the location of the video image in three-dimensional space, creating strongly ambivalent plays between the animated dummy as mirror (of the viewer's body in real space) and surrogate (of the artist as performer). Emphasizing a migration towards real space rather than any resolution into sculptural form, this work articulated the image's occupation of the material conditions it would ostensibly transcend. In this context, and where the 'fact or condition of being present' may be understood as 'the state of being before, in front of' (*OED*), the presence of the figure in these installations is manifested as a closeness felt *in* distance, as a *division* and *tension* in relation to the proximity of an object and its animation. Here, then, in pressing the image towards 'physical' space, Oursler foregrounds the divisions and limitations of video's incursion into 'the real', rather than a synthesis or resolution of relationships between media and spaces. In doing so, Oursler's work engages with a doubling of spaces and bodies – and so implicitly with problematics that stand in relation to the participant's encounter with virtual agents in immersive virtual reality environments, including CAVE. In the context of these strategies, Oursler's approach to the figure, in particular, may be seen to emphasize a double movement: a closeness, achieved in a direct emotional address in which the projection strikes a charged and specific position in relation to the viewer; and a distancing produced in the spatial dynamic in which its auditor is approached. Extending the implicit psychological positioning of the viewer before the work in *Grand Mal*, then, Oursler's early dummy installations, including *Crying Doll* (1993), *White Trash/Phobic* (1993), *Getaway #2* (1994) and *Judy* (1994), were, he has suggested, conceived as 'empathy tests or traps' (Oursler in Kelley 1999: 53). Purposely 'scaled to the size of a doll or elf' to elicit a sentimental identification on behalf of the viewer, *Crying Doll* thus demands the viewer's attention and emotional investment through, Oursler recalls, 'its superhuman ability to never stop weeping, which in turn becomes horrifying to the viewer, who must eventually turn away' (Oursler in Rothschild 1999: 22). At the same time, *Crying Doll* works against any sense of a unified form or seamless illusion. Exploiting, he notes, 'our natural instinct to see oneself in every perceived situation' (Oursler in Rothschild 1999: 22), *Crying Doll* exposes props and mechanisms of its operation: the untransformed materials comprising its seemingly unfinished body; the wooden support; the projector focused on its face, as if surveilling rather than animating its activity. In time, the figure also reveals its repetitions; it cries *again*, further asserting its operation in a series of separations. Indeed, in this mechanism, *Crying Doll* articulates conflicts between its projected and 'found' components: its looped image suggests an animation of materials that precede it and remain stubbornly inert; yet its material form and fixity lend 'meaning' to its distress. Here, the very elements that assert the dummy's occupation and functioning in the same space as the viewer also divide it from and before the viewer, extending its emotional gesture, articulating the dilemma of its migration into the real space and spectacle of its exhibition. In this respect the composer Tony Conrad, one of Oursler's collaborators, observes that:

> These are not unified individual works in the modernist sense; each is an art piece which has made a break for it, has *escaped the Frame*, but then – hobbled by the tether of video (its cables, the implied – even if not visible – framing the edges of the video image) – it fails, importantly, to stand free, and instead is pinned in place, projected flat, a crushed soul, skewered in the din.   [Conrad 2001: 150–1, original emphasis]

It is an aspect of this work Oursler frequently amplifies, too, in emphasizing the dummies' lack of mobility: trapping them under furniture; pinning them to the floor. Where for *Crying Doll*, as well as *Hysterical* (1993), *Full Moon* (1993) and *MMPI Test Doll* (1992), the figure is suspended on a wooden or metal pole, for *Getaway #2* the dummy lies on the floor, its head (and projection) seemingly stuck beneath the corner of a mattress. *MMPI (Red)* (1997) is similarly immobilized beneath an upturned chair, while the head of *Pinned* (1995) is painfully fixed to the floor under the foot of a chair leg.

The rise of Multiple Personality Disorder, MPD, in the USA during recent years and its connection to media have informed my plans for the production of the installation for the Kunstverein in Salzburg. The installation will take the form of a number of figures which 'transform' into one another in a rough line a cross the gallery. The progression of interrelationships can be traversed by the viewer/ participant who is also invited to sit within the group structure and interact with it by working a remote control camera. The figures/ objects are sparsely constructed dummies/scarecrows and dolls, piles of dirt and pieces of furniture which represent various aspects and manifestations of MPD within a fictitious individual. A number of these figures/objects are given voice and expression by means of

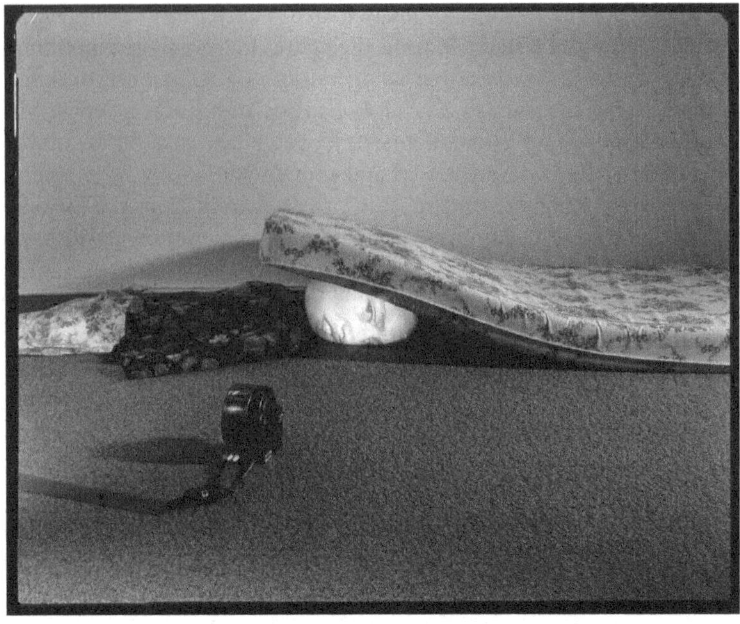

Figure 6.5 Tony Oursler, *Judy* (1994). Detail

projecting video images upon them. Thus a composite image can be perceived by the viewer/participant, much like all the characters of a drama performing independently at the same time (while in reality one would experience only a few aspects of the illness at a time).

[From Tony Oursler, 'Proposal for *Judy*, an installation at Salzburg Kunstverein', 1994]

It is in the articulation of such dilemmas, too, that the affective 'presence' of the dummies is advanced. Where in the single-channel tapes, Oursler suggests to Kelley, '[c]onversion from real to video space was a big part of my process', these installations also perform a reversal of this movement. Thus, where Oursler's installation serves to literally and metaphorically support the projection's *virtual* act and identity, so it also manifests and traps this 'virtual character' in 'real' space. It is a tactic that exploits and amplifies the spatial complexity of these installations' operation to articulate 'the portion of space before or around someone or something' (*OED*). Indeed, the figures in the dummy installations invariably appear to seize and multiply the *spaces before*, asserting, in their relationship to the onlooker, the 'presence' of their virtual spaces to their material support, just as these supports are dramatized by, and seemingly become *present to*, the virtual character's state of distress. In this way, its own divisions amplify the sense of the dummy's 'being before' the viewer, as its 'virtual identity' and emotional gesture are performed in oscillation between 'real' and 'video' spaces.

Furthermore, and seemingly giving vent to the emotional consequences of their manifestation in 'material conditions' for which they appear ill equipped, these figures' verbal statements deftly occupy positions between their own animation and a construction – or reflection – of the viewer's attitude, who, it seems, may share or be responsible for the situation in which they find themselves. In giving voice to this permeability between figure and visitor, Oursler's installations are charged with refusals, rebuttals and feigned transgressions, which, in the early doll and mannequin projections were invariably stated 'by' the figure itself. Thus the dummies implicitly direct their frustrations towards the visitor in reflections upon the indignity of their position. Trapped under an upturned armchair, the doll-like figure of *Judy* (1994) repeats: 'Fuck you, fuck, fuck, fuck, you fuck . . .' (Malsch 1995: 15). In *Flowers (Undermind)* (1994), the features of a face – an eye, a mouth – can be seen dispersed across a display of cut flowers, as it mouths: 'You suck. I'm going to turn you into the wall, the floor; you are nothing. You should have never been born. No. No. No' (Malsch 1995: 19). For the critic Deborah Rothschild, these installations perform a 'media introjection', a process she extrapolates from the psychoanalytical term indicating the internalizing and reproduction of behaviours from the subject's surrounding world. Thus, in absorbing the media, these inanimate objects at once display the 'living characteristics' of the onlooker, while prompting a corresponding recognition of 'our assimilation of thoughts and behaviours from television and film' (Rothschild 1999: 12). In this context, Rothschild cites the critic Peter Schejeldahl's response to *Getaway #2*, that comprises a head animated by a looped projection on to a pillow, with a prone body formed from loosely stuffed jacket and pyjama trousers tied at each end, which:

> simmers with disconsolate fury at the injury of its helpless condition and the insult of being trapped in public view. Occasionally its restless eyes fix the visitor and it speaks, 'Hey, you. Get out here. What are you looking at?' After pausing for mournful reflection, it tries again. 'I'll kick your ass,' it hazards with measured venom but not much conviction.   [Schejeldahl in Rothschild 1999: 30]

–   So why do they move, then?

+   To approximate life's relationship to technology. The effigy becomes

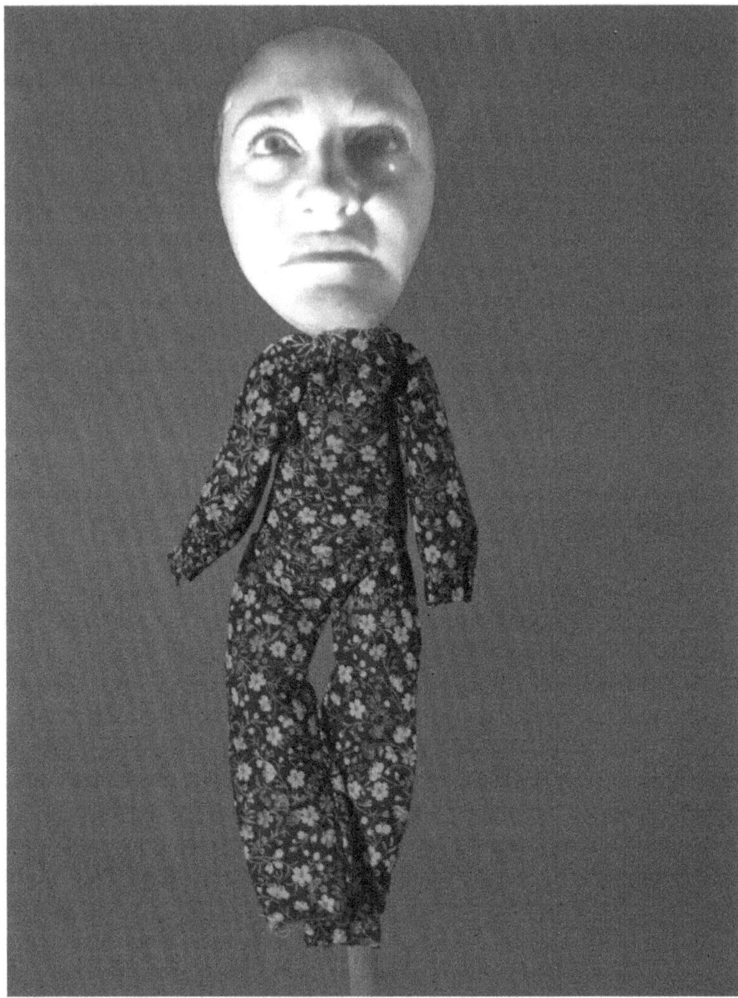

Figure 6.6 Tony Oursler, *Crying Doll* (1993)

the focus of ridicule: '. . . look at that stupid Dummy with its camera-tunnel vision, something really important could be happening right over here and it would never know it in a million years . . .' But, on the other hand I don't think we should underestimate the capability of a Dummy. That's the tricky part.

–   Like the so-called Phallic Camera that's getting so much press these days.

+   Personification of the camera as well as other technologies is not much more than a cheap marketing ploy. I have a little more faith in people than that; one can tell the difference between their sexual organs and a camera or any other vision shifting device. Ask those who have a micro-camera inserted into their urethra for pathology detection.
−   Evidently you see this gear in that light − as a tool for pathology detection. As a means of asking the viewers to position themselves in relation to some form of pathology.
+   Exactly, no pain, no gain. The Dummies have no faces. They exploit our natural instinct to see oneself in every perceived situation. Dummies have the skill of seasoned panhandler. The viewer may ask: 'Can we accept such a pathetic invitation to empathy?'
    [From Tony Oursler, 'Conversation about Some Recent Work', 1991]

It is here, too, that in his step into installation Oursler furthers his address to the place and function of media as 'mimetic systems' (Oursler in Conrad 2001: 174), a term he reports borrowing from '[p]harmacology, psycho-mimetic drugs, drugs that mimic portions of our mental state' (Oursler in Neri 2001: 56). In this regard, *Window Project* of 1991, which shortly preceded his first use of projections on to dummies and mannequins, provides a clear equation between the development of work in which '[v]ideo no longer acts as a window to look through but is somehow made physical' (Oursler in Kelley 1999: 72) and his positioning of the viewer through allusions to psychological systems, psychiatric conditions, predispositions and malfunction which are implicit in the dummy installations. Consisting of three discrete performances to camera by three performers − the writer and performance artist Karen Finley, the artist and poet Constance DeJong and musician Kim Gordon of *Sonic Youth* − back-projected on to outward facing windows of the gallery, *Window Project* sought 'to counter the passive situation associated with video viewing' (Oursler 1995: 52). Writing Karen Finley's performance *Test*, solely on the basis of his memory of the Minnesota Multiphasic Personality Inventory (MMPI), a series of questions designed to provide the basis of an empirically derived assessment of a subject's psychopathology, Oursler furthered this by integrating a series of statements that reflexively mirrored and interrogated the viewer's attitude and place in the work. Filtered through Oursler's recollection, however, the MMPI becomes a systemic reference whose 'inaccuracy in representation' reflects on Oursler's investment in this 'system' while testing the viewers' recognition of themselves in what remains of this diagnostic procedure. Facing the gallery window from the street, then, Finley presented the viewer with twenty-one statements, including:

1. When in a crowd I feel lost.
2. I like to see all the way to the horizon.
3. I feel connected to others when I watch TV.
4. The people who used to live here are still watching us.
5. God was responsible for the diseases that made them sick.
6. We are pioneers in a dangerous place.
7. Things are the same as they have always been.
8. At certain times killing can't be prevented.

[Oursler 1995: 54]

It is the extension of this engagement with the viewer in the division of the 'media entity' across virtual and real spaces that leads to Oursler's emphasis on its *absences*, which in turn becomes an engine of these experiences and articulations of presence; a mechanism operating in the viewer's continual return to invest in the dummy's *lack*: its *claim* and provocation to presence in its *absence* from *this place*. It is to this end that Oursler's dummies invariably 'act out' and articulate the problem of installation itself, as their trespassing into the dilemmas of materiality works to amplify their occupation of a kind of negative *space before*. In hypothesizing the dummies' conversations Oursler has thus emphasized their negative relationships to the spaces of their installation and to viewers themselves, and so their performance of an ineluctable separation or gap in their invitation to emotional identification. He emphasizes that:

> It's part of their design: provocation through absence. How they relate to each other, to us, is by psychological dependency. If they could speak they might say something like:
> D 1. I occupy space yet I can't perceive that space,
> D 2. I can't occupy your space yet I can perceive it,
> and on like that. Each 'surveils' the other, incapable of self-reflection.   [Oursler 1991: 62]

Such a failure of the figure to fully occupy *its own spaces* is aligned, too, to an 'economy of the uncanny' – a process by which these works 'make space' for the viewer only to disturb the onlooker's position as they act out a 'being before' that questions in whose place and presence the 'media entity' is performed.

Absence, performance and the uncanny economy

It is in this overt identification of the viewer as a term within a dynamic system, too, and the production of these absences or lacunae, that these installations engage with 'the uncanny' as part of their layering of systems and effects. In relation to presence, in particular, these installations provoke a self-reflexive perception of the projected figure's 'doubling', or 'liveness', or an 'aliveness' ghosted in a process analogous to that which the writer Nicholas Royle identifies as 'an economics of the uncanny' (Royle 2003: 26). Identifying the uncanny with an eclectic range of tropes and phenomena manifested widely in popular culture, art and philosophy, Royle defines its root and effect as a disturbance of boundaries and identities. He proposes:

> The uncanny is a crisis of the proper: it entails a critical disturbance of what is proper (from the Latin *proprius*, 'own') . . . It is a crisis of the natural, touching upon everything that one might have thought was 'part of nature': one's own nature, human nature, the nature of reality and the world. But the uncanny is not simply an experience of strangeness or alienation. More specifically, it is a peculiar commingling of the familiar and unfamiliar.   [Royle 2003: 1]

Following Freud's prescription of the *unheimlich*, Royle's account begins in reference to the experience of 'curious coincidences', of being 'fated' or that of witnessing 'forms of what might appear merely mechanical or automatic life', while 'conversely or likewise, it can be felt in response to dolls and other lifelike or mechanical objects' (Royle 2003: 1–2). In these encounters, Royle argues, 'the sense of the uncanny has to do with a sense of a secret encounter . . . it disturbs any straightforward sense of what is inside and outside. The uncanny has to do with a strangeness of framing and borders, an experience of liminality' (Royle 2003: 2). While evidently resonant in relation to Oursler's staging of 'media entities', as well as these works' allusions to 'psycho-history', and so conditions and diagnoses that imply interpenetrations between media systems, volition, identity and 'the real', Royle accounts for the uncanny as a broad range of phenomena that encompass but is not limited to Freud's account of the *unheimlich*. Indeed, it is a phenomenon resonant also to the 'returns' of 'presence', place and the body in the work of Hershman and Hill and to the encounter with one's own 'presence at a distance' in Sermon's telepresence installations. Identifying Freud's claim of the capacity of psychoanalysis to 'lay bare . . . hidden forces' (Freud in Royle 2003: 24) as symptomatic of precisely the phenomenon Freud seeks to account for through the concept of the *unheimlich*, Royle notes that 'it is perhaps now becoming possible to see psychoanalysis as a branch of the uncanny, rather than vice versa' (Royle 2003: 24). Where 'the uncanny' 'overflows' psychoanalysis, Royle continues, so by dint of its potential to produce or reveal the inhabitation of texts and meanings by alterity '[a]nother name for uncanny overflow might be deconstruction' (Royle 2003: 24), especially in its demonstration of 'how difference operates at the heart of identity, how the strange and even unthinkable is a necessary condition of what is conventional, familiar and taken for granted' (Royle 2003: 24).

Exemplifying the uncanny figure of 'the double', then, in prompting a recognition of the capacity of media 'to transform matter, space and time, inanimate to animate' (Oursler 1997), Oursler's installations, like Hershman and Hill's works, evidently trouble the 'proper place' of object, artwork and viewer, inviting the 'uncanny' attribution of volition, purpose and identity to signs and representations. In Oursler's works, the tension, specifically, within these installations between the figure's direct emotional address and a deconstruction of its form and representations also drives towards this effect. Indeed, where 'nothing is hidden'; where the mechanisms of the representation and media system are laid bare, the efficacy of these figures' emotional gestures and their manifestation as 'media entities' work to reveal a commingling of viewer and object – an effect captured precisely in Royle's construction of an uncanny that is 'construed as a foreign body within oneself, even of the experience of oneself *as* a foreign body' (Royle 2003: 2, original emphasis). Following Freud's proposition that the uncanny is concerned with 'the theory of a quality of feeling', Royle concludes, '[t]he uncanny is not what Freud (or anyone else) thinks. It has to do with a sense of ourselves as double, split, at odds with ourselves' (Royle 2003: 6), for '[t]he uncanny is (the) unsettling (of itself)' (Royle 2003: 5). Indeed, following Gordon C. F. Bearns's proposition that *the presence of what ought to be absent is* uncanny' (Bearns in Royle, 2003: 88, original emphasis), 'presence' 'itself' is performed in the uncanny: in a 'return' of that 'which was never properly there' (Royle 2003: 84) to effect the 'uncanny overflow' Royle describes. In turn, this binding of the perception of the figure to the perception of the self, which Oursler repeatedly thematizes, examines the viewer's experience of their co-presence with these 'media entities'; their sense of 'being before' a figure and disturbance of the self. In these installations, then, 'media systems' are configured as technological, social and personal spaces in which behaviours, emotions and psychological topologies are simultaneously repeated by the projection and rehearsed by the viewer.

In tandem with this, Oursler has also explicitly deployed the tropes of the uncanny in overt plays on the projective figures' performances of their steps towards the viewer. Thus, *Underwater (Blue/Green)* (1996) incorporates that which Freud identifies as perhaps 'the crown of the uncanny . . . being buried alive, only apparently dead' (Freud 2003: 150). In doing so, *Underwater (Blue/Green)* presents a head projected on to a fibreglass model in a tank of water. Following the logic of Oursler's 'empathy tests', the head's projected performance attempts to give meaning to the conditions of its display as it repeatedly acts out its potential drowning by desperately attempting to hold its breath. Deborah Rothschild thus cites the critic Sarah Ward's report that in this piece '[t]he face, desperate for air, puffs out its cheeks, moans through closed lips and looks upwards towards freedom. It is only an illusion, but the urge to reach into the tank and rescue this poor disembodied head is overwhelming' (Rothschild 1999: 31). In this way, *Underwater (Blue/Green)* attempts to act out an impossible step from the virtual to the real, provoking a response that may be read after Freud's general proposition that 'an uncanny effect . . . often arises when a symbol takes on the full function and significance of what it symbolizes' (Freud 2003: 150).

Extending this, from 2003 Oursler initiated a series of projections on to overtly abstracted three-dimensional forms, including *Pet* (2003), *Coo* (2003), *Big Eye* (2003), *Baby* (2003), and *Blob* (2004), that articulated this crossing of spaces in relationships between video and bodily space. Rather than invite the viewer to project towards the circumstances of the dummy's dilemma, as in *Underwater (Blue/Green)*, *Blob* provokes a somatic connection: a bodily identification of internal states. *Blob* is a body pared down towards a collapse of recognizable features, yet one designed, Oursler emphasizes in his essay of the same name, to remain 'a character, an irreducible entity' (Oursler 2005). In setting itself apart visually, however, *Blob* plays out a migration towards the viewer's bodily space. *Blob*, Oursler continues, 'never stops moving, moving all around with no place to go':

> The blob's movements are alien yet oddly familiar. Pulling and stretching. Like peristaltic movement. Like the way things move through your body by contractions which result in locomotion. You understand this is linked to your bowels and intestines, because even though this motion is involuntary, it is conscious on some level. It is essentially a wave, the universal form of energy transmission divided into peaks and troughs like a bad ocean. Unending waves, wave after wave, wash away your shape. Now formless, You are the blob.   [Oursler 2005]

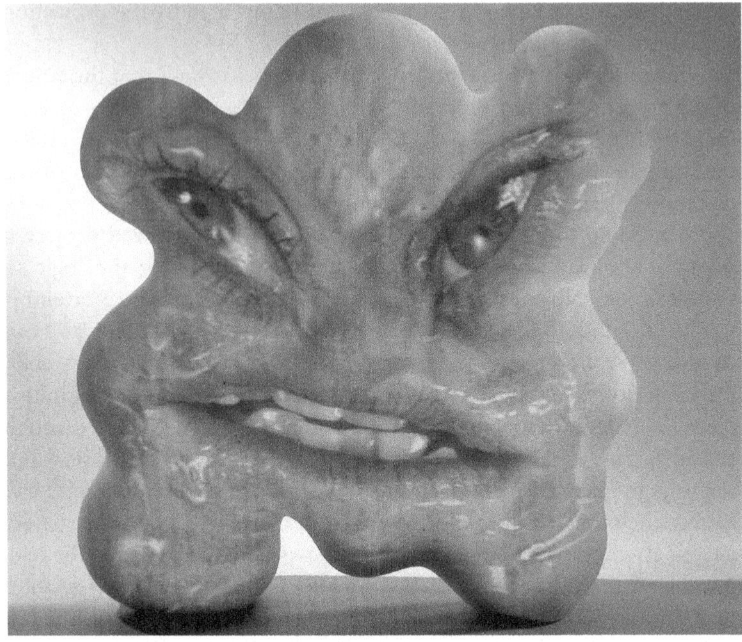

Figure 6.7 Tony Oursler, *Blob* (2003)

Here, *Blob*'s difference acts as a foil to the viewer's sense of its physical intrusion. Indeed, where this somatic connection takes its effect, so the viewer's sense of 'its presence' is articulated in the difference and division between the visual and the physical: *Blob* is *seen* to occupy the space before, precisely as it is *felt* to disrupt or intrude upon the viewer's sense of their own physical separation and integrity. In this sense, too, it is the viewer, in their awareness of the uncanny physical 'intrusion' of this visual sign, that performs 'its' presence, and this affect, leading to Oursler's provocation that 'we' have become 'it'.

With its transparent skin, the blob exposes its muscles, organs, blood flow. The banal workings of the organism are revealed in fragile detail. How embarrassing. To encounter the blob is to see the simple, low ambitions that sustain life with no greater purpose. The blob can only and merely exist, it is useless. Whatever happens inside the blob should be hidden, should remain private.

The blob can be funny like any mutation, a dead end creature in the chain of evolution. And in the food chain it has no niche, no other life form feeds on the blob. It's a disturbing creature because it is unique. A Monster that could kill you like a cancer, a devolution of cells. Here is the nightmare scenario: a terratoma analogous to you, an evil negative offspring replaces you the host. A formless double, the blob kills you when it takes up residence within.

When you gaze at the blob, your eye no longer has a focal point because the blob has no focal point. You see right into it. You may keep losing your sight in a myopic blur. In this way the blob can escape even though it moves very slowly and with no apparent direction.

[From Tony Oursler, 'Blob', 2005]

Yet Oursler's articulation of the presence of these media entities does not end in this address to the spaces of the image's display. Indeed, this work also gives emphasis to the differences in times marked by the virtual image's movement towards the viewer. Here, again, this work foregrounds the disjunctive relationship between the material conditions of its installation and its production of mediated and virtual spaces and times. Thus, with regard to time, the art critic Achille Bonito Oliva argues in his contribution to a major catalogue of Nam June Paik's work, *Nam June Paik. Eine Data Base* (1993), that video installation necessarily 'documents' 'a twofold time. Twofold because of a double possibility of measurement, one dictated by the internal cadence of the technology and the other by the encounter between the technology and materials that are steady in themselves and the public, either still or in movement' (Oliva in Paik 1993: 16). It is in the context of this multiplication that Oursler's empathy tests invariably use time-looped video, so deferring attention back to the material conditions of video itself, its operation in real-time recording and playback. In this way, for example, in *Getaway #2* and *Underwater (Blue/Green)*, the repeating structure of Oursler's projections provide for a key part of their effect, amplifying its 'absences', its separation from the 'real time' of viewing. Stressing, again, the limits of the virtual image's occupation of real space, this gesture also sets an important limit, or interruption, to the work's engagement of the viewer, disrupting their identification with the projection, interrupting their cathartic experience or anticipation of closure. With regard to the perception of 'presence', too, this articulation of incongruent times may be read in relation to techniques of presence evident in live theatrical performance.

Thus Oursler's strategies may be set against tactics for performance that emphasize process and disjunction, memory and anticipation. Jon Erickson, writing in *The Fate of the Object* (1998), observes the articulation of the performer's presence in disjunctive temporal relationships between the body, action and language, noting: '"Presence" in the theater

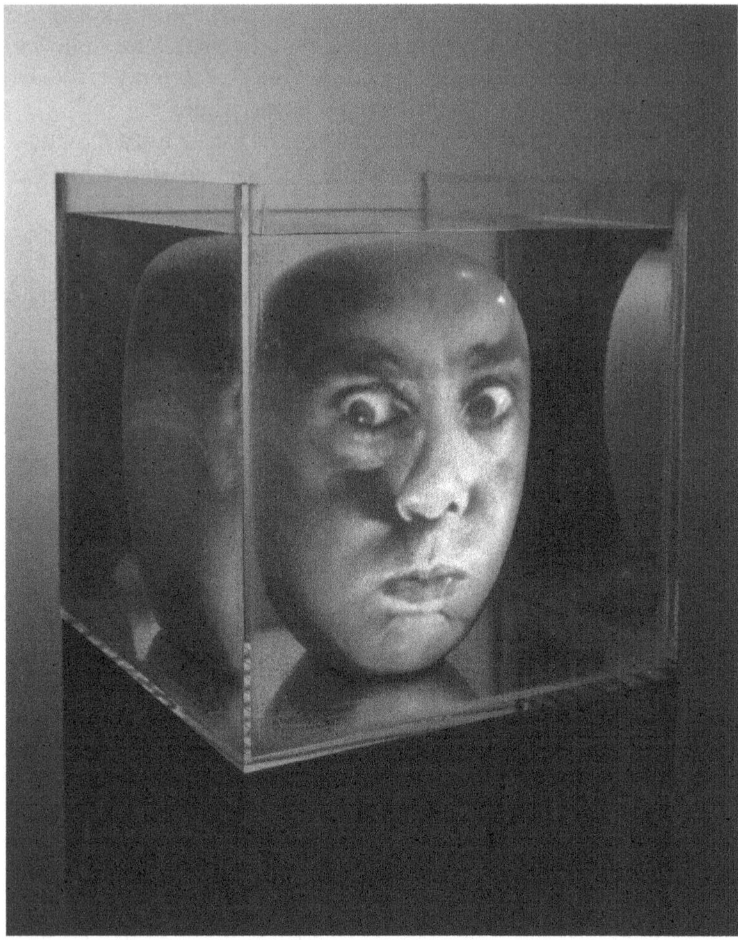

Figure 6.8 Tony Oursler, *Underwater (Blue/Green)* (1996)

is a physicality in the present that at the same time is grounded in a form of absence. It is something that has unfolded, is read against what has been seen, and presently observed in expectation as to what will be seen' (Erickson, 1998: 62). Erickson concludes, '[p]resence has an inverse relationship to language', arising in the moment where the body is *there* and yet '[o]ne is holding back the articulate meaning that the audience is expecting' (Erickson, 1998: 62). For Tim Etchells, it is precisely such lacunae in performance that heighten a perception of performer presence – and reveal its construction – by throwing emphasis on the work of viewing itself. Etchells notes that in witnessing performance:

> I am aware of people on a number of levels, like I'm seeing past one layer of
> what they are doing to another layer and then may be to another. Perhaps
> there's something important about this experience that we have, of seeing
> layers of information, the feeling that we are seeing through, from one layer
> to another to another. As watchers, we aggregate all of that information
> and we make a kind of map that allows us to say: there's somebody there.
> None of those layers is quite enough on its own – presence is to do with the
> combination.   [Etchells in Giannachi and Kaye 2006]

In this context, amplifying the work of the 'reader' through layering
or veiling – and even in the implicit obstruction from view of that which
is promised or *should be seen* – may, Etchells proposes, drive the reading
and so effect of 'presence'. He concludes that: 'presence is so much about
reception. It's about reading. And reading is a complicated act. One of
the things we do as readers of signs and situations – and of all things – is
that we respond to absences – and we fill absence' (Etchells in Giannachi
and Kaye 2006).

It is such an articulation of presence in lacunae produced by
silence, or in the *gap* or refusal, too, which finds an extreme expression
in the presentation of animals within dramatic performances. Thus,
for Romeo Castellucci of the Italian performance company Societas
Raffaello Sanzio, the animal offers a presence that is disruptive of the
representational apparatus of the theatre precisely because of its performative alertness yet inability to answer for its own symbolic significance.
Writing of 'The Animal Being On Stage', Castellucci remarks that:

> On stage, the animal is comfortable (being not perfectible) in the confi-
> dence of its own body; at the same time it feels uncomfortable in its sur-
> roundings. The device of technique cannot be used by the animal, as it
> already possesses the greatest device: to be alienated on stage, immobile, in
> an alert state.   [Castellucci 2000: 26]

In Raffaello Sanzio's performances the animal's very lack of 'technique', its *refusal* of the rhetorical questions its presence raises, inter-
rupts the 'theatre itself' by opening a space before its representations.
Analogously, in Oursler's installations, not only do the dummies
present a disruptive movement between representational schemes in
the interplay between virtual and real objects, but they are continually interrupted, replayed, repeated, and so brought to a repetition or
silence they themselves cannot account for. In turn, this throws
attention towards the *expectation*, towards the flow of time that
prompts an amplification of phenomena of presence in much of the
work considered in this volume. In the viewer's experience, too, this

repetition, which marks the projection's unreality, its failure to 'arrive', in *Underwater (Blue/Green)* the failure to drown, in *Crying Doll* the refusal to rest, heightens the spectacle of its performance, its effort towards migration. Indeed, it is the loop, the *compulsion to repeat*, that prompts the viewer to move ahead, dissociate and then return to the effect of presence, an effect that may be amplified, rather than diminished, in this exchange – or economy – in which presence is performed. Thus, in his response to *Getaway #2*, again reproduced in Rothschild's survey of Oursler's work, Peter Schjeldahl's experience seems to mirror just such a phenomenon:

> Even realizing that the looped tape speaks whether anyone is near by or not, I couldn't shake a sense of being addressed personally. I caught myself retreating out of intimidated respect for the creature's feelings. Then I had to laugh at myself. I went back – get a grip Peter! – And sat on the floor to contemplate my own emotional response, a tossed salad of pity and fear.   [Schjeldahl in Rothschild 1999: 30]

In these desynchronizations, the object's heightened presence becomes the focus of Schjeldahl's attention and the instrument by which the installation provokes an interrogation of the self who views. In the manner of the 'uncanny economy', Schjeldahl's response follows Royle's description of the disturbance of the relationship between viewer and viewed: 'One tries to keep oneself out, but one cannot. One tries to put oneself in: same result. The uncanny is an experience of being after oneself, in various senses of that phrase. It is the experience of something duplicitous, diplopic, being double' (Royle 2003: 16). Here, 'presence' returns in the 'media entity's' performance of its own disappearance, in its disarticulation, in the very visibility of its illusion and pretence, and so in a heightening of the viewer's experience, in reflecting the figure, of *being before oneself* in the perception of presence. It is a performance of presence in and through media that disturbs the sense of integrity of the one who looks, calling into question the differences and oppositions between 'the real' and its definition in virtual systems and representations.

Simulation in real space

Through an attention to the signs and practices of presence, Oursler's staging of media entities serves to interrupt and articulate the viewer's negotiation and performance of media spaces and processes. In this respect, Oursler's work makes a phenomenological exploration of the circulation and exchange of the signs of presence, and so of aspects of self and identity, through practices of media consumption. Suggesting that 'media space has transposed realism to create a new space of everyday life' (Oursler in Ardenne 2005: 45), Oursler's installations intrude upon the viewer's sense of their own psychological separation and integrity from seemingly illusory and ephemeral phenomena. Indeed, one of the roots of these projections' uncanny effect is their exposure of the mobility of the signs of presence and the close link between presence and simulation. In Oursler's work, this position is perhaps illustrated most clearly in his series of works in 2001 that incorporated antenna-like forms, as well as references to the hardware of transmission. Following the creation of his major installation and performance, *The Influence Machine* (2000), that marked a culmination of his *TimeStream* project, these works projected talking heads on to opaque and translucent screens supported by various combinations of antennae. Providing a physical expression of Oursler's observation in his essay 'Pop Dead Pictures', that '[w]e are antennas, all that stuff moves through us. Different parts of our body, organs, bones conduct themselves differently and can be measured' (Oursler 2002: 165) pieces such *Buzz* (2001), *Endfire Array* (2001), *In the Sky* (2001) and *Wavefront* (2001), articulate mobile relationships between the viewer, the physical apparatus and projected, speaking entities, producing a sense of identity and personality in movement. Such work emphasizes exchange, mobility and mutability in the performance of presence, to pose fundamental questions over the nature of action, identity and self in the relationship with media forms.

Here, too, Oursler's work elaborates questions raised by research and practices in new media, telecommunications and human–computer interaction. Writing of 'The Cyborg's Dilemma: Progressive Embodiment in Virtual Environments', Frank Biocca argues:

> Rather than seeing social presence as a partial replication of face-to-face communication, we should more generally see social presence as a simulation of another intelligence. The simulation is run in the body and mind of the perceiver, and models the internal experience of some other moving, expressive body. It is a simulation because the simulation occurs whether or not the moving object has intelligence or intentionality, whether the 'other' is a moving human being or an animation composed of nothing more than moving patterns of ink. The definition above suggests that social presence applies to the mediated experience of all forms of 'intelligence'. This perceived intelligence might be another human, a non-human

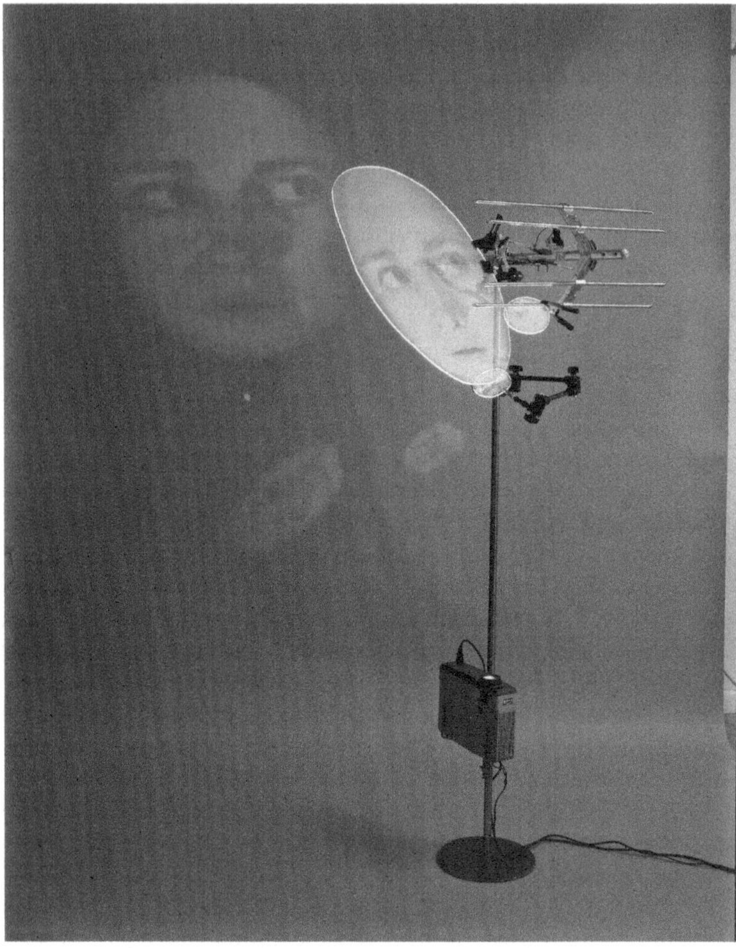

Figure 6.9 Tony Oursler, *Endfire Array* (2001)

> intelligence such as an animal, a form of artificial intelligence, an imagined
> alien or a god.   [Biocca 1997]

In the context of Biocca's analysis, these installations' approaches to the viewer may be read as acting out and exploring precisely the place of such simulations within the mechanisms of presence. Indeed, where the figure of the dummy articulates its lack of centre, or dramatizes its absences, while heightening the drama of its attempt to occupy 'its' spaces, so it acts out the mobility of these signs, the fluidity between the viewer and the viewed, to effect the presence of its simulations. In this process, and as this work's uncanny effects suggest, it is the viewer who ghosts the system, and it is their presence that is performed in this doubling, as these 'mimetic technologies' reproduce and refract the signs of the viewer's place in and out of media.

disjunction The Builders Association

Founded in 1994, and directed by Marianne Weems, The Builders Association's large-scale multimedia theatre productions have emphasized the 'interface between live and electronically mediated presence' (The Builders Association 2002) through work in which, typically, '[n]o performer . . . is ever really fully present in an unmediatized way. There is always some encroachment' (Kaye and Weems 2005). In doing so, the company has explored the performance of presence in the theatrical enactment of media processes, embedding the actor's performance into layered and responsive soundscapes, architectonic designs or mobile and mediated sets that emphasize passages between live, mediated and recorded channels of address. In foregrounding these transitions and exchanges, in particular, The Builders Association's work has located and amplified 'performer presence' in the dynamic interleaving of virtual and real architectures and spaces for performance. In these explorations, too, the company's work has foregrounded narratives of dislocation from and reinvention of contemporary place in performances articulated and underpinned by formal and thematic addresses to the problematic of a *being there* enacted in media forms and networks. Beginning with *Master Builder* (1994), which incorporated a full size 'house' onstage embedded with triggers to cue sound and video, the company's work has engaged with these questions not only through narrative and visual design, but architectural approaches to the integration of the performer into mediated and simulated spaces and exchanges. Developed through a distinctive process in which all elements of production – including live performance, the composition of soundscape, projective video and mediation, set design, lighting and text – are evolved simultaneously and in explicit conversation with one other, the company's productions have also incorporated original scenarios and scripts including *Imperial Motel (Faust)* (1996) written by John Jesurun, *Jump Cut (Faust)* (1997) and *Jet Lag* (1998), created with the architectural partnership Diller + Scofidio. More recently, *Super Vision* (2005) and *Continuous City* (2008) have further advanced and complicated the company's articulation of the actor's presence in juxtapositions and transpositions between 'live' and 'mediated' spaces and performances: in *Super Vision* through the integration of actors into complex and hyperreal simulations of theatrical sets created by the visual design company *dbox*; and, in *Continuous City*, in the animated and mobile fragmentation and dispersal of live, mediated and recorded images across the 'real' spaces of theatrical performance.

MARIANNE WEEMS In every performance, in all of our shows, for me it is about the performers being really isolated physically, but we are mediating them electronically and so what the audience sees is the network that is joining them all. [In *Super Vision*] none of the performers ever really look at each other. What is being staged is the network.

[New York City, November 2005]

Located and unlocated: *Master Builder* (1994)

From its outset The Builders Association's work has engaged directly with an articulation of the performer's presence in transitions between 'real' and 'virtual' spaces. Drawing in conception on the architectural deconstructions of the artist Gordon Matta-Clark, The Builders Association's first production, *Master Builder* (1994), articulated performative and electronic interventions into an overtly architectural installation. Here, in the event from which the company derived their name, The Builders Association presented a 'three-storey house' (Kaye and Weems 2005) constructed in an otherwise empty New York warehouse space in midwinter, in which Weems embedded a treatment of Ibsen's *The Master*

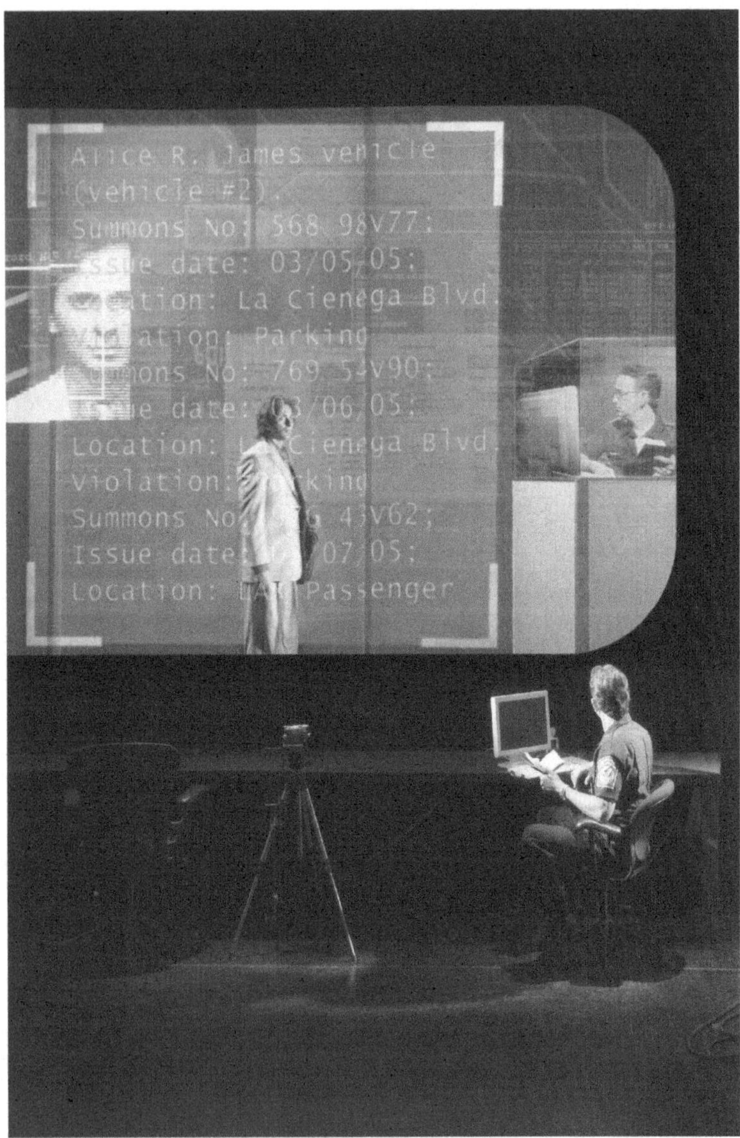

Figure 7.1 The Builders Association, *Super Vision* (2005). On stage, left to right: Rizwan Mirza in projection and live; Joe Silovsky on stage and in live mediation

Builder. In this production, in collaboration with the architect John Cleater, Weems's responded to concerns in Gordon Matta-Clark's practices, and evident across contemporaneous 'theoretical' architectural projects by Vito Acconci (Acconci 2005), Bernard Tschumi (Tschumi 1994b), Peter Eisenman (Eisenman 1986) and others, that posed questions over the performance and occupation of place and location. Such architectural work, Weems suggests, 'had very little to do with actual buildings and much more to do with bodies and the perception and manipulation of space and how space is a system that is ideologically configured' (Kaye and Weems 2005). Approaching Cleater's design, in this context, as an architecture the performer's interconnected activities might act out, disrupt and transform Weems's established a key point of departure for the company's future work, recollecting that:

> It was a dream-like, super-voyeuristic experience. And the house was lined with video and sound triggers, which the actors activated. After that, and in each succeeding project since then, my interest in physical edifices has receded, and what has emerged is the interest in the electronic network and how that too is a kind of architecture.   [Kaye and Weems 2005]

Here *Master Builder* also signalled the company's early emphasis on the exploration and delivery of narratives of place, character and event; an emphasis in counterpoint to the then predominant postmodern theatrical engagement with multimedia, reflected in Weems's observation that '[n]arrative has been imploded by "experimental theatre" to the point of meaninglessness ... My company's interest has been in reinstating narrative in a structural sense while at the same time incorporating technology' (Weems in Chalmers 1999: 60). Yet, characteristically, in The Builders Association's work, narratives are conveyed through the media and technology of which these narratives speak and often implicitly critique (Gibbs 2008b), so producing ambivalent and uncertain relationships between the import and perspective of their performance and its stories. This ambivalence, too, defines their engagement with the actor's place and presence within these media.

In these respects, The Builders Association's approach to both narrative and the actor's presence has continued to have affinities with the theory, tactics and implications of the architectural practices Weems identifies with *Master Builder*. Thus Bernard Tschumi's highly influential early theoretical architectural projects, exemplified by *The Manhattan Transcripts* (Tschumi 1994b), set out equations between architectural design, 'real' and 'textual' spatial configurations and narrative form, while cinematic narrative provided a guiding concept for important aspects of his first large-scale built project, *Parc de la Villette* (1983–87) (Tschumi 1987: 12). Importantly, though, for Tschumi, far from resolving 'the meaning' of his architectural projects, such narrative references served to amplify a paradox in architecture's operation; that, in articulating both 'real' (felt) and 'signifying' (coded) space, architecture is realized in disjunctions between the user's bodily experience of *being in* a space and their 'reading' (or 'concept') of those spaces. Analogously, from 1983, Vito Acconci's architectural practice turned his approaches to installation, video, film and performance towards interventions in political, social and other contextual narratives of site, in projects that challenged the stability of the meanings and uses of architectural forms and the places they occupy. John Cleater, who was taught by Tschumi at Columbia University, subsequently training at the Karl Chu Studio, and who has collaborated with architectural practices including Acconci Studio and Asymptote, points to analogous crossovers in his commitment to The Builders Association's theatrical work, noting that:

> my work with The Builders Association and simultaneously with Asymptote Architects has a common interest in how one experiences the threshold between physical and virtual spaces. In my work with Asymptote, as with The Builders, there is [a] given that we are going to be up to date with the latest technologies and how they get infused into space, whether it's theatre space or real architectural space.   [Cleater and Kaye 2007]

Such implicit connections between The Builders' approach to theatrical design and place and architectural ideas and practices also provided the basis for Weems's later collaboration with the architectural partnership Diller + Scofidio for *Jet Lag* (1998), as well as the company's close collaboration with the design and media studio dbox, founded by James Gibbs, Matthew Bannister and Charles D'Autremont. Extending from *Jet Lag* (1998), *Alladeen* (2002) and the design and implementation of virtual sets in *Super Vision* to Gibbs's contribution as dramaturge for *Continuous City* (2008), the involvement of dbox in The Builders Association's work built on their early interest in the articulation of time and narrative in architecture. Thus, in relation to dbox's extensive work in virtual modelling, as well as in their interest in theatrical projects, Gibbs notes that in their architectural training 'Matthew Bannister, Charles D'Autremont and I were all interested in narrative . . . We got excited about the possibilities of trying to maintain narrative using architecture, or using architectural language and that pushed us more towards representation and drawing' (Gibbs in Kaye 2007: 562). At the same time, Gibbs has noted that the resolution of architecture into narrative is probably unattainable. In this context, and after Tschumi's pursuit of narrative forms to unsettle relationships between the reading and experience of space, The Builders Association's engagement with media has never consistently sought to resolve the presence of media processes and forms *into* narrative, but rather to filter their work's narrative emphasis through visual and media design, an emphasis reflected in the company's positioning of the actor's performance across distinct spaces and media.

For *Master Builder*, then, while preceding this collaboration with dbox, an emphasis on relationships between design and narrative, and the positioning of the performer at the threshold and exchange between 'real' and 'virtual' (or mediatic) spaces, is apparent, while the actor's presence at the architectural site was a primary engine of the performance. Here, too, this project pursued an explicit link between the question of the performer's location across real and virtual architectures and a performance and amplification of performer presence to an audience. *Master Builder* thus begins in a transposition of Gordon Matta-Clark's radical interventions into existing architectural spaces towards a dynamic integration of theatrical action and set, providing for the de-structuring and eventual physical division and opening of the house construction itself. In its conception and design, *Master Builder* specifically referenced *Splitting* (1975), a 'building cut' in which Matta-Clark had dramatically intervened into the structure of a suburban house in Passiac NJ, first by dividing it into two, then raising the two separate halves of the building back and away from each other. Documenting the result in multiple forms as a film, *Bingo X Ninths* (1974), a bookwork *Splitting* (1974), and through various exhibited photographic collages, including *Splitting 32*, which Weems and Webster had proposed to Cleater as the basis of the *Master Builder* design, Matta-Clark also conceived of his architectural interventions, and *Splitting* in particular, as performance, noting in a contemporaneous interview with the critic Liza Béar that:

> The way I experienced it as a performance was through my interest in hanging out, or hanging on . . . the suspension or suspense of it . . . Putting your shoulder to a part of the building, pushing it and having it give way reminds me of silent film comedies, which is the kind of humour I like.   [Matta-Clark in Béar 1974: 34]

Cleater correspondingly approached the design of the house and *Master Builder* performance as 'a kind of research as an architect. It

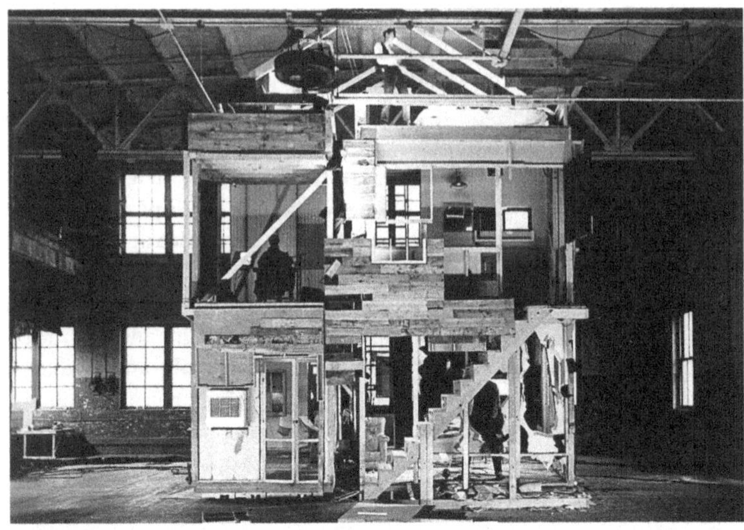

Figure 7.2 The Builders Association, *Master Builder* (1994). In house. Attic: Emma Strahs; upstairs room: Jane Smith; downstairs right: Jeff Webster

was a kind of temporary architecture' (Cleater and Kaye 2007). Where Matta-Clark's photo-collage emphasized the bilateral division and lifting of the house, The Builders Association, Cleater recalls, 'cut it in half and rotated it – eventually. It was built in sections and separate pieces and we didn't realize that we were going to want to literally split the thing at the end of the performance until after it was built' (Cleater and Kaye 2007).

JOHN CLEATER Jeff [Webster] and Marianne [Weems] came to me with the idea of translating the psychological breakdown that happens in [Ibsen's] *The Master Builder* to a physical breakdown of the set – and we talked about, you know, Matta-Clark's actions and incorporating all that into the actual set as well as incorporating ideas of the de-perspective of the stage – an interest of ours seen in Giotto's paintings. The set was built in a way that, rather than forcing a perspective, the walls kind of go apart from each other. It is the opposite of forced perspective, so if you are standing at one point it looks as if the walls are continually going in space and they never would meet. And at the same time, raking the floor.

NICK KAYE So there wasn't a single unifying point for the perspective. How was the floor raked?

JOHN CLEATER It was raked in a conventional way, while the walls went back in an unconventional way, so it was confusing. It created an illusion that people were moving up and down rather than back and forth. I was really interested in playing around with these ideas between Giotto and Matta-Clark and it all came together for me in a particular way. . . . And also there is a Buster Keaton aspect, I think it is *One Week* (1920) – the film that delivered a house in a kit and he gets the numbers screwed up and puts it together wrongly so you end up with the kitchen on the outside. So we did that. We built it on a kind of rotating pedal – there were several parts of the set that were playing around with this inside-out idea.

[Hudson NY, November 2007]

Drawing on ten different, mostly colloquial and contemporary translations of Ibsen's text, which came to comprise roughly two-thirds of the performance, and incorporating a sub-plot around agoraphobia in which David Pence shadowed Jeff Webster's performance of the title role, Weems's narrative structure played towards twin culminations enabled by the splitting of the house into two. In designing this manipulation and opening of the house's spaces, and while explicitly referencing *Splitting 32*, Weems recalls the influence of drawings by Piranesi, of Giotto's organization of pictorial space across distinct rooms and separation of figures by walls, as well as Buster Keaton's *One Week* (1920), in which Keaton receives a kit house by post only to build it, in part, inside-out. Here, too, Cleater's treatment of the house presaged the company's emphasis on exposing and articulating electronic media's presence and operation on stage, whereby cameras, screens, and the operation of, for example, chroma-key, as well as the work of the technical crew, are exposed to the audience's view. *Master Builder* thus began with one of Cleater's collaborators in constructing the house, Joel Chichowski, setting out tools with which it had been built, and describing 'what they were, and where they came from – how they were made' (Cleater and Kaye 2007). Subsequently, and after Matta-Clark's exposure of architecture's structures through division, disruption and removal, *Master Builder* unfolded in a dialogue between the completion of the performance and the unmaking of the house. In this process, the actors' physical engagement with this material structure was extended and amplified through 'media interventions that were embedded within this architecture' (Rubin 2007) triggered by MIDI switches set throughout the house and integrated into Cleater's design by the artist Ben Rubin, who also created the video content. Thus, as the disruption of the house unfolded, the actor's engagement with a set that 'was in a continual state of self-destruction' (Rubin 2007) was amplified in transmissions from real to virtual spaces that articulated an ongoing

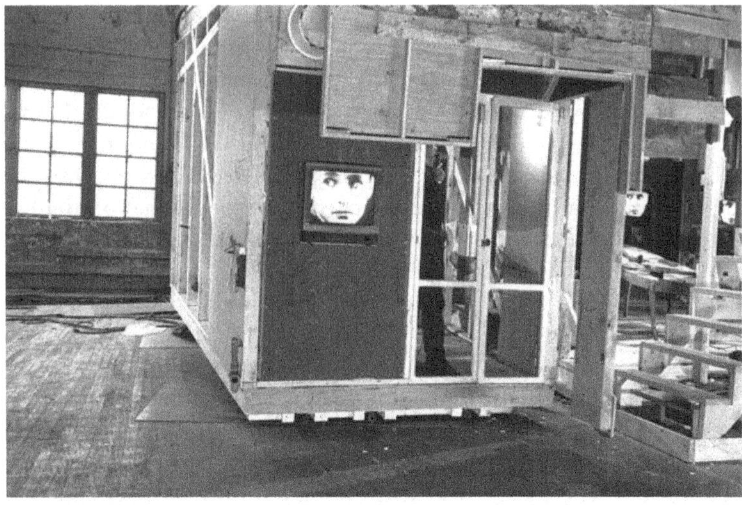

Figure 7.3 The Builders Association, *Master Builder* (1994). On video: Emma Strahs

negotiation between the materiality of the house and its definition as a 'media object'.

BEN RUBIN We built a number of sound triggers into the set. There were places where Jeff [Webster] is flying into a rage as the Master Builder – he smashes his hand into the wall and it creates this huge thunderous crashing sound. You can play that sort of thing with someone sitting offstage with a sampler and matching the gesture, but part of the experiment in *Master Builder* was to find out what happens when actors really play the set like an instrument, so that sound was not triggered by a technician offstage but by the impact of the hand on the wall. . . . In *Master Builder* we had also built all kinds of speakers into the set, so that sounds came not only from the main front speakers, but were woven into the whole structure of the piece. Part of what we were exploring with *Master Builder* was to make the house, the set, into a kind of media object. And the way that we infused this media into it, it kind of became a character: its various parts were articulated.

[New York City, November 2007]

For Rubin, this integration of media served to support the actors' sense of their physical habitation and location in the set; a departure that defined the ground for a key aspect of the company's practice in which, wherever possible, media are played 'live' to facilitate interactive and performed exchanges between 'real' and 'virtual' processes and spaces. In *Master Builder*, Rubin thus recounts, the performer's triggering of video and sound served to further facilitate their material relationship with the house and its technologies, such that 'the experiment for us was more what happened in the mind of the actor when the actor knows that he or she is really in control of this media' (Rubin 2007). Here, too, *Master Builder* echoed Matta-Clark's dramatization of the theatrical nature of architectural site and his physical engagement with site and structure, exemplified in his filmed actions, such as *Clockshower* (1974), which drew inspiration from early silent comedy (Simon 2007: 126).

JOHN CLEATER It had all kinds of different things going on. We had one sidewall, which was borrowing from the Buster Keaton scene where he is leaning out of the windowsill upstairs and his wife is leaning on the windowsill downstairs. Then the whole facade falls and it rotates. I built a kind of rotating pinwheel. . . . The house was built so the pin was right in between the two floors – it was on a rod or steel pipe. I came up with as many different ways of the house either shifting and sliding – part of the side of the wall when you leaned on it would peel off to the side and would kind of come back. What I tried to do was make it so when the parts of the set were being physically manipulated they were happening from other rooms – so we had the peeling idea, the rotating idea, we had inversion, inside and out – where the kitchen could be on the outside. We had pieces that just got knocked and then we had the whole set split in half and rotate over. We tried to do as many different kinds of things as we could.

[Hudson NY, November 2007]

Extending this dynamic play, at the end of each performance and with the physical edifice of the house opened, the reconfigured structure of *Master Builder* remained as an architectural installation exhibited in its own right, offering its audience the opportunity to enter the house set. In doing so, visitors found themselves activating the media and site in which Ibsen's text has already been enacted, so underscoring *Master Builder*'s performative engagement with architecture while further exposing the performance's mechanisms.

In these various ways, *Master Builder* operated through its performers' simultaneous occupation of multiple systems and spaces. Indeed, while media are embedded into the 'house' in order to amplify the actors' engagement with the materiality of the building, their triggering of video and sound in their interactions with this physical architecture realizes otherwise hidden connections, systems and electronic networks, which augment the reading of their presence and position within the physical structure. For John Cleater, a key interest in the performance was precisely the slippage between actions, spaces and causes expressed both in the manipulation of the building and in the triggering of the network, as he notes: 'I was really interested in how one thing would happen in one room, but it would affect the change in another room' (Cleater and Kaye 2007). In *Master Builder*, it follows, the mediatic system, the network by which the information flows through the building, is a function and expression of the actor's physical intervention into the 'real' building itself. In facilitating this performance *Master Builder* is thus realized in an interleaving of the located and the 'unlocated', in performances that realize mutually reinforcing 'real' and 'virtual' systems, processes and spaces.

BEN RUBIN What are unlocated in *Master Builder* are the links. That was a lot of what we were playing with in that piece. We would have Kyle [DeCamp] in one room, stage right, in the lower part of the house, and up above, on a higher level, stage left, is Jeff [Webster] in another room – and the image of Kyle is coming to Jeff on a screen in Jeff's area and the voice of Jeff is coming into Kyle's area. Now we would play on these sorts of things, where you know that there is a transmission link somewhere – there is a physical connection – that you can't see. Even though there are wires all over the place, you can't really discern where that signal is actually travelling. I think part of the energy of *Master Builder* was always pulling the actors away from each other but creating these media links between them – and again the house became this tool for those communication channels. The channels are always the hardest to see.

[New York City, November 2007]

This emphasis on the systematic transposition of actions across material ('real') and mediatic ('virtual') architectures is linked directly to The Builders Association's engagement with presence, and specifically to a disturbance of the actor's place effected in this medium's generation of 'its own' spaces across the 'real' spaces of theatrical performance. 'Media space,' the artist Tony Oursler has suggested, 'is a conglomerate of virtual spaces' (Oursler in Humphries 2007), a space whose boundaries and identities are multiple, permeable and contradictory. In this view, 'media space' is produced in a collocation of spaces in paradoxical or dissonant relationship: in a layering of one space in and over others.

It is this 'media space', and its production in the 'real spaces' of theatrical performance, that *Master Builder* implicitly enacts and amplifies. In this context, the key figure in *Master Builder* is *disjunction*: 'a lack of correspondence or consistency' (*OED*) between terms that are nevertheless structurally bound one to another. Set against Tschumi's definition of the intractable 'internal contradiction' defining architecture's operation between 'the concept of space and the experience of space' (Tschumi 1994a: 15–16), this term further extends the spatial metaphor in which The Builders' work may be read. Transposed into the relationship between 'live' and 'mediated' acts and spaces, 'disjunction' suggests restless and contradictory relationships between interdependent but distinct orders of representation and experience, while its theatrical performance offers the realization of a kind of palimpsest in which real, virtual and simulated spaces and events negotiate a writing over, reconfiguration and translation of each other. In this respect, too, the production or enactment of 'disjunction' reflects a moment Derrida identifies with 'The Hinge', an articulation of 'a single word for designating difference and articulation . . . This word is *brisure* [joint, break] – broken, cracked part. *Cf.* breach, crack, fracture, fault, split, fragment . . . The hinge, the *brisure* [folding joint] of a shutter. *Cf.* Joint.' – Roger Laporte (letter)' (Derrida 1976: 65). Such a performance of disjunction, and the implication of a moment or act which is neither 'here nor there' but operates and is produced as the *hinge* or *joint* on which these mutually exclusive spaces or terms nevertheless depend, leads to an emphasis on threshold and transition, rather than *difference* or *opposition*. Set in this context, the actor's presence in *Master Builder* is articulated in the performance of conjoined and dislocated spaces: in the acting out of disjunctive spatial orders; of multiple sites; in the direction of attention towards the 'unlocated' *slip*. It is a moment, also, that is resonant to Oursler's articulation of the video image's functioning in real space and the subject's experience of the 'merging' and simultaneity of real and virtual spaces in CAVE.

An analogous emphasis is evident, too, in Matta-Clark's practice and in particular his emphasis on the disjunctions and transpositions between found and constructed spaces. In Matta-Clark's work, architecture's relationship to its 'real sites' is articulated in the *disruption* of built forms and their orderliness, rather than through that which architecture can capture, represent or make material. Thus, in his various performed and sculpted interventions into found architectural sites, including *Bronx Floors: Thresholes* (1972), *Splitting* (1974) and *Conical Intersect* (1975), which were subsequently exhibited as film and photographic images akin to contemporary performance documentation and

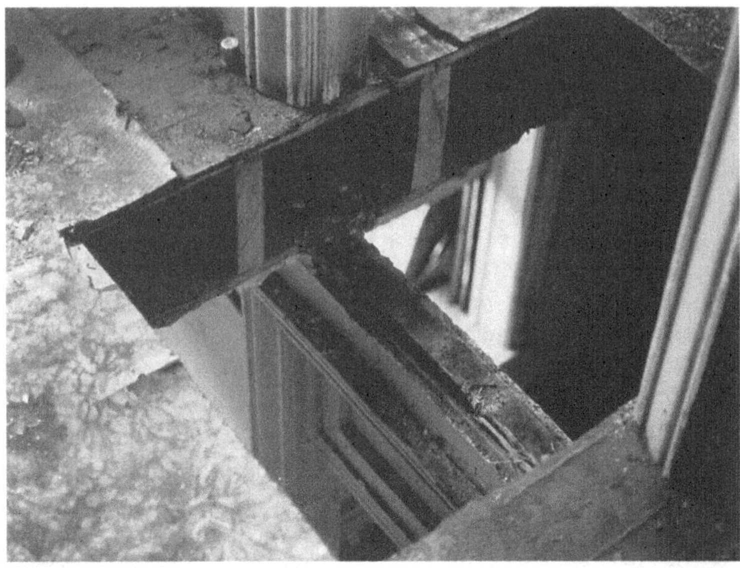

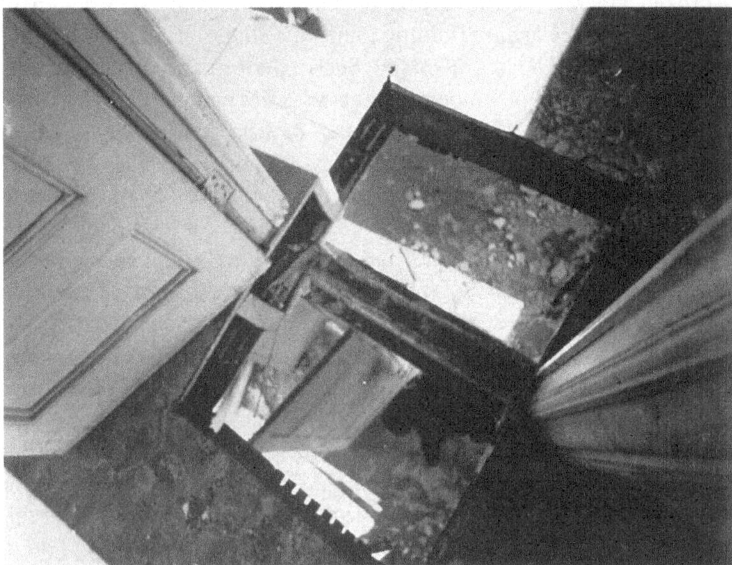

Figures 7.4–5 Gordon Matta-Clark, *Bronx Floors: Thresholes* (1972). © 2009 Estate of Gordon Matta-Clark/Artists' Rights Society (ARS), New York; DACS, London

conceptual art, Matta-Clark's interruptions of the orderliness of built forms pressed towards the irruption of apparently 'negative' 'empty', seemingly 'intangible' and yet paradoxically 'real' spaces into the unity of architectural design.

While Matta-Clark himself drew attention to his interest in performance, these photographic works place emphasis on *the gaps*, the negative 'unlocated' *differences* that Matta-Clark's interventions produce. As his series *Bronx Floors* (1972) demonstrates, these actions produce vertiginous, mobile spaces and shifting positions and perspectives prompted by the articulation of different but connected spatial orders. Such works appear vertiginous because no one perspective entirely subsumes the others, even as they define and reflect one another. It is this, too, that produces the characteristic restlessness of Matta-Clark's work, expressed in the sense of shifting perspectives within individual pieces. While radically different in form, *Master Builder* similarly worked against a settled perspective or a single vantage point in its articulation of a performance of 'presence' acted out in dissonances between real, theatrical and media spaces. As the live performer's actions cross thresholds between material and electronic sites, their 'presence' is realized in disjunctive relationships between spaces and processes: in their actions' simultaneous articulation of *different* and conjoined spatial orders, which, in turn, qualify and inform the narratives they unfold.

Media places: *Jet Lag* (1998), *Alladeen* (2002), *Super Vision* (2005)

DAVID PENCE In this piece, probably more than half the time I'm being shot live by a camera, and these live images carry a great deal of power. There are some quite dramatic close-ups. So much so that I have to think in terms of moderating my performance – in other words, doing less. Anyway, during let's say sixty or sixty-five per cent of my time on stage I can move very little. My whole performance is right here – the camera in close on my face – and for me it is a really interesting challenge to keep the character activated and flowing and yet be expressed through a range of what might be an inch and a half of head movement. Yet it's interesting also that there are moments when I break away from the camera and can use my whole body. In other words, it's not only film, and it's not only theatre. It's a hybrid.

[New York City, November 2005]

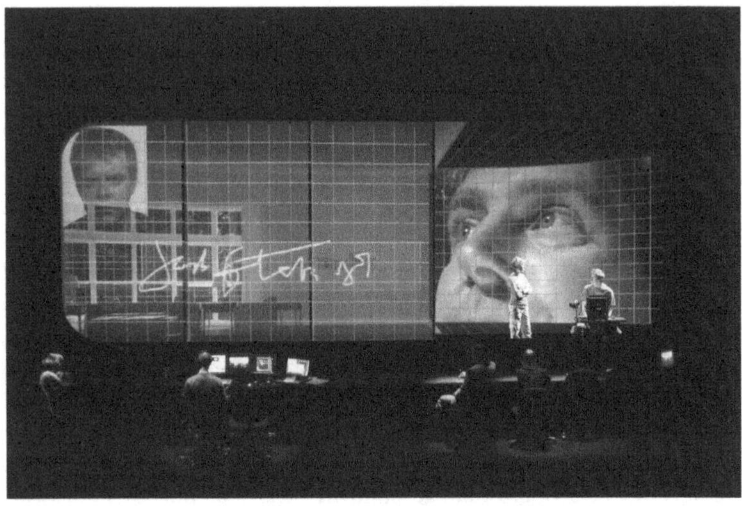

Figure 7.6 The Builders Association, *Super Vision* (2005). On stage, left to right: Kyle DeCamp, David Pence live and mediated in close-up

Where *Master Builder* located performances across real and virtual spaces, architectures and systems, in the company's subsequent work this positioning of the actor simultaneously 'in' and 'out' of place provided for an exploration of the impact of media and the 'speed' of contemporary communications (Virilio 1995) on experiences of presence. In this process, the location of the actor's performance in disjunctive systems and spaces formed a paradoxical locus for the articulation of the performer's 'liveness': of the performance and perception of the 'present tense' enactment of theatrical and media spaces.

Extending *Master Builder*'s articulation of performances across the thresholds between spaces, in the subsequent *Imperial Motel* (*Faust*) (1996) and *Jump Cut* (*Faust*) (1997) the company further foregrounded disjunctions between 'live' performance and its articulation of media and mediation. Designed by Cleater in such a way that 'we could see live performance happening in one space and then video, or some other kind of aspect, showing up in another space' (Cleater and Kaye 2007), *Imperial Motel* incorporated a 'remaking of F. W. Murnau's 1926 silent film *Faust* using live actors' (Wehle 1999: 6). Here, the company set a large video screen, some 6 ft high and 18 ft wide, above the main theatrical space and behind a gantry permitting performers to stand before its projections, while in a room below alluding to the eponymous hotel performers re-enacted scenes from the film. Approached as an 'armature of some video-like ideas' (Cleater and Kaye 2007), the design for *Imperial Motel* at once juxtaposed performances in theatrical and filmic spaces whilst facilitating the live performance of chroma-key, in which actors presenting to camera on stage before a 'blue screen' were simultaneously integrated into complex screened images projected on to the walls of the room or the gantry screen above.

JOHN CLEATER The idea was there were these two main playing spaces on the stage and they weren't necessarily connected – there might be a bar and a motel room, a bedroom – so we were referring to a few different spaces in different versions of *Faust*. There were these disparate things happening live on stage and this real interest in . . . putting the blue screen set up on display so that you saw how it actually worked. You would see the camera, the set-up; you would see the blue screen so the backdrops would change from a wallpapered motel room to just a blue room – it was just a series of these panels that were pulled out so each space would have a different background. So the idea was that you would see the whole set up – you would see the action here going on and you would see an action on the other side of the stage – then that came together seamlessly on this film above.
[Hudson NY, November 2007]

In these ways, *Imperial Motel* opened the audiences' view to the mechanisms of this 'live' mediated performance, whilst emphasizing the actors' displacement from 'theatrical' into ostensibly 'filmic' spaces. In doing so, the actor performs spaces bound together in relationships of difference, performing 'here' (in the theatre; on the screen) and yet simultaneously *from* or *towards* this position in an articulation of a 'live' transmission and transition. In this context, Weems's direction has sought to amplify the actors' attention to their 'liveness' in performance *through* media, over and above their attention to the production of images *in* the media, an attention further supported in *Jump Cut* (*Faust*) by the sound designs of Dan Dobson and video created by Christopher Kondek being played in direct exchange with the theatrical performance.

What holds it together is the *presence* of the actors and the awareness of everyone. Like a musician, each person must be fully sensitive to the nuance of each moment while at the same time aware of the larger structures – the rhythm, the tempo, where the piece is driving, where it can be more relaxed, what is coming next.

Each person must be *attuned* to each other, connected and aware of what's happening.

Dan [Dobson] and Chris [Kondek], Yvette and Kelley have to watch what's happening on stage, and the actors have to work with them and each other.

[Marianne Weems, handwritten pre-performance note to the company, *Jump Cut (Faust)*]

Such prompts and exchanges between the network of 'live' 'theatrical' performances and their transmission and circulation through mediation is integral to Weems's focus on the responsiveness and reciprocity between performers presenting to and *before* each other and the audience. Here, rather than construct electronic mediation in opposition to the theatrical performer's 'liveness', Weems approaches the '*presence* of the actors and the awareness of everyone' as augmented in the media itself. As a consequence, the 'real time' screened image of the performer performing ('live') troubles the place in which the present-tense of action is constructed and perceived: here, rather than simply eliding 'liveness', mediation announces it.

It is an analogous troubling of 'place', too, that is articulated in The Builders Association's subsequent narratives, performance modes and designs. In this development, and following *Imperial Motel* and *Jump Cut (Faust)*, their key trilogy of performance works, comprising *Jet Lag* (1998), *Alladeen* (2002) and culminating in *Super Vision* (2005), set tensions between place and placelessness, the located and unlocated, thematically at the fore of the company's work. Focusing on the construction of place theatrically and thematically in or through electronic media, this trilogy engaged with passages between 'virtual' and 'real' places and their implications for contemporary experience, identity and location. Created in collaboration with the New York-based architectural partnership Diller + Scofidio, *Jet Lag* thus offered two narratives of place constituted in the dislocating affects of the 'speed' of contemporary communications. Rooted in 'real' events, the piece, Elizabeth Diller and Ric Scofidio recall, arose in response to a citation by the critic Paul Virilio:

He spoke of a 'great American heroine' . . . who kidnapped her fourteen-year old grandson and travelled with him from New York to Amsterdam, then Amsterdam to New York, back and forth 167 times over a period of six months in the attempt to elude pursuit by the boy's father. The father wanted his son to see a psychiatrist. After six months of continuous air travel, the grandmother finally died of 'jet lag'. [Diller + Scofidio in Chamlers 1999: 57]

Where this journey, they suggest, 'simulated domesticity for her grandson while in perpetual motion', *Jet Lag*'s twin narrative mirrors this in reverse, through a protagonist who 'fabricated the bravado of movement while in constant stasis'. Diller + Scofidio continue:

> A British sailor [whom Jessica Chalmers renamed Roger Dearborn] joined a round-the-world yacht race. Dearborn was so driven by the promise of media attention that he entered the race ill prepared. The sailor ultimately took two journeys. One took place only in the media: Dearborn sent radio signals falsifying his whereabouts as if he were actually circumnavigating; the other was his actual journey, which consisted of sailing in circles for six months in the South Atlantic, unable to admit his failure. He ultimately died, possibly a suicide, by drowning.   [Diller + Scofidio in Chalmers 1999: 57]

These stories articulate paradoxical *movements in place*: an ungrounding of location and a sense of stasis produced in the journey itself. Thus the grandmother's constant travelling is subject to a 'deferred time' (Chalmers 1999: 60) and place produced, Diller + Scofidio suggest, in 'the boredom of the airport space, which is neither here nor there' (Diller + Scofidio in Chalmers 1999: 58). In parallel, Dearborn simulates a powerful narrative of his journey though 'real space', a terrain that, for him, lacks all co-ordinate. In their subsequent collaboration with the London-based company **moti**roti for *Alladeen* (2002), the performance of multiple places and times was further explored through the experiences of call centre operators working from the Indian subcontinent to the United States. In this address to the individual as an agent acting out the meanings of 'being there' in networked time and space, the company characteristically exposed their processes of mediation, as performers located live on stage were simultaneously re-presented in the cinematic space above, integrated into a series of transforming images and narratives. Such a division and dispersal of identity was also reflected in the fabric of *Alladeen* itself: the project, devised across two continents, encompassed a theatre performance, a music video and web site; in performance, the stage was divided between cinematic and theatrical spaces; its subject matter, a making visible of the simulation and subversion of a 'global' (North American) identity simulated by the Indian call centre operators. In this process, the performance of place, identity and time was charged with the political and social implications of crossing 'first' and 'developing' world spaces and sites. Here, far from collapsing distance and difference, the ubiquity of networked communications offer a further myth of transformation as questions of presence are explored through the performance and reception of identities across multiple and dispersed media sites.

However, it is the third of these pieces, *Super Vision* (2005), in which the architectural imperative is foregrounded through the

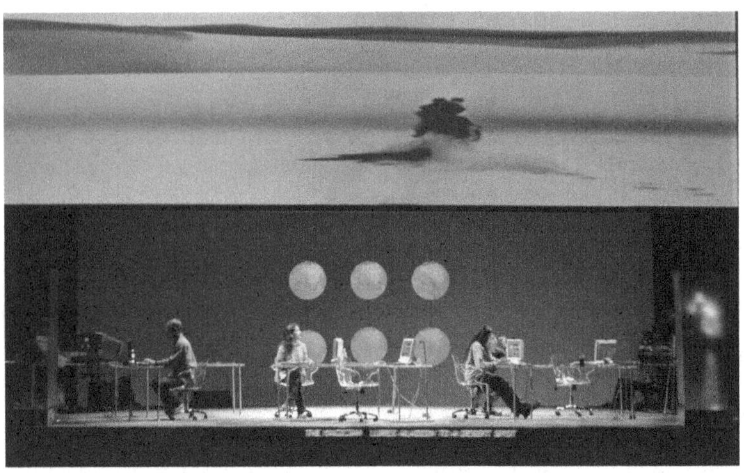

Figure 7.7 The Builders Association and **moti**roti, *Alladeen* (2002)

company's collaboration with dbox that most explicitly embedded the thematics of presence into the operation of the performance. Presented within responsive virtual sets and dbox's simulations of 'real' spaces that also encompassed systems for the performer's mediation and integration into the projected environment, *Super Vision* explicitly operated across spatial thresholds. Interweaving three thematically related narratives, through a text developed in collaboration with Constance DeJong, *Super Vision* engaged with identity theft, 'dataveillance', with virtual and 'natural' place, and with dispersals of subjectivity and identity. Indeed, *Super Vision* begins in a visualization of the digital shadow or doubled identity constructed in the surveillance of 'real bodies' and the consignment of personal information to the 'datasphere', a visualization performed in this collocation of real and virtual architectures.

The three narratives of *Super Vision* are:

1. A father covertly exploits his young son's personal data to meet the demands of the family's lifestyle. This ploy escalates beyond the father's control, until he is compelled to disappear.

2. As he crosses successive borders, a solitary traveller gradually is forced to reveal all of his personal information, until his identity becomes transparent, with no part of his life left outside the boundaries of data surveillance.

3. A young woman, addicted to the white noise of constant connection, maintains a long-distance relationship with her grandmother.

[The Builders Association, November 2005]

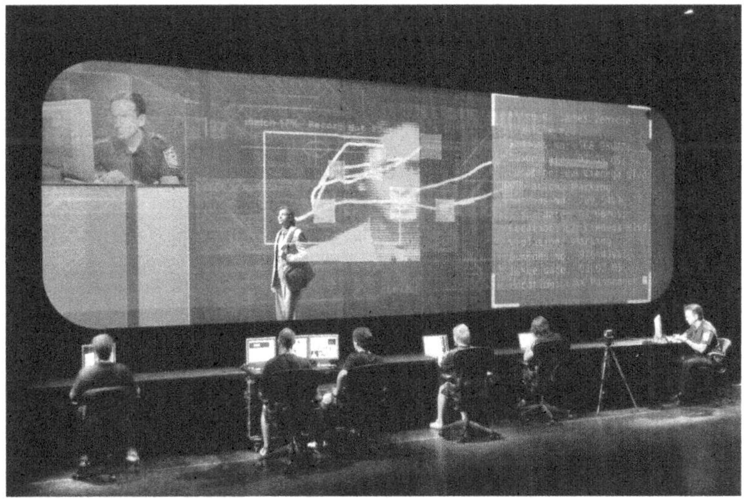

Figure 7.8 The Builders Association, *Super Vision* (2005). On stage, left to right: Joe Silovsky mediated live; Rizwan Mirza live and in close-up. Fore stage, far right: Jo Silovsky. At table: Neal Wilkinson, Jeff Morey, Hal Eager, Kate Stannard

Eliding oppositions between screen and stage space, the virtual architectures of *Super Vision* define media spaces for live performance. Thus the family room to which *Super Vision* opens is explicitly constructed in a layering, through projection, of real, simulated and recorded spaces, which its actors' live and mediated performances variously traverse. It is an organization of places for performance, too, that explicitly enacts 'media space' as palimpsest, as the performance proceeds through a continual writing over of real, virtual and simulated spaces and events. In this context, in a counterpoint of the production of media spaces in the performance of *Master Builder*, the actors' physical presence and performance intrude into *Super Vision*'s virtual architectures by providing for the irruption of 'real' embodied spaces into this simulated staging even as these projections reconfigure or render these spaces in transition. Here, too, the simulation of 'real' spaces foregrounds a further paradox of the 'live' performance of electronic media: that the visual effect of layered high-definition projections does not easily succumb to documentation, remediation or reproduction by other means, so implying a quality of the 'unique' and the 'live' in the occasion of its performance.

MARIANNE WEEMS In the family scenes there is a nice layering of the real body and then the completely manufactured living room environment, and then the real photographed environment (the 'back yard') seen out the windows behind them. And of course there's the insertion of the video boy actor moving between the animated and the photographed environments – and the live actors relate to the video boy as he moves between those various planes.

JAMES GIBBS It is impossible to capture the fidelity of the imagery when you collapse it down to a single DVD – what is up there on stage is actually beyond HD-TV resolution. On the other hand, if you just take any one of the virtual elements on their own, outside of the performance, they mean almost nothing. The performance is in all those elements at play, together, live.

[New York City, November 2005]

In this dynamic, 'presence' is articulated in the actors' performance at the threshold of – and disjunctive relationships between – 'live' theatrical and 'mediated' performances. It is an approach and reversal evident in *Super Vision*'s most overt play between 'real' and simulated performance. In the opening scene, integrated into the projections in which the sets and location are constructed, the young son, John Fletcher, Junior, is represented through a seemingly interactive projection; a video-child animated in a series of exchanges with his fictional parents and extended scenes with his mother (played by Kyle DeCamp) that bring the mediated and recorded forward towards a claim to the 'real' space and 'present' time of 'live' performance. In the family scenes, in which, as they progress, it becomes evident that the father, played by David Pence, has appropriated and exploited the digital identity of his son, behaviour towards the virtual boy becomes the fulcrum of the Fletchers' relationship and the motor to the father's departure. In these scenes the 'presence' of the virtual boy 'on stage', whose projection on the mobile fore-screen renders his image translucent, is articulated in the rhythms of the performers with whom he apparently interacts. In this process the boy's recorded performance provokes a sense of spontaneity and unity, a 'presentness' to the theatrical space reinvented by his co-performers. In contrast, the father's performance is seen simultaneously on stage and in 'live' mediation, and so in an explicit division and multiplication of his present-tense performance. Here, Pence's simultaneous location across the real and virtual spaces in which *Super Vision* is articulated thematizes his emotional displacement from his son while amplifying his actions and removing him from the apparent unity and consistency of the virtual boy's 'theatrical' performance.

KYLE DECAMP In this piece with The Builders I find myself making choices located in how *not* to reproduce what's already going on via

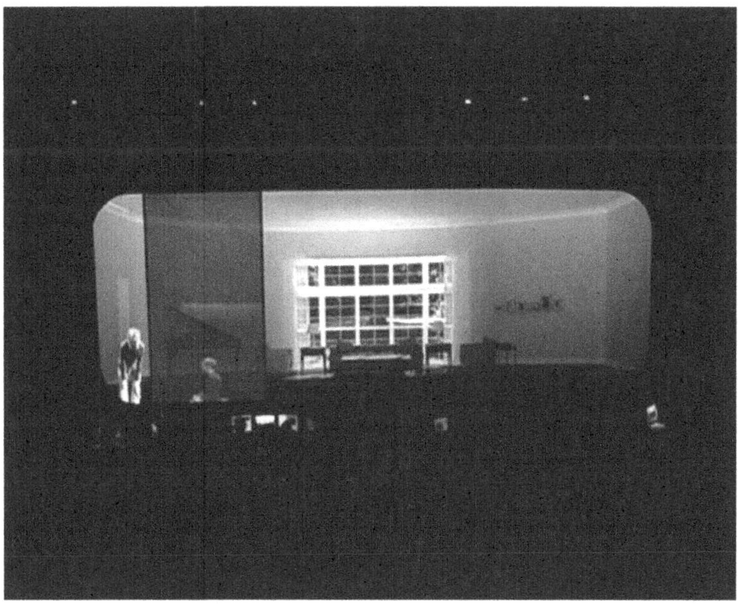

Figure 7.9 The Builders Association, *Super Vision* (2005), the virtual boy. On stage, left to right: Kyle DeCamp; Owen Philip. Video still

other mediums that hopefully add to the dynamic dissonances on stage. There's a lot of illusion and affect that I don't have to create in my performance: in Dan Dobson's sound score, in the projected imagery of the house and its movement, in the narrative information and flow – they're all facets of how the story is told. I have to do a different kind of work as a performer in relation to the video-child, because he's a flat projection, and the same every night. What a remarkably consistent little performer he is! So . . . somewhat ironically for me, it's the warmth of my performance that effectively animates him, although he appears to be an 'animation' on screen. . . . I animate our interactions through my moment-to-moment responses, and play it differently every night. I quickly discovered where I could inflect emotion, rhythmic pauses, overlaps, and play around with the movements between his projection, the moving projection screen and myself. It sometimes feels like this very human play between a mother and child – even though he's a projection – is as real if not more humanly warm and 'real' than the relationship between the wife and husband, in a way that I hope resonates metaphorically within the story.

[New York City, November 2008]

In this context, rather than emphasize mediation's elision or erasure and so *absenting* of the actor, *Super Vision* foregrounds the 'live' transmission and circulation of its various performances, as, for example, David Pence (the father, John Fletcher, Senior), Moe Angelos (the grandmother) and Tanya Selvaratnam (the young woman, Jen) perform simultaneously towards 'live' and 'mediated' frames and spaces, amplifying awareness and perception of their actions and presence *there* (on stage) and *here* (in projection; in the 'mediatic' system). In turn, it is this articulation and traversal of 'real' and 'mediated' spaces that provides the context for the animation of the virtual boy: presented in projection, the boy occupies in a single image the spaces his 'live' counterparts traverse; his 'presence' is not *in projection* but performed in his reversal and mirroring of the actors' transitions.

Here, too, the performance of the virtual boy plays on paradoxical relationships between presence and the signs of theatrical representation and mediation. In the first instance, his co-performance with Kyle DeCamp might be read in the context of Phillip Auslander's celebrated critique of 'liveness as a pristine state' (Auslander 1999: 53), in which he observes the effect of 'mediatization' across a range of popular cultural forms. Proposing that 'mediatization' conventionally announces itself in *the absence* of the 'real' or 'live' event, Auslander's reading implicitly critiques influential ontologies of 'the live', in which, for example, the theorist Peggy Phelan locates performance in its 'disappearance' and so in an eventhood and ephemerality that evade reproduction (Phelan 1993: 146–66). In this sense, Auslander's analysis attends first to the operation of language, leading him to argue:

> That the mediated is engrained in the live is apparent in the structure of the English word *immediate*. The root form is the word *mediate* of which *immediate* is, of course, the negation. Mediation is thus embedded in the *im-mediate*; the relation of mediation and the im-mediate is one of mutual dependence not precession … Similarly, live performance cannot be said to have ontological or historical priority over mediatisation, since liveness was made visible only by the possibility of technical reproduction.   [Auslander 1999: 53–4, original emphases]

Auslander's position is shadowed by the idea that 'presence' is neither available in the performance of 'liveness', nor in opposition to the mediated. Indeed, 'liveness', the claim to the performer's undivided occupation of the present tense of time and space, is defined in the interdependence and so contamination of liveness *in* mediation and vice versa.

In *Super Vision*, then, DeCamp and the virtual boy's mutually reinforcing performances invite recognition of the interdependence of these effects. It is an overlapping produced, too, in their mutual performance of the signs of dramatic character. Indeed, within the apparatus of theatrical representation, and through the dramaturgical and narrative structures that define *Super Vision*, the virtual boy shares with his 'live' counterparts the performance of the theatrical sign; that which Kier Elam characterizes in *The Semiotics of Theatre and Drama* (Elam 2002) as the product of the theatrical relationship itself, whereby the act on stage is read as a signifier of the 'class' (or case) of that action rather than the act itself. Here, in their differences, DeCamp and the boy announce each other's performance of the sign, drawing attention to the theatrical conceit and framing in which their exchange must be understood. In turn, these constructions offer not so much the 'opposition' of the 'live' to the 'mediated' as exchanges between modes of mediation in which theatrical signs are produced, circulated and transformed. It is this circulation, too, that the electronic network facilitates and articulates: thus, on stage, The Builders Association perform the signs of 'live presence' in and against its 'screening'; simultaneously, on screen, in 'real time' 'live' mediation, *Super Vision* takes its cue from and provokes performance on stage. In this movement of performance and the spectator's eye from the live to the mediated to the live, the 'real/live' performance of the actor is, again, articulated in the 'unlocated' links that blur and contaminate these distinct orders of space, media and representation.

It is in this exchange, too, that the movement and division between places also becomes the locus of individual performances. Thus, where the 'electronic network' through which *Super Vision* operates and is performed separates performers from each other, so the actor's simultaneous performance to live and mediated spaces may also divide their action from itself. In *Super Vision*'s third narrative, this division provides a thematic underpinning to Moe Angelos and Tanya Selvaratnam's performance of a long-distance relationship between a grandmother in Sri Lanka and a young woman in New York. Looking out towards each other, with Angelos playing to camera 'off stage', but in view of the audience, the grandmother and Jen conduct a series of exchanges marked by erasures and mistaken memories. In making visible the multiple sites 'on' and 'off' stage and camera in which this performance is enacted, this exchange exemplifies *Super Vision*'s operation in movements or oscillations of attention between the located and unlocated, between the 'live' and the 'mediated'.

MOE ANGELOS I am looking at a monitor almost the entire time. And since I am doing a 'webcam performance' it is sort of 'real', because

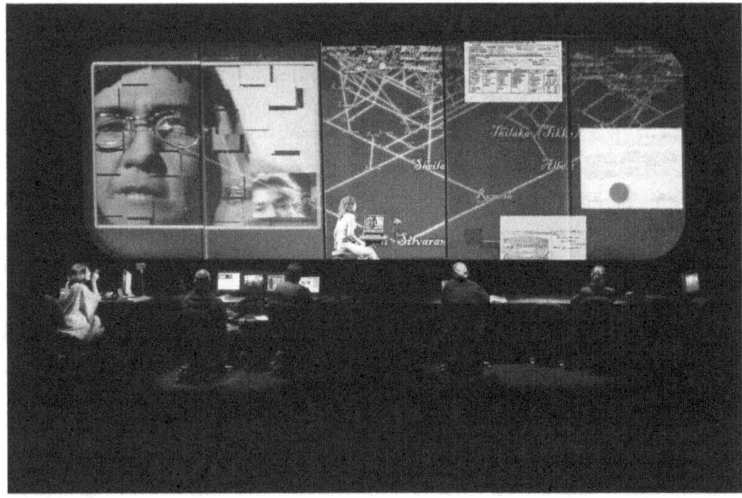

Figure 7.10 The Builders Association, *Super Vision* (2005). On stage, left to right: Moe Angelos, live and mediated in close-up; Tanya Selvaratnam, mediated to window and live; Moe Angelos, mediated to computer screen

that is what you do when you are chatting to someone on a webcam. You are sitting at your computer, looking at this little eye that is the camera, and you are watching them and they are watching you. So my situation replicates reality in a certain way ... On my monitor is a very long shot from the back of the house, so I can see the whole stage; I am seeing what the audience sees, basically. When I am projected I can see myself.

NICK KAYE How does watching yourself in mediation affect your performance?

TANYA SELVARATNAM I am doubly aware because I am looking at myself to see how I look on camera – and I am also trying to be unconscious of myself ...

MOE ANGELOS [I]t is strangely voyeuristic, or narcissistic, in a certain way, because I am just looking at myself in the same way as when we walk past a mirror. It's the same thing. I am sitting there, and I catch myself looking at myself – watching to see where I am: am I framed properly?

[New York City, November 2005]

In *Super Vision* 'presence' is performed in spaces of difference: in the mirroring and amplification of David Pence's performance to camera; in the presence of the operators – and performers – at the desk before the 'stage space' they intervene into; in the traveller's multiplication before and behind the screen. Here, and echoing the other rhythmic structures that carry the performance forward, the signs of presence 'flow through the system' (Cage 1965) and are subject to repetition, simultaneity, variation and recapitulation. Articulated in such movements and transitions between 'real/live' mediated and recorded spaces and performances, this presentation of the performer also constructs the sense of dissonant unity and uncanny distance that characterizes The Builders Association's work, whose visually full and media-rich aesthetic at first belies the lacunae in which its systems operate, and which in turn informs their address to themes of place and locality. 'Presence', here, is not assigned to any one aspect of performance but enacted in vacillations, translations and transitions between media, in the crossing of thresholds and the construction of the live in the mediated. In this layering and modulation of projection, duplication and mediation, *Super Vision*'s performance amplifies that which technologies of reproduction would seem to defeat: the performance of the signs of presence across the absences of the screen.

MARIANNE WEEMS This complicating the presence of the performers has always been our direction, and this piece in particular succeeded. And it was also made very palpable for the audience – you could feel that the performers were really being extended into the media and vice versa, because of the way that they are lined up on a one-to-one scale ... Again, what came first in *Super Vision* was the idea that we are dragging another body behind us – this electronic network that is extending out of us in some way or flying around us constantly – and how to make that palpable and visual. The more it seemed like the performers were really being invaded by that – or overlapping with the electronics – the more interesting it became.

[New York City, November 2005]

In *Super Vision*, place, too, is expressed in this crossing of spaces. Indeed, for The Builders Association, the impact of media on site and location forms an explicit part of their engagement with presence; with the subject's occupation of and construction in 'real' and 'virtual' times and spaces. In its penultimate scene, *Super Vision* reveals John Fletcher, Senior, now set against the backdrop of the Arctic, having left the family. Echoing references in the first family scenes, a flock of birds appear in the distance, slowly gathering and moving towards the still figure of the father. Travelling north to escape the datasphere, and to occupy a 'real' place, the appearance of a flock of birds in the distance, then coming closer, relates visually to dbox's recurrent motif of mobile images of data that link and overlap scenes, and that threads its way through the performance. Here, the web of virtual imagery, the web environment and the data environment constitute the place of departure and arrival. The birds appear, and then they are gone. This place 'is' information, code, data, media.

Transition and location: *Continuous City* (2008)

It is this return of the experience of place in disjunctive relationships between media forms and layering of spaces, too, that underpins The Builders Association's most recent work. Thus in *Continuous City* (2008), this approach to performance, place and 'live' theatrical presence comes to articulate an occupation of place defined in the intersection and relationship between networked systems. Indeed, this performance is itself comprised of a layering of networks – real, virtual and represented – within which the experience and meaning of distance and performance of identity and presence are explored in occupations of places always already displaced by the network.

MARIANNE WEEMS *Jet Lag*, and in many ways *Alladeen*, are about the erasure of geography and that sense of – I think the simplest way for me to put it is how the First World is pulling away from the rest of the world and part of the sense of privilege is that *placelessness*. That it is only because of travel and wealth that we are able to blur these locations, and that is how networking works: you have to have a certain level of privilege to be within the network. So part of this project is about recuperating a sense of place or at least investigating what location could be, even if it is a kind of nostalgic idea that somehow people still feel location or they imply location.

[Berkeley CA, October 2007]

Taking, in an early point of departure, elements of Italo Calvino's novel *Invisible Cities* (1972, trans. 1974) Weems's initial research for *Continuous City* also engaged with the economic, political and social distance constructed on the outskirts and margins of mega-cities and a corresponding exclusion in the removal from these places constructed in the suburban architecture of gated communities. Emerging through

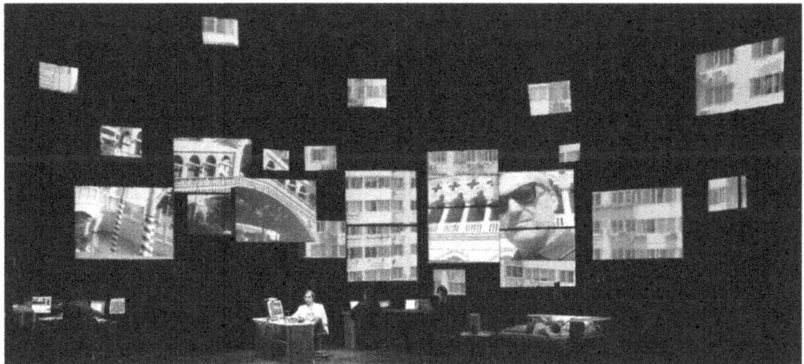

Figure 7.11 The Builders Association, final rehearsals for *Continuous City* (2008), Krannert Centre, University of Illinois in Champaign–Urbana, September 2008. On stage: Rizwan Mira. On screen: Harry Sinclair

this process was an engagement with experiences of periphery, a theme translated through the eighteen-month development of *Continuous City* towards an address to the meaning of geographical and emotional distance in the ubiquity of networked technologies, and the analogous circulation, in built architectures, of signs of place and belonging.

> *Continuous City* is a meditation on how contemporary experiences of location and dislocation stretch us to the maximum as our 'networked selves' occupy multiple locations. From Shanghai to Los Angeles, Toronto to Mexico City, *Continuous City* tells the story of a travelling father and his daughter at home tethered and transformed by speed, hypermodernity and failing cell phones. The characters they interact with pursue their own transnational business, from an internet mogul exploiting networking across the developing world to a nanny who blogs humorous stories about the people and places within her universe.
>
> The show also reaches directly into each city the production visits through a participatory website and on-site filming to create a global and local production. *Continuous City* is about people far from home, *Continuous City* is where we live now.
>
> [The Builders Association, April 2009]

In this performance, then, a father (Harry Sinclair) travels internationally to promote a new social networking company, 'Xubu', communicating via the web and his cellphone variously with his employer, J.V. (Rizwan Mirza), his young daughter Sam and her live-in nanny

Deb (Moe Angelos). As the narrative unfolds, the father is in continual but disrupted contact with J.V., Sam and occasionally Deb, from Somalia, Guadalajara and Shanghai, while seeming, at times, to be in Paris, Venice, London or New York, although these latter locations are 'real' simulations: 'Little Paris' in Tianducheng, China, in which the Eiffel Tower is reproduced in a *faux* Paris for 2,000 residents; 'Thames Town', a simulated Georgian and Victorian village one hour's drive from Shanghai. Projected across a suite of up to thirty-seven screens of varying sizes, which continually open and close to receive single or varying numbers of multiple projections, the father's communications envelop the theatrical space in a material representation of the layers of the network and a mobile rendering, in theatrical space, of the fluidity of the multiple windows of the desktop.

In *Continuous City* these networks also intersect with a staging of 'real' and 'fictional' local and 'family' networks. Thus, in advance of each performance, Moe Angelos ('Deb') will visit the venue for the performance to produce a blog reflecting on the immediate locale, interviewing members of the local community and grounding her performance through a 'real' online narrative that will subsequently be presented as her character's reflections on 'living in' this location. This layering of the fictional 'Deb' and the 'real' Moe Angelos is echoed, too, in Rizwan Mirza's presentation of J.V., which is punctuated by Mirza's performance of 'live' teleconferences with family members residing in Delhi and London. Offering J.V./Rizwan Mirza in seemingly 'real time' conversations, this sequence also poses questions over the signs of liveness and authenticity of Mirza's subsequent interactions with performers presenting on screen as well as the boundaries of each performance of *Continuous City* itself. It is a question rendered more complex by the different qualities of performance at play on stage and on screen, which variously contrast Harry Sinclair (the father) performing to camera on location in the 'real' ('simulated') places to which he refers, the capturing and replay of contributions by members of the public to the *Continuous City* networking site, which invites comments and reflections on places of personal significance, and the informal, long-distance, interrupted exchanges with dispersed family members.

RIZWAN MIRZA In the development process of *Continuous City* last year at UC Berkeley we experimented with pre-recorded and edited conversations with my family members in New Delhi and in London. That sparked the idea of attempting to incorporate live, real-time online video conversations during the performance. What we discovered was that video-conferencing technology wasn't what

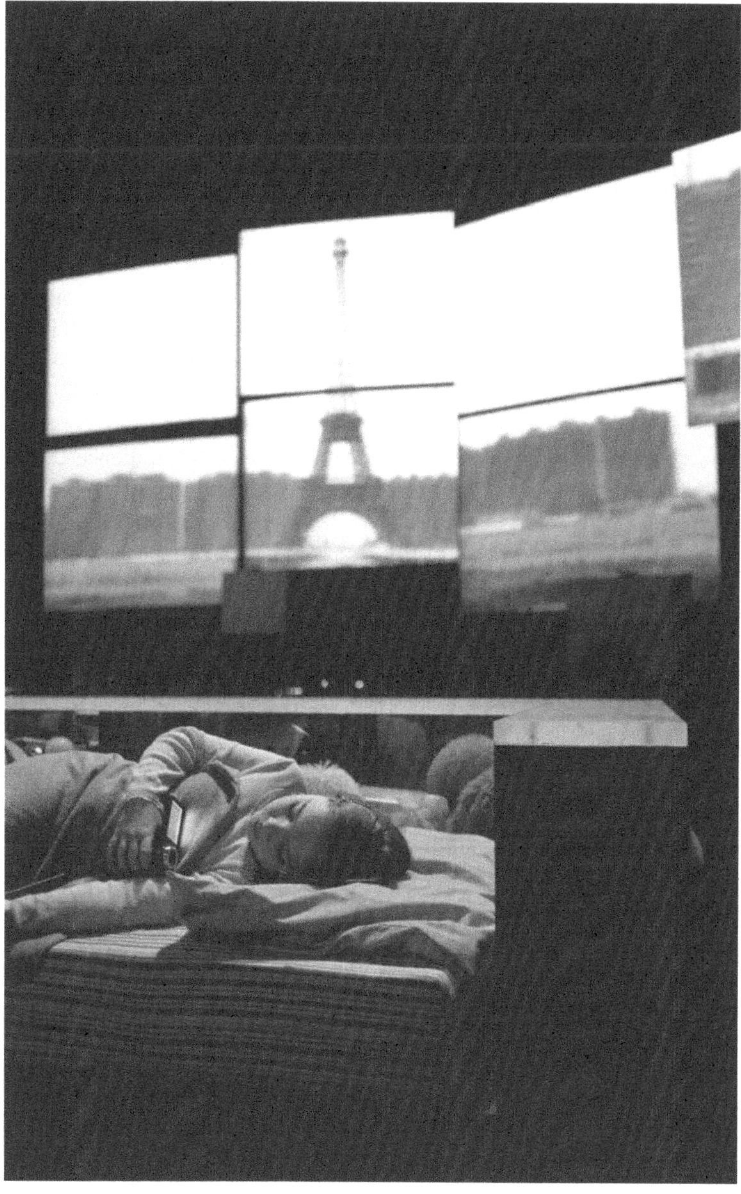

Figure 7.12 The Builders Association, *Continuous City* (2008). On stage: Caroline O'Neill

we see in the movies! There's quite a bit of lag and drop-outs, audio challenges. To depend on that would be to take a big risk in front of a live audience but we like to take risks! My actual family members would play J.V.'s family members but talk about actual family situations that were happening at times. And that's very exciting. *Continuous City* is about a non-real company – Xubu, which has a real web site but is a web site for the show itself, not Xubu. The site connects real people in a virtual community. J.V. the character interacts with the actor's actual family, who tell the actor true stories but referring to him only as the character. We would bring up contemporary news items, like discussing Obama's speech that night. Being in that space has the anxiety of whether the technology is going to work or not at that very moment: there were times my family used my real name, which was hilarious because even they got confused about how to be present – and who knows if the audience caught that or not! Live on stage five nights a week in different parts of the world with internet connections that may or may not be available in the theatre! – so all of these factors have to be pushed aside to be present in that moment. I do think that that anxiety leads to an edgier energy in the show. Part of what we do in our work is to play with ideas of time and space, the virtual often becoming the 'real' and the real changes shape and texture.

[Champaign–Urbana IL, August 2008]

Counterpointing this layering of networks is a reversal and extension of the virtual boy's performance in *Super Vision* in the figure of a six-year-old actor, Caroline O'Neill, and later alternated between O'Neill and the eight-year-old Olivia Timothee. Indeed, for Weems the positioning of a child performer as the fulcrum of the performance evidently offered a centring of the performance thematically and formally, as well as with regard to perceived qualities of 'presence', in a strategy that also implicitly echoes Societas Raffaello Sanzio's incorporation of child performers in works such as *Genesi: From the Museum of Sleep* (2001) among others (Giannachi and Kaye 2002: 152–6).

MARIANNE WEEMS When we went to Krannert we found a little girl with a lot of technique – she seems to have had a lot of stage time in her short six-year life – and very little self-consciousness. The thing that was the most successful was when I had her doing something else on stage – for instance, she has a web game that she plays, a network called Webkinz. So we set her up so that she could play the game *and* she had to talk to Harry [Sinclair] – the father – on camera. All I said

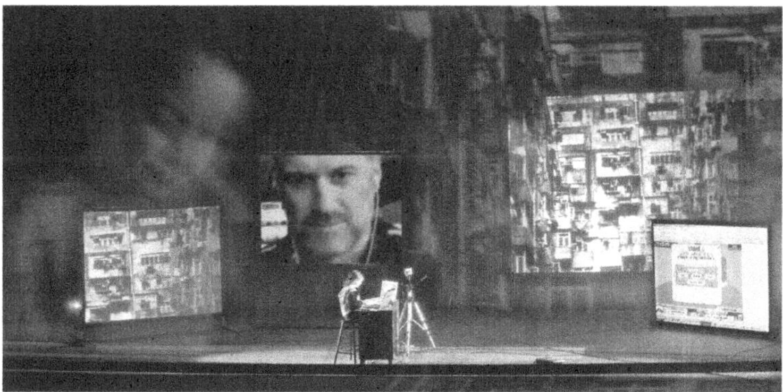

Figure 7.13 The Builders Association, work in progress for *Continuous City*, Krannert Centre, University of Illinois in Champaign–Urbana, July 2007. On stage and screen: Caroline O'Neill; on screen: Harry Sinclair

to her was: Caroline, go away and play the game and when you have a line look in the camera and say it to Harry. And she did it in this unbelievably seamless, totally unselfconscious way. She did exactly what I asked her. It wasn't like with an actor where you get some resistance and you have to discuss whether they should do it or not or how they should do it. She did it exactly like I asked her to, and nothing more and nothing less. It was a very pure experience. She is almost like – I can't believe I am about to say this – but it was like having an animation on stage, because the way she did it was so unselfconscious.

[Berkeley CA, October 2007]

In these various constructions and layering of networks, mediations of place and qualities of performance *Continuous City* brings forward and develops key underlying themes and practices within the company's work as a whole, linked also to the early architectural sources and concerns that informed *Master Builder* with regard to the *location* of mediation and media practices. Indeed, here the company's vocabulary and practice interrogate and extend issues of the affect of media on location and place raised not only in architecture but in video art and video installation. Thus, for the artist and architect Vito Acconci, tensions around place and location reached to the core of his own influential video art and installation as he proposes that:

Video installation is a conjunction of opposites . . . On the one hand, 'installation' places an art-work in a specific site, for a specific time (a specific duration and also, possibly, for a specific historical time). On the other hand, 'video' (with its consequences followed through: video on broadcast television) is placeless: at least, its place can't be determined . . . Video installation, then, places placelessness.   [Acconci 2000: 376]

In its engagement with networked place *Continuous City* explores the affect of enacting and so locating the media's production of 'placelessness'. In doing so, the company directly extend their core concerns for the definition of place and identity in movements between the located and unlocated – and so for the performance of presence, of *being there*, in the gaps and absences produced in the operation of network media. In *Continuous City* this act of location is articulated in a further amplification of the multiple and disjunctive relationships between 'real' and 'virtual' spaces. Thus, eschewing *Super Vision*'s play on the synthesis of material and simulated sets and architectures, *Continuous City* purposely extends the virtual spaces of the screen across and through its theatrical spaces. It is a design that provides a key emphasis in this work's address to the experience of these places: an aesthetic identified in the process of the performance's development by James Gibbs as the sense 'that our relationships that are mediated by these technologies are discontinuous; are not seamless' (Gibbs 2008a).

The 'continuous city' is realized in a layering of networks, in which signs and performances of 'being in place' circulate. Here, an occupation of 'the city', and a realization of identity and relationship, are subject to the circulation and exchange of signs momentarily occupied, of particular places and positions temporarily located. In the 'seamfulness' of *Continuous City* the locus of place, and so identity, remains the interdependent, disjunctive and mobile relationships enacted between media forms, realized here in the actors' traversing and definition of their 'presence' in their performances' layering of these systems and places. In this context, the performance of presence is articulated and realized in the move *across* networked spaces, in the layering of one networked 'place' or 'act' upon another; in the seam or the slip, where the signifiers of place and space cross, intrude and define one in the other. 'Being there', in this context, is produced in the contamination of one system, media, and so location by another; amplified in an enactment of transitions, in acts of migration across signs and spaces. Consistently with Weems's early approach to the electronic network 'as a kind of architecture', presence, in these networks, is a function of incongruence: of a temporary and disjunctive placing of 'placelessness'; of a hybrid exchange whereby one system or network, for the moment, is enacted, and so located, in another.

8

pervasiveness Blast Theory and
Mixed Reality Laboratory

Since the late 1990s Blast Theory, led by Matt Adams, Ju Row Farr and Nick Tandavanitj, have developed mixed reality performances and installations investigating the 'social and political aspects of technology' (Blast Theory 2005). Their work, known for blurring the boundaries between spectator, participant and performer, between the performance and its social and personal contexts, and between 'real' and 'digital', is hybrid in nature, often utilizing, concurrently, strategies drawn from performance, theatre and games. The former was already apparent in *Kidnap* (1998), in which two volunteers were selected from several hundred applicants, kidnapped and put under surveillance for a period of forty-eight hours. The latter became prominent through *Desert Rain* (1999), their first collaboration with the Mixed Reality Laboratory and Professor Steve Benford at Nottingham University, which, inspired by Jean Baudrillard's *The Gulf War Did Not Take Place* (1991), attempted 'to articulate the ways in which the real, the virtual, the fictional and the imaginary have become increasingly entwined' (Blast Theory 2002). In its entwining of multiple locations, contexts and actions Blast Theory's work has also consistently engaged with concepts, practices and experiences of presence, often through a radical dispersal and layering of the places of individual action, performance and reception. Importantly, too, Blast Theory's collaboration with the Mixed Reality Laboratory brings together in their performances and installations distinct and complementary aims, as works such as *Day of the Figurines* (2006) among others achieve a range of aesthetic and experimental outcomes. In this chapter, and in the interviews interpolated into this analysis, the question of presence is explored also in these connections and differences.

Following *Desert Rain*, Blast Theory and the Mixed Reality Laboratory developed a number of performance works, which, consistently with other pervasive games (Montola 2005), extended conventional computer games in one or more of three dimensions. Spatially, they often operated through location-based experiences, which responded to players' positions and movements and that were frequently designed for a specific site. Socially, they built on the primarily social use of personal devices, such as mobile phones, and the establishment of new forms of interaction between players and non-players, such as spectators in public settings. Temporally, they operated by finely interweaving game experiences with the patterns of daily life, once again building on the particular character of devices such as mobile phones that enable communication with others at many times and in many places (Flintham *et al.* 2007; Adams *et al.* 2008). An example of spatial expansion is *Can You See Me Now?* (2003), which utilized the global positioning system (GPS) to track each performer's movements through the city and then map these on to the movements of their avatar through a virtual model of this city as part of a game of chase with online players (Flintham *et al.* 2003). An illustration of social expansion is *Uncle Roy All Around You* (2003), which explored the boundaries between the fictional world of a game and the physical reality of a city, implicating bystanders on the city streets in the narrative of the game (Benford 2006). Finally, *Day of the Figurines* (2006) and *Rider Spoke* (2007) explored temporal expansion. The former involved up to 1,000 players using SMS to share 'twenty-four hours' in the life of a virtual town that was extended over a period of twenty-four days in real time, leading to a fine-grained embedding of the performance into their everyday lives. The latter, a location-based game for cyclists, encouraged players to cycle around London, record memories on to a hand-held computer, and listen to the responses of preceding participants, thus building, over time, a 'mixed reality' author-generated city map intertwining past memories with performative encounters in found and designated sites.

While all these works engage with performance and experiences of presence, *Day of the Figurines* is particularly suited to a study of this field in that the piece took place over a prolonged period of time, thus affecting not only a player's sense of their own presence, or their sense of the presence of others within their own engagement in the performance,

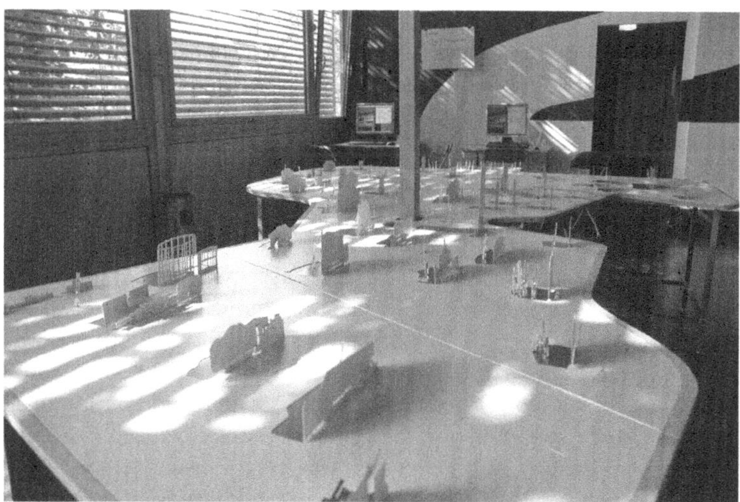

Figure 8.1 Blast Theory, *Day of the Figurines* (2006). The board displayed at
Hebbel am Ufer, Berlin

but also their experience of presence in this temporal expansion. The
piece was developed by Blast Theory in collaboration with the Mixed
Reality Laboratory as part of a larger research project, IPerG, funded by
the European Commission's IST Programme, and comprising a number
of European institutions, including Fraunhofer Institute, FIT and Sony
NetServices. IPerG's principal research objective was the investigation
of pervasive games, that is, games that 'are no longer confined to the
virtual domain of the computer, but integrate the physical and social
aspects of the real world' (Magerkurth *et al.* 2005: 2) by 'interweaving
digital media with our everyday experience' (Capra *et al.* 2005: 89). That
questions around presence played an important role in the project's
initial stages is evident from the fact that an early IPerG paper addressed
the question of how to design pervasive games in order 'to support successful interaction between players and characters that are virtually and/
or physically present, including mixed presence for the same player'
(Waern *et al.* 2004: 3). The paper also cited other issues relevant to presence, such as the role of spectatorship, the fact that games should be able
to be interrupted rather than totally immersive, and that they should be
socially acceptable and combine characters and players in role-playing
and narrative games.

IPerG researchers, further elaborating Carrie Heeter's study of presence in virtual reality (Heeter 1992), also distinguished between personal
presence, 'the self-experience of one's presence', social presence, 'the

other's experience of one's presence', and environmental presence, 'the environment's notion of one's presence' (Benford and Capra 2005: 27). While in a physical environment these aspects were considered to be inseparable, in a pervasive game, the team argued, 'it may be necessary to differentiate between players, spectators and bystanders, respectively those not involved'. The paper also drew attention to the importance of distinguishing between player roles through 'tags, dresses, etc.' and pointed out that 'in case of games that are played out in the real and in the virtual, the challenge is to make the players visible *both* in the real and in the virtual space', while, finally, the expression 'player presence' was coined to support the 'identification and localisation of the player in the multilocation game space' (Benford and Capra 2005: 27, added emphasis). 'Required for personal presence', a 'precondition for social presence' and 'important for the game mechanics' in terms of environmental presence, 'player presence' was to be represented by the *role* and the *action potential* of a player because 'indicating player actions enhances the level of social presence and facilitates interaction' (Benford and Capra 2005: 28, added emphasis). Although later papers abandoned direct references to presence and focused instead on the aesthetics of the interface's design (Crabtree in Capra and Benford 2007) and the synchronization of temporal trajectories in the game (Giannachi and Benford 2008; Benford and Giannachi 2008), the role of 'player presence' and the identification of a 'mixed presence' are likely to play an important factor in the design of future narrative-driven interactive networked experiences.

Dispersing place, time and action: *Day of the Figurines* (2006)

Day of the Figurines was a massively multi-player board game for up to 1,000 participants which players could interact with remotely via SMS through their mobile phones from anywhere in the world. The world premiere took place in Berlin at Hebbel am Ufer, as part of Trampoline, from 28 September to 21 October 2006. On this occasion the game was run for twenty-four days for 141 players.

The game took place over a period of twenty-four days in a virtual setting based on an imaginary British town within which players could visit a number of destinations, be allocated missions and dilemmas, and interact in real time with other players. To participate, players

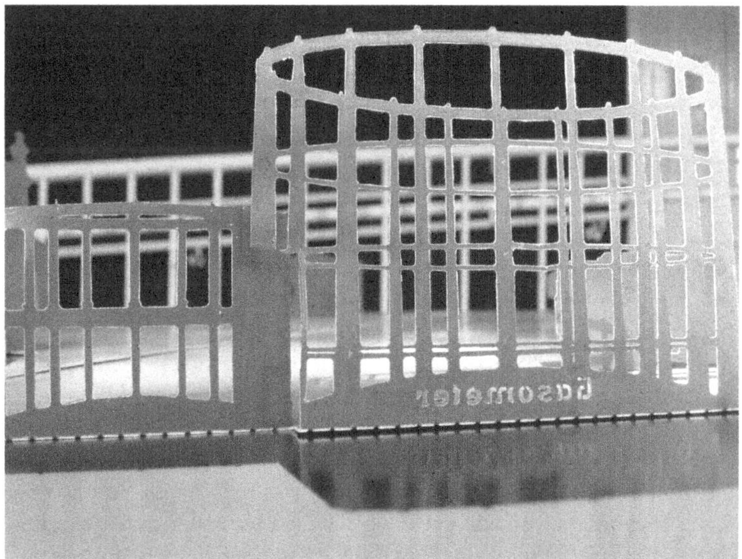

Figure 8.2 Blast Theory, *Day of the Figurines* (2006). The gasometer displayed at Hebbel am Ufer, Berlin

visited a physical space, which could be a museum, gallery or art centre. Here they found a large-scale white metal model of an imaginary town at table height. This acted as a tangible interface or 'framing device' which shaped the participants' experience (Crabtree in Capra and Benford 2007: 9, 17), established the board as the site of a spectacle, and positioned participants as spectators. On the board there were fifty cut-up destinations representing locations within an archetypical 'British' town, including a twenty-four-hour garage, a Big Chef, the Blue Cross, a boarded-up shop, a hospital, a nuclear bunker and the 'Rat Research Institute'. Each of these destinations was shown on the table in the form a white silhouette of bare metal, in a shape cut out from the surface of the table and bent up vertically, then lit to produce a corresponding shadow on the table itself. Beneath the table, two sets of video projections were also directed up through holes in its surface, to be reflected back on to the board by mirrors mounted horizontally above it, so enabling the table to be visibly augmented with projections of live information from the game. This augmentation system was turned off periodically (usually hourly) to allow the game operators to move each figurine as they updated the physical game board. In addition, and for each figurine in turn, the augmentation system projected a line from a 'player's' current position on the board to a new position produced as a result of recent activity.

To enter the game, participants took up an invitation to select a figurine from a separate neatly arranged display of 100 such pieces on a second, smaller square table. Assisted by an operator, they were invited to give their figurine a name and answer a few questions about their identity. Before leaving the space, they were given some basic instructions about the game, which explained how to move, speak, pick up and use objects, find other players, receive help, or even leave the game. From the moment of registration the game contacted the participant through SMS. Soon after registering, players received a first message in which the game asked for directions. If the participant answered the call and chose a destination, they found themselves repositioned as 'performer', and the figurine was moved toward the designated location. Once the new destination was reached, they could encounter other players with whom they could exchange, in real time, SMS. They might also encounter objects, ladders, cups of tea, saveloys, fleeces, among other things, and be presented with dilemmas and missions in the form of multiple-choice and open questions, some formulated in real time by the game operators. Each element, including objects, had a specific temporal constraint under which, in game time, it became available to participants. It might also have a timeout after which a default answer or action was assumed, to keep the narrative moving on.

GABRIELLA GIANNACHI How would you describe what happens around the board as both a real space and a trace in players' memories?

MATT ADAMS As with several previous Blast Theory projects (such as *Kidnap* and *Desert Rain*) our approach – somewhat ironically – is to create a high threshold to participation. Here, players must visit the board to join the game even though there is no practical need for them to do so. The induction of players into the game is a journey towards the board and the picking of a partner, namely their figurine, to accompany on the first part of their journey. The figurines are the size of a thumbprint, made of plastic and brightly coloured. The need to get close to them in order to see them properly (especially their facial characteristics) pulls potential players down to the table on which the figurines stand in serried ranks of a hundred waiting to be chosen. Visitors take great pleasure in choosing their figurine and regularly take portraits of themselves with their figurine once they have selected one. The figurine acts like a cartoon: it is crude and symbolic and thus permits a deeper level of identification than a more realistic portrayal. As an operator places your figurine on to the board, complete with handwritten name tag, these two elements, which are both verging on blankness and simultaneously aesthetically very rich, act in two ways. They provide a firm characterization of the town and of the player/figurine's place within it. And they provide enough scope for the player to interpret the town highly subjectively. Together these two experiences are designed to inform the rest of the game, even if the player never visits the board again. They establish the game in three spaces: on the board, in the player's head and on the phone. These three fields of play are in different physical locations, process time differently and construct experience differently. *Day of the Figurines* invites players to move between them.

[E-mail, 16 January 2007]

As time went by, with each day of real time corresponding to one hour of game time, the town underwent a series of subtle changes – 'pubs open, shops close, the car park gets deserted' – and the participants' health deteriorated – 'temples are grazed, ankles get twisted, armpits start to smell' (Adams 2005a) which gave the sense of the passing of time within an overarching narrative. Participants, who were refugees in an alienating town, learned that by eating and drinking certain foods, by advising others on how to do so, or by completing missions and answering dilemmas in the 'correct' way, their health could be restored and even improved. They also discovered that objects could have more than one function, and learned that, to survive, they must share objects and knowledge. Through this, participants learned that they were in a game with specific rules of play. Although Blast Theory published some basic instructions, which were available to players as cards and on the web, it was only by engaging with the game that players gained knowledge on how to survive. In fact, *Day of the Figurines* did not entail a conventional dramatic or game conflict, a 'contest of powers' (Salen and Zimmerman, 2004: 80), nor result in a clear quantifiable outcome – players did not clearly win or lose (unless they died, of course). Rather, the game's pace was more lifelike, and so uncertain. Despite the challenges of missions and dilemmas, the piece followed less formal play activities, which allowed a focus on 'social interaction and emergent behaviour' (Adams 2005b) that may have been influenced by players' everyday life circumstances.

Feedback from the initial test at the Laban Centre in London revealed and subsequent questionnaires and log analysis confirmed

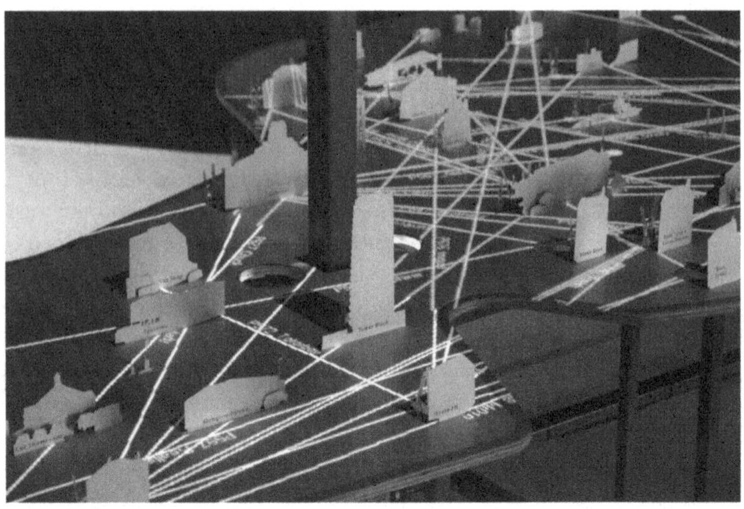

Figure 8.3 Blast Theory, *Day of the Figurines* (2006). Augmented board showing all recent figurine movements simultaneously. Sonar, Barcelona

(Benford and Capra 2005; Benford 2006) that the majority of players had adopted an episodic mode of play and dipped in and out of the game over the course of twenty-four days, sometimes not playing for several days before re-engaging again. In the initial version of the game, the board was divided into squares and players would travel from destination to destination one square at a time, a process that would frequently take hours or even days. The spatio-temporal structure of the game was subsequently revised through the introduction of a 'hub' model of movement. In this new model, on journeying from one destination to another, figurines stepped out into streets, which were represented by a central meeting point called the hub. Here, they were allocated a new interaction, either a pre-scripted game event message or a dilemma that required a multiple-choice response. Once this was completed, they moved on to their destination. Consequently, and in direct contrast to the impression given by the game board, all destinations in *Day of the Figurines* were equidistant. The physical board contained several hub regions on the city streets into which figurines were moved while they were in the central game hub. So there was a deliberate difference between the geography of the board and the actual spatio-temporal structure of the game which affected players' perception of their presence in the game (see also Benford and Giannachi 2011).

Player presence and the present moment

In elaborating the subjectivity of time the philosopher Paul Virilio notes that Ludwig Boltzmann 'identified *the present* with the presence of a *living* observer at a certain place and time', thus relating 'the apperception of passing time with metabolic aliveness' so that the 'aliveness of any animate organism (animal) is the alertness or vivacity, or in other words the schema of temporality of being, the *metabolic speed* with which the observer acquires information' (Virilio 2000: 51, original emphasis). The reading of presence as linked to the experience of the present moment, physiologically, or even metabolically speaking, may be seen as originating from Martin Heidegger's *Dasein*. This, Heidegger claims, is an 'entity in its Being which we know as human life' or, better, an entity 'in the *specificity* of its being' (Heidegger 1992: 6E, original emphasis) which predominantly takes place 'in speaking with one another in what one thus spreads around in speaking, there lies the specific self-interpretation of the present, which maintains itself in this dialogue' (Heidegger 1992: 8E). So, famously, '*Dasein* is that entity which is characterized as *being-in-the-world*', which means 'dealing with the world; tarrying alongside it in the manner of performing, effecting and completing, but also contemplating, interrogating, and determining by way of contemplation and comparison' (Heidegger 1992: 7E). For Heidegger, being-in-the-world is characterized as *concern* (*Besorgen*, 'provision') as well as '*being-with-one-another*, being with Others: having the same world there with Others, encountering one another, being with one another in the manner of *being-for-one-another*' (Heidegger 1992: 7E, original emphases). Indeed, it is this emphasis on process and '*being with one another*' that underlies aspects of Gary Hill's approach to presence as process, or that which *persists*, in the approach to and enfolding of 'otherness' or difference.

Analogously, *Day of the Figurines* interfered with players' *Dasein*, their experience of presentness in time, the subsequent location of their *besorgen* (providing) of objects, food, drink, help, but also information, knowledge, self-reflection. In doing so, the game affected participants' 'metabolic aliveness' by *augmenting* their ability to *act* in the moment and so offering them the possibility of cohabiting different worlds at the same time. This led to a degree of contamination between everyday life and the game. For example, feedback from the Singapore game revealed that players admitted to occasionally addressing messages from the game before answering those sent by friends because, in a player's own

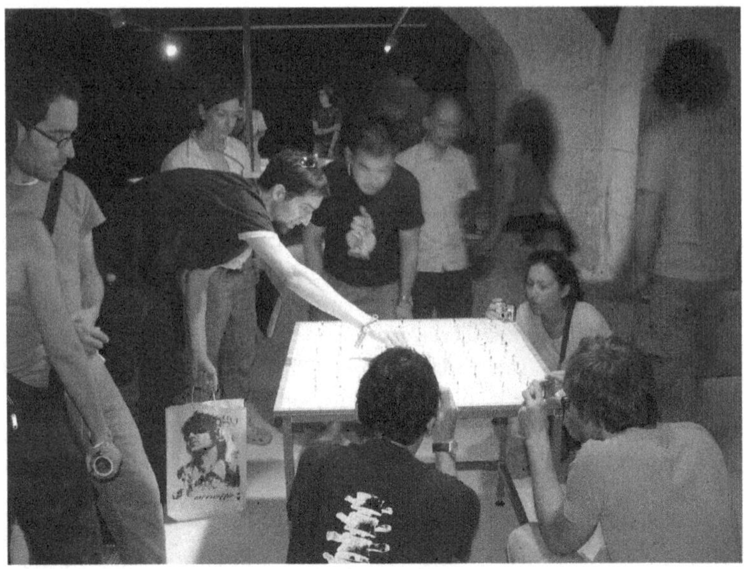

Figure 8.4 Blast Theory, *Day of the Figurines* (2006). A player chooses a
figurine at Sonar, Barcelona

words, '*Day of the Figurines* conversations were more interesting than
real ones.' This, according to a variety of players, depended on 'the information received', 'which is more urgent? The real friend or where I am
in the game?' 'the topic and the reason' (in Capra and Benford 2007: 40).
For some players, the team noted, 'their figurine's behaviour reflected
their own actions and mood in the real world' (Benford 2006: 40), so
much so that 'aspects of players' personalities, real-world activities and
situations' had the tendency of 'bleeding through' into the world of the
game (Benford 2006: 43). This 'bleeding through', producing a degree of
fluidity between the game and the everyday contexts of playing, between
art and technology, and between 'real' and represented, was a fundamental mechanism of the piece.

MATT ADAMS Does *Day of the Figurines* use both real and virtual
  space, in your opinion?
STEVE BENFORD At the heart of *Day of the Figurines* lies a virtual
  space, a fictional town that exists in the minds of the players, that
  is framed by the game board, and that is brought to life through
  the text messages that they exchange. In contrast to location-based
  pervasive games that are based on positioning technologies such as

GPS, *Day of the Figurines* does not attempt to establish any explicit mapping between this virtual space and the real spaces of its players. In particular, players are not required to move to particular locations in the real world in order to access locations in the virtual. However, this is not to say that *Day of the Figurines* does not make interesting use of physical space. The game board provides a powerful physical manifestation of the virtual city, showing the movements of the players through its various destinations. There is a sense in which *Day of the Figurines* inverts previous location-based games in that a physical space is constructed as a display, as an output device in human interaction terms rather than as an input. Beyond this, it is interesting to consider the potential impact of a player's physical location on their experience of the game and on their interactions with it. Players may receive messages from the game and frame their responses within different physical locations, which may influence their actions, in terms of their mood, connections they may make between their current physical and virtual space, not least the input of others who are present and who may share and comment on the messages.

[E-mail, 24 January 2007]

Theatrically, *Day of the Figurines* unfolded according to a pre-scripted narrative, which allowed participants the possibility of a passive, 'voyeuristic' mode. The relationship between action and stillness, the reciprocal progression and halting of the game were central to this dimension. In this regard, Manfred Pfister identifies a distinction between different notions of time in drama, which is crucial here. Pfister states that there are fundamentally two conceptions: in the first, 'chronological progression is concomitant with constant change and one in which time is seen simply as duration – that is, the chronological prolongation of a static condition' (Pfister 1991: 289). Pfister contrasts this with temporal structures in modern drama, particularly in works by Maurice Maeterlink, Samuel Beckett or Peter Handke, in which static conditions often prevail and, in Pfister's words, 'actions degenerate to no more than iterative activities designed to pass the time' (Pfister 1991: 290). While in French neoclassical tragedy the linear form prevails, in Shakespeare linear progression is often combined with cyclical rhythms (Pfister 1991: 290), a structure also operating in Beckett's *Waiting for Godot*. Interestingly, as Dougald McMillan and Martha Fehsenfeld record in their study *Beckett in the Theatre* (1988), when Beckett directed *Godot* he identified a number of small units, which he called 'W', for *Wartestellen* (waiting points) (Pfister 1991: 115–19), or, in his

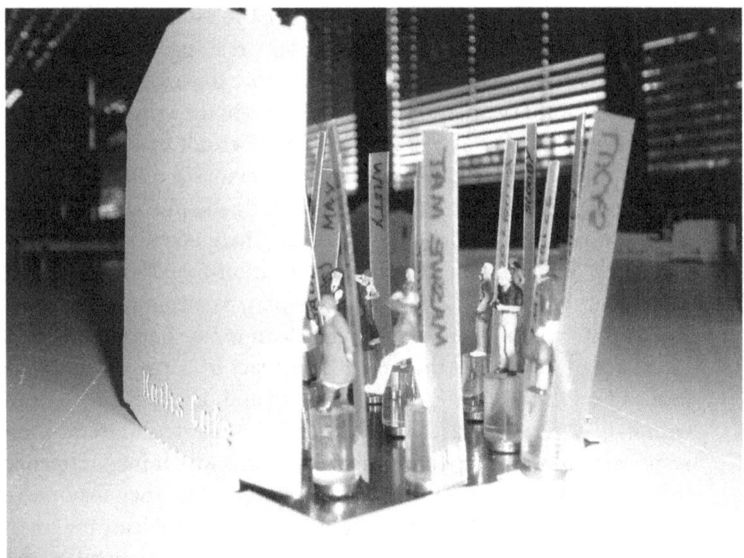

Figure 8.5 Blast Theory, *Day of the Figurines* (2006). Kath's Café displayed at
Hebbel am Ufer, Berlin

words to the director, Alan Schneider, 'moments of stillness' (Pfister
1991: 397–8). The relevance of these moments in the play is fundamental, in that the *Wartestellen* contribute to the creation of the sense of
circularity that characterizes the piece, and intensifies the sensation of
absence produced, among other elements, by what one is supposed to
be waiting for.

Day of the Figurines adopted conventions that at first seemingly
align with naturalist traditions. Thus, the chronological unfolding of the
story allowed for progressive development and change. However, in *Day
of the Figurines* performance time was a slowed-down version of the fictional time span, in the sense that the story's twenty-four hours occurred
over a period of twenty-four days, and so this progressive development
was continuously interrupted, if not disrupted, by the flow of everyday
life. Indeed, players were deliberately kept waiting to allow for this
fluidity between everyday times, events, contexts and the game to take
place. Adams notes: 'the choice of slowness in *Day of the Figurines* is so
accentuated that it violates almost all game design rules because it is cen-
tered on and causes complete disruption to play' (Adams in Adams *et al.*
2008). Here 'these gaps allow players to conduct their daily life or, more,
they force daily life to assert itself in the interstices between each game
event. At one level this constantly breaks game immersion but it also

intertwines the two states in an unusual way. Your experience of "now" is therefore always contingent and in some sense removed' (Adams in Adams *et al.* 2008).

GABRIELLA GIANNACHI How did using SMS affect the aesthetic of the piece?

MATT ADAMS *Day of the Figurines* is a tension between a lack of information and a surfeit of information. The core of the work is the sending and receiving of messages that cannot exceed 160 characters in length. Not only is each message very short but it is also relatively expensive. Every message must fully warrant the cost of its transmission. This formal constraint inhibits the richness of the game world in many respects: as designers we can include very little information about each individual player (typically less than twenty characters), about places that are visited and objects found. *Day of the Figurines* is a game about not knowing, about being in the dark. This then forms a thread throughout the narrative. Players are not told what the town is called or why they are there. The goal of the game is 'to help other players' but this is a moral direction rather than a concrete game goal. It is not clear how to help people nor is there a visible metric that measures players' progress within this framework. Even the geography of the town is slippery: Cartesian space has been replaced by a virtual topography in which every destination is equidistant from the others. Non-sequiturs and unconnected fragments predominate in the events that players experience. And the asynchronous, time-delayed nature of SMS means that by the time a player hears about anything it has happened several minutes previously. The work is the diametric opposition of the high-speed, adrenaline-fuelled world of 'twitch' console games in which time is measured in sixtieths of a second.

[E-mail, 16 January 2007]

Day of the Figurines also operated as a performance, and encouraged players to choose between what Peter Thomson, after Richard Schechner (1966), describes as 'result' and 'set' time (see also Benford and Giannachi 2008; Benford and Giannachi 2011). Thomson notes how games usually fall into one of two categories with respect to temporal organization: set time in which 'a time limit is pre-established, and the score of the completion of this *set time* is declared the result of the game' and result time, as in tennis, where 'the game continues according to its own internal logic until a result is reached, and the clock has no direct bearing on it' (Thomson 1970: 64–5, original emphasis). Thomson also shows that 'plays normally use *result time*, which is to say that it is the completion of the story rather than the running out of time that brings them to an end', but that some forms of entertainment adopt both models, so that in boxing, for example, the spectator 'is held in tension by the possible imposition of result time on set time' (Thomson 1970: 65). *Day of the Figurines* operated within a set time, in the sense that the game lasts ten hours a day, for twenty-four days, and players, via the allocation of missions and dilemmas, which have to be completed within a given time span, are able to control smaller units of set time within the overall time the game puts forward. Furthermore, there were 'timeouts' associated with missions and dilemmas, so they too involved an element of set time as well as result time. The game, however, also operated through result time in the sense that, if a player died, for example, the game stopped for them and if missions were completed before the set time the game moved on. This coexistence of set and result time played on players' anticipation and created a 'dramatic' tension that affected participant's sense of their own presence within the game.

STEVE BENFORD How important is it when individual players die and how should this be handled? Is it like death in a conventional computer game or does it have a different impact or significance in *Day of the Figurines*?

MATT ADAMS Even in this highly subjective and individualized form, death is a critical part of the work. That death is final in the game is unusual – most games permit players to be reborn, in some cases, within seconds – and some players are shocked by that finality. But, because the game plays with the boundary between the player and their fictional *alter ego* in a slippery manner, death can perhaps seem even more disruptive. From our observations of the games played so far, players shift between a fictionalized voice that is appropriate to their persona (an old lady, perhaps) and their own voice, between carefully structured messages and those closer to conventional SMS. Because the game is long and slow, because players drop in and out of the game at will, because game play is infrequent, this fluidity between self and actor is emphasized. This confusion between the self and other identities may happen unconsciously and be inadvertent or it may be deliberate but the paucity of information possible in an SMS allows it to happen very easily. These bifurcations happen repeatedly in electronic communication spaces (witness the variety of different user names that most regular net users have) and massively multi-player online games are just one of the most widespread cultural developments that derive their potency from the pleasures involved. But in those games the boundary between self and role-play is established through a range of steps or codes such as sitting at the PC, logging in to the game, an ever-present three-dimensional avatar and so on. In *Day of the Figurines* these steps are dramatically reduced and so the potential elision is that much greater. It is only when a player dies that this blurring is brought to an abrupt halt.

[E-mail, 16 January 2007]

Yet *Day of the Figurines* was also, and perhaps most important, a game. This further complicates the distinction between set time and result time. Noah Wardrip-Fruin and Pat Harrigan note that typically multi-player games engage viewers in a duality where they are both themselves and in role-play. This duality is reflected in the game's use of time which consists of play time, 'the time the player takes to play', and event time, 'the time taken in the game world', with action games tending to proceed in real time, and strategy and simulation games either speeding or slowing down the game (Wardrip-Fruin and Harrigan 2004: 131). However, there is a distinction, Wardrip-Fruin and Harrigan note, between 'the adventure game that creates coherent worlds that the player must explore in a coherent time and the action game that favours unexplained jumps in world and time by way of unconnected levels and rounds' (Wardrip-Fruin and Harrigan 2004: 132). Thus in *Sim City*, for instance, 'play time' is faster than 'event time' such that 'an event time of a year takes a few minutes of play time' (Wardrip-Fruin and Harrigan 2004: 134). In *Day of the Figurines*, however, play time was highly subjective, with players adopting their own episodic modes of play, often affected by events in their own life. Although play time may be interpreted as the time the game is accessible for play (usually from 12:00 a.m. to 10:00 p.m.), it is more accurate to describe it as the relationship between this time (which has a specific real-time duration) and the time the player is engaged with the game (which varies from day to day, and from player to player).

MATT ADAMS How does *Day of the Figurines* fit the debates within the practice of human–computer interaction [HCI]?

STEVE BENFORD Our studies of *Day of the Figurines* shed light on several contemporary issues in HCI. First, we are concerned with understanding how players interweave the experience of playing the game with patterns of their daily lives. It appears from their feedback, and also from an analysis of log files of messages sent to and from the game, that the majority of players exhibit an episodic style of play, sometimes playing intensively and sometimes not playing at all for several days before returning again. This raises new challenges for HCI. When and how should the game interrupt players? How can it avoid flooding players with too many messages, especially while they are disengaged? Such questions resonate with ongoing research into context-aware computing in which computer systems try to adapt to the situation of the user. *Day of the Figurines* deepened our understanding of context including when and where people prefer to engage with a mobile experience.

A second issue concerns the ways in which people interact with and through the medium of texting. Previous studies of text messaging in HCI have either focused on improving the efficiency of text input, comparing various text input techniques, or have explored the social use of text messaging, for example revealing how texting among teenagers involves elements of gift-giving behaviour. In contrast, *Day of the Figurines* provided us with the opportunity to explore how people experience and engage in a narrative that is delivered and constructed through text messaging. Here, for example, we explored new techniques for making maximum use of the limited bandwidth of each text message by aggregating information about several events into a single SMS.

A final issue concerns the role and design of the augmented game board in *Day of the Figurines*. As computers increasingly find their way into public settings such as museums, galleries, theatres and even the city streets, so interaction designers are becoming more aware of the need to design interaction for spectators as well as for the direct users of an interface. The augmented game board in *Day of the Figurines* has been explicitly designed to be a spectator interface, intended to attract new players, to reveal aspects of the game that would normally be hidden, and to frame the introduction to the game. Studying the design and actual experience of the game board should help in deepening our understanding of designing spectator interfaces.

[E-mail, 24 January 2007]

Theatrically, the game was experienced as duration, one in which the experience of the 'now', however, was continuously displaced. On the other hand, performatively, it was practised within seemingly independent temporal blocs that may either be 'set' or contingent on the result of a given task or mission. Once the tasks were completed, players may readopt a spectating mode. As a game, however, *Day of the Figurines* was engaged with episodically, with the players themselves deciding when and how long they wished to play for. At this level, the game interacted and even interfered with players' everyday lives. To understand the overall framework connecting these different temporal structures it is useful to consider the concept of temporal trajectories. Inspired by Edmund Husserl's analysis of the subjectivity of temporal perception and his vision of time as a flow of presence, rather than a succession of measurable successive 'now' points, Francisco Varela explains that time has a three-part structure constituted of 'now', 'retention' and 'protention'. Retention is described as belonging to the past even though it is happening now, whereas protention is 'the expectation or the construction of the future' (Varela 1999). This suggests that players continually negotiated their nowness or presentness within the artwork, whether theatrically, performatively or ludically, by choosing between, or being steered within, a number of possible temporal trajectories (Benford and Giannachi 2008; Giannachi and Benford 2008).

The roles of the game

The principal mechanism by which players were asked to interact with the game was role-play. *Day of the Figurines* at once drew inspiration and departed from the variety of types of role-play that form this genre. Role-playing games (RPGs) span from tabletop RPGs, which are usually played around a table (for example, *Dungeons and Dragons*) and in which players 'perform their characters in a more or less immersed manner'; live-action RPGs, 'where players dress up as their characters and act them out in surroundings simulating the game world'; online RPGs (for example, *Multi-user Dungeon*) which take place through the internet; and pervasive RPGs (Heliö in Montola and Stenros 2004: 66). Most RPGs thus lack the winning conditions and fixed rules that characterize other game worlds. Whereas most games function within the parameters of a 'magic circle' defining a 'special place in time and space created by the game' (Salen and Zimmerman 2004: 95), RPGs operate by deliberately blurring the boundaries of the magic circle (Montola 2005: 1) as defined by Johan Huizinga (1971). This distinctive feature is responsible for the contamination between the everyday and the game at the heart of *Day of the Figurines*, and informed the way presence operated fluidly between the world of the game and day-to-day events and circumstances.

Day of the Figurines was a pervasive form of RPG. However, because participants' first encounter with the game was through the board, and the fictional environment was experienced through SMS, the game also

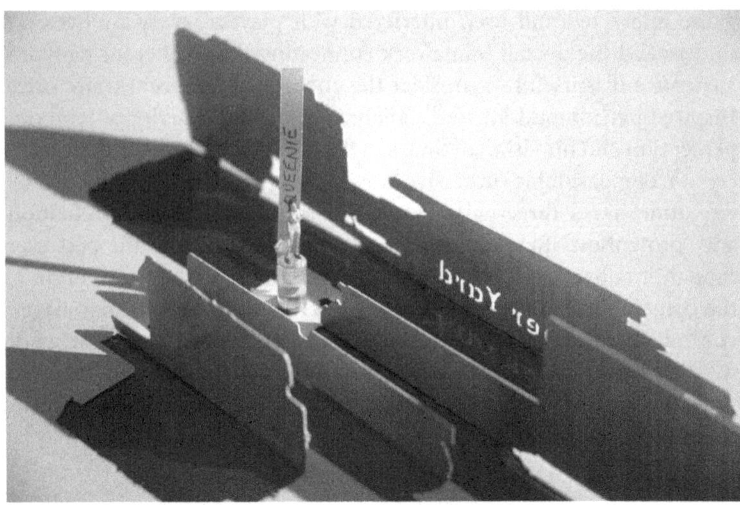

Figure 8.6 Blast Theory, *Day of the Figurines* (2006). A figurine displayed at
Sonar, Barcelona

included features of tabletop and online RPG. In 'conventional' RPGs,
participants assume the roles of characters, which then act within or
co-create the narrative in which they are implicated. Players determined
their own character's actions, and these actions succeed or fail according to the specific rules of the game. Within the context of these rules,
players may improvise more or less freely. In *Day of the Figurines*,
however, players often redefined their roles and the rules by which they
played, for example by adopting fake characters, as in the case of the
player Hassan in the Berlin game, who pretended to be a doctor and
started treating other players:

Say hello Paul. I'm a doctor. Now, what seems to be the trouble?
Sent 18:52 GMT, Tuesday 17 October
14:05 p.m., PAUL said: 'Hi I'm feeling bad. Can't figure why.'
Received 19:07 GMT, Tuesday 17 October
Say I see. Tell me, do you think you might have eaten something that has
disagreed with you recently?
Sent 19:12 GMT, Tuesday 17 October
14:06 p.m., PAUL said: 'Probably the opposite. Haven't found a decent place
to eat at since this morning.'
Received 19:23 GMT, Tuesday 17 October
Say, hmmm, that could be the problem. Still, it's best to be careful. Do you
mind if I examine you?
Sent 19:27 GMT, Tuesday 17 October

Players also ganged up against each other to 'enhance' what they perceived to be a slow game, to the extent, in the Singapore game, that other participants began to circulate warnings about a handful of dangerous players who behaved, literally, like killers on the loose. Floss here warned other players:

> 11:36 p.m., MIDNITE said: 'floss no din hear abt it. Who killed who?'
> *Received 08:43 GMT, Saturday 23 December*
> Say it was DJ Raj and Dr No. They killed five people at kaths cafe earlier today. They beat them to death with planks of wood. They're still on the loose!
> *Sent 09:00 GMT, Saturday 23 December*

Similarly, Bernard, also from the Singapore game, pointed out:

> say It's Dr No and DJ Ray. Already 5 were killed. Let's meet at 9:40 at the Allotments. SPREAD THE WORDS,
> *Sent 10:13 GMT, Wednesday 20 December*

continuing, shortly, with:

> say Hi tinman. I have been looking for you. Will you help me stopping the killings?
> *Sent 09:17 GMT, Thursday 21 December*
> 09:40 p.m., TIN MAN said: 'sure! Wat to you have in mind'
> *Received 09:20 GMT, Thursday 21 December*
> say I dont know. DJ Ray is dangerous. I saw him killing Ms Bisquit.
> *Sent 09:26 GMT, Thursday 21 December*
> say we have to find more people supporting us and then attacking him all together ... ?
> *Sent 09:27 GMT, Thursday 21 December*

Live action role-playing games (LARP) are quite improvisational. Players do not simply describe their characters' actions but act them out. As indicated by Montola, 'LARP is role-playing, where physical reality is used to construct diegeses, in addition to communication, both directly and arbitrarily' (Montola 2003). Whereas 'in LARP the game is superimposed on a physical world', which is used as a foundation in defining the game world, 'in tabletop role-playing the game world is defined predominantly in verbal communication' (Montola in Donnis *et al.* 2007: 94). *Day of the Figurines* 'took place' within a 'virtual' game world that continuously superimposed itself on players' everyday lives. This game world, however, manifested itself as a tension between the memory of the board, a site experienced in the past, and players' own

exchanges of communication and actions, which, because of the artificial delay imposed by the game between sending an action command
and receiving the notification that the action has taken effect, would
become manifest only in the future.

GABRIELLA GIANNACHI What do you think is the function of role-
play within this piece with particular reference to SMS?

STEVE BENFORD *Day of the Figurines* is a role-playing game and
its players are invited to create and maintain a character within
a fictional world. However, there are some interesting ways in
which role-play in *Day of the Figurines* may differ from role-play
in more conventional online environments. The game will often
interrupt players, potentially taking them unaware and arguably
giving them less time to step into their characters than they would
get with more traditional role-playing experiences where they can
actively choose and prepare for the moment they assume their role.
Furthermore, rather than sitting down at their PC and console
in the familiar environment of their home, players may play the
game in a wide variety of locations. Some players have reported
that aspects of their current context, ranging from details of their
current location in the real world to their current mood affect
their figurine's actions. Perhaps the most extreme example of this
involves showing messages to other people in their current location and involving them in framing responses to the game. As a
consequence of these various factors, there may well be a greater
blurring between the players' real selves and their fictional roles in
Day of the Figurines.

[E-mail, 24 January 2007]

In RPGs players identify with their own characters emotionally and
tend to see themselves as the sole protagonists of the work. John Kim
notes that 'the actions of the other characters may be interesting and
relevant, but they are not where the power of the story lies', so much so
that RPG players do 'not derive emotional impact primarily from the
performances of others, but rather from her own performance' (Kim in
Montola and Stenros 2004: 36). Characters are often put together loosely
and players are known to modify their characters during the game by
'more or less consciously' filling in the blanks or improvising (Hardy in
Donnis *et al.* 2007: 27). Montola noted that *Epidemic Menace* (2006), a
prototype game built to experiment with mixed-reality gaming within
the IPerG context, in which participants fought a virus spreading across
a campus, lacked characters but had 'functional roles emerging from the

interaction with various gaming devices', resulting in players adopting 'minimalist role-play' (Montola and Stenros 2004: 98). In *Day of the Figurines* players similarly started their role-play by choosing a figurine and giving it one or more cartoon-like features. These were highly subjective, often 'minimal' descriptions, such as 'with a face like a slapped ass', 'with six fingers on his hand', 'looking for something' in the Berlin version of the game, or with a 'fat belly', 'carrying a brown suitcase', with 'extreme mood swings' in the Singapore version. These distinct features attributed by players did not necessarily bear any relation to the appearance of their actual figurine or actions during the game. As indicated in an early report on the game, although players often played a role which 'may have been an exploration of an aspect of themselves' or 'a particular character that they could use as a sort of template for how to behave that might be different from the way they normally behaved' (Tallyn in Benford 2006: 116–17), their actual use of their own roles, during the twenty-four days of the game, was often episodic and occasionally inconsistent. Throughout the game, players frequently abandoned their chosen role-play, usually to identify themselves to other players, to create a more interesting or topical role or, in the case of the player Hassan discussed above, to discuss events taking place outside of the game world, an impulse evident also in Constance's sudden query in German 'Rich, bist du's?' (Rich, is it you?) in the Berlin game. In an analogous exchange, Tin Man attempted to catch Miss Biscuit out in the Singapore game:

> Say Miss Biscuit hello. Are you a volunteer at the museum?
> *Sent 04:38 GMT, Sunday 10 December*

Then, two days later, Tin Man entered into a similar conversation with another player:

> Say gel i say you today at the museum.
> *Sent 08:03 GMT, Tuesday 12 December*
> 12:30 p.m., through pursed teeth, you force the chemically enhanced brew towards your stomach. You feel a little more warmed and alert.
> *Received 08:07 GMT, Tuesday 12 December*
> 12:30 p.m., Gel said: 'tinman u saw me at d museum?' You are feeling extremely well.
> *Received 08:07 GMT, Tuesday 12 December*
> Use coffee
> *Sent 08:08 GMT, Tuesday 12 December*
> Say gel yah, You were with amaranta at the rotunda
> *Sent 08:09 GMT, Tuesday 12 December*

12:30 p.m., through pursed teeth, you force the chemically enhanced brew
towards your stomach. You feel a little more warmed and alert.

Received 08:12 GMT, Tuesday 12 December

12:31 p.m., You are feeling hot to trot.

Received 08:13 GMT, Tuesday 12 December

12:31 p.m., GEL said: 'tinman yeah but no idea who r u:p'

Received 08:14 GMT, Tuesday 12 December

Say gel i am the guy in black polo t. Dont know if you rem

Sent 08:16 GMT, Tuesday 12 December

As can be seen from the examples above, in *Day of the Figurines*
players' role-play was the result of a complex interweaving of embedded
and emergent game features. The frame of the game, or 'magic circle',
was blurred and the game often caught participants unprepared, such
that they responded out of character, as themselves, or blurred game
and life contexts by more or less deliberately using one to affect the
other (Tallyn in Benford 2006: 117). It was precisely by adjusting role-
play according to circumstance, by moving between different modes of
participation, spectatorship and performance that players were thus able
to negotiate their presence within the game.

Pervasive presence

Spatially, *Day of the Figurines* functioned by relocating participants
within a pervasive form of board game/RPG that was at once a physical
entity *and* a virtual environment. Although the board seemed to have a
certain geographical configuration, all destinations were in fact equidistant and could be reached within the same amount of time. Temporally,
the game functioned by mapping twenty-four hours, the 'day of the
figurines', over twenty-four days. Participants were required to negotiate clock time with event and game time, and within that to play both by
'result' and by 'set' time. Although participants were given the impression that they were in distinct temporal hubs, they were in fact caught
in a number of temporal trajectories (Giannachi and Benford 2008). The
experience of the present moment, Heidegger's *Dasein*, was stretched
across these trajectories so that player presence, that is, their role and
action potential, was always simultaneously referring back to the past
(the role they created for the world of the board game) and pointing to
the future (the delayed point in time at which their action would affect
the game). Significantly, it was precisely at the level of this interruption,

or 'suspended' protention, that this game's use of player presence operated.

GABRIELLA GIANNACHI How would you describe the differences between your own experience of engagement, immersion and presence within *Day of the Figurines*?

STEVE BENFORD For me, like some other researchers in virtual reality, immersion is a technical term that refers to the extent to which an interface technology blots out sensory input from the real world to replace it with input from a virtual world. Thus virtual-reality head-mounted displays tend to be immersive, whereas the mobile phone interfaces used in *Day of the Figurines* are not. Presence on the other hand can generally be thought of as the feeling of being there that is actually experienced by a participant. Immersion may contribute to presence, but so may many other factors, including the ease with which participants are able to imagine or project themselves into a virtual world. There were moments when I did feel highly present in the world of the *Day of the Figurines* even though I was only experiencing the world through short text descriptions. I think that this was to due to the way in which the framing of the experience and the nature of the messages provided space for my imagination to fill in the details. Engagement, on the other hand, I see as being something different again. For me this is about sustained participation in an experience, and, in the case of *Day of the Figurines*, is about the way in which I repeatedly returned to the experience over an extended period of time. So I felt an ongoing engagement with the experience and occasional moments of presence but without being immersed by the technology.

[E-mail, 24 January 2007]

IPerG researchers claim that 'player presence', meaning the 'identification' and 'localization' of a player in a 'multi-location space', their 'role' and 'action potential' (Benford and Capra 2005: 28), might enhance the level of social presence and facilitate interaction. In *Day of the Figurines* players are asked to create a role and identify a figurine. Interestingly, the two may not coincide. While the figurines operated at the level of the board, visualizing a player's presence within it, their roles were the main tool by which players interacted with the game. Players may have thought of themselves visually as their figurine, but were seen within the game world as the salient features of their role(s), that is, their 'character'. Just as the board operated as a catalyst, attracting visitors to the game by literally pulling them down towards it, SMS forced viewers

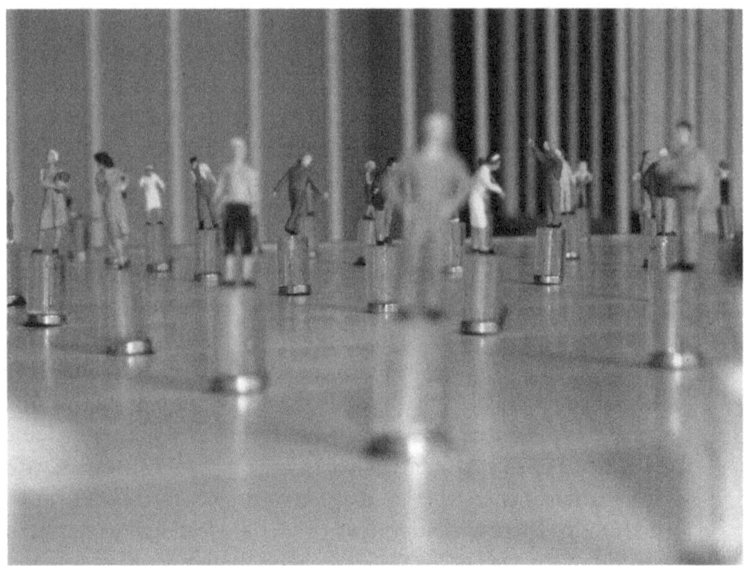

Figure 8.7 Blast Theory, *Day of the Figurines* (2006). Figurines displayed at
Hebbel am Ufer, Berlin

to refocus on their mobile's interface to the (if only temporary) exclusion of the world around them. It is this physical movement between
everyday life and the game, this act of refocusing, repositioning oneself
in space but also in time – between the memory of the board and the
virtual game world – and the subsequent anticipation of the effect of
one's actions, that informed the way the participants' presence was acted
out within the game.

In *Day of the Figurines* this act of refocusing was induced nar-
ratively. Participants wrote first-person messages, such as 'Go Kath's',
and received second and third-person messages such as 'you've arrived
at the Bins, fag butts between upturned crates' or 'SENGA said: "DAVE
you\'re looking good today. KATHS CAFE does good tea."' Whereas first-
person messages gave players the impression that they could effect an
action, or, in the case of example cited above, initiate a journey, second
and third-person messages respectively let participants know about
their status in the game or informed them of what they themselves or
others were saying or doing. Through the use of first, second and third-
person messages *Day of the Figurines* steered participants in and out of
the game world, and, within that, it relocated them between the more
or less active roles of spectating, acting and playing. Throughout this
process, participants were continuously presented with another world,

that of the game, within which they were also present. Adopting IPerG researchers' terminology, player presence, as expressed through participants' role and action potential, occurred at the moment during which players were asked to face themselves as an other and took place as the process of addressing that request during which they became that other only to then return to themselves and, in an act of suspended protention, wait for the effect of their presence to become manifest. What was here in front of or before the 'self', that is, *prae-sens*, was both the role, including its action potential, and the trace of the figurine the player was about to adopt, however loosely, to act inside the game world. The participants' role and their figurine thus acted respectively as a medium and an icon facilitating the delivery of the game's subjects back to themselves as objects and, vice versa, by moving between first, second and third-person messages, reminding them that those objects *were* them. Pervasive presence, in this context, is not only the player's own capacity to become present, through their manipulation of role and action potential, but also their ability to do so in time. It is the *prae* of *prae-sens* itself that was multiplied here such that the processes that defined the movement between the self's perception of itself as subject and object occurred pervasively in both time and space.

9

conclusion Presence and recovery

The artwork, performances, applications of technologies and experimental practices explored and analysed in this volume position the viewer, participant or performer *in action* as the locus and agent of presence. In doing so, these works and processes engage with the enactment and emergence of phenomena of presence in processual and mobile exchanges, in acts *towards* the other and *towards* the elements of 'a work' formed in time. In turn, rather seek to unify 'a work' within the 'present tense' and so advance its claim to fixed place, presence or authority – and so a unique *difference* – these artists and technologies *implicate* the viewer, participant or performer in relational *acts* of presence and an emergent process. Here, too, 'presence' arises in processes of doubling and in the intrusion and overlapping of one place, position and realm on another: in imbrications between 'self' and 'other'; in uncanny separations of and returns to a sense of where 'I am'; and in the implication and discovery of the 'real' in the virtual. 'Presence', here, *is* both the phenomenon and 'medium' 'of' 'the work' – and so the means by which these various installations, performances and technologies realize and interrogate the action, position and formation of 'their' viewers, participants and performers. Furthermore, these works and processes exemplify and advance an interrogation of presence precisely in their effect and form as temporary ecologies; in *acts of presence* in which the viewer or participant is implicated and in traversals rather than entrenchments of positions and places. It is here, too, that these strategies present most directly a performativity of 'presence'. Approached as an *act*, 'presence' is shown in each of these works and applications to operate in its own recovery: in *performative* realizations and evocations of authority, identity, place, and location; in a *being there* that has no final foundation or stability but is nevertheless affective. Here, too, both as a phenomenon and in its representation, presence remains always *in advance* or *before* itself: always in emergence.

It is in these contexts that the artworks, technologies and experimental practices considered in this book emphasize, first, the performative and processual character of 'presence', rather than identifying these phenomena with a closed or given forms, or with any fixed or given position. Here, too, these works converge around this articulation of phenomena of presence while radically diverging in means, forms, technology and media. Thus, Lynn Hershman Leeson's work positions the visitor as agent and catalyst within a field of interrelated signs and remains that are spatially and temporally dispersed, yet in whose 're-enactment' – or re-reading – the 'presence' of event, site and identity persist. Indeed, in response to Hershman Leeson's development of *Roberta Breitmore* and her replaying of *The Hotel Dante* in Second Life and Mixed Reality installations, it is explicitly in the viewer and participant's positioning between 'real' and 'virtual' spaces and past, present and future acts that the work and the sense of 'presence' it provokes are effected. In relation to this emphasis, Gary Hill's video and video installations emphasize an unfolding and modulation of the experience of an image in time, which, *over time*, displaces the visual towards a sense of 'visceral physicality' realized in the perception of the body in multiple tenses and through a veiling or overlaying of spaces. In breaking down the 'present tense' of experience to produce a sense of a layering of spaces and 'real', replayed and recorded times, Hill's work provokes experiences of implication and agency that are integral to the viewer's paradoxical sense of the unfolding of the 'physical' presence in their encounter with virtual and mediated bodies.

In Paul Sermon's telepresence works, this multiplication of sites and spaces is given a further physical form and a direct technological expression. Thus Sermon deploys telepresence systems to amplify the spatial differences in which a participant's actions take place, so confronting each 'viewer' with their 'own' presence at a distance to be experienced in uncanny returns. By these means, Sermon's work multiplies the spaces in which participants act precisely in order to heighten their sense of 'being there' *before* themselves. Analogously, in CAVE, a participant's experience of 'presence' within a virtual, projective environment may be seen as a function of their mediations *in action* between 'real' and 'virtual' worlds. In this context, participants' experiences of presence are affected and modulated by the framing and layering of behaviours between virtual agents (or avatars) and between virtual agents and human performers, and so in collocations of 'real' and 'virtual' behaviours and spaces. For Tony Oursler, an implicitly related emphasis on the disembodied image's occupation of the material site and 'real' space of the viewer produces encounters with 'media entities' that amplify and test their auditor's investment in and identification with experiences of presence in relation to media forms. Here, it is the viewer's implicit identification with media forms and processes – and so their own 'mirroring' or 'doubling' of these systems – that amplify these 'entities'' 'presence' in and before the works' real and virtual spaces.

Finally, in The Builders Association's large-scale multimedia productions it is in movements between 'real' and 'virtual' spaces and architectures for performance that 'performer presence' and 'liveness' are advanced, modulated and explored. Far from articulating such spaces as in opposition or in different relationships with regard to 'presence', The Builders Association locate the slip, disjunction and exchange between these orders of space *in their performance*, as the locus of the effects, practices and implications of presence: of a 'being there' defined and shaped by contemporary technologies. In turn, it is in the simultaneous 'occupation' of multiple spaces and times that, in *Day of the Figurines*, Blast Theory and the Mixed Reality Laboratory implicitly locate the performance and experience of a 'pervasive' presence. In this work, the participant's presence is augmented in their capacity to act in different spaces, locations and tenses in both real and virtual environments – an experience of 'presence' amplified in the effects of simultaneities of electronic networks and communications systems.

It is this unifying emphasis on the enactment of presence, too, and the role of the 'participant' in realizing the work, that foregrounds processes of making, realization and performance as a mode and analytical framework across the range of forms considered here. Indeed, in this context, the commentary and detailed exposition of process by the artists interleaved into the analysis this volume presents, gains a further significance. Approaching presence as phenomena that are always already in emergence and in process, it is precisely the emphasis upon acts of unfolding, of revealing, and of changes and accumulations over time, which provide further connections between these works and processes in their address to the performance of presence. Stressing phenomena over object, time and change over fixed form, and enactment and 'making' over resolution, it is also in these approaches towards an unfolding of 'presence' that these artists' works obtain their formal eclecticism and interconnection.

Here, too, and within the recent history of art and performance, another recovery and qualification might also take place, in so far as the bodies of work detailed here are resonant of the broader development of practices across theatre, visual art, media and new media. As these various cross-media engagements with the performance of presence suggest, the expression of performance – and 'presence' – by technical means in performance, media and new media practices has invariably operated in an articulation of the unfolding of 'presence' rather than, in a narrow sense, an implicit opposition between the 'absences' of 'mediation' and representation and an otherwise 'radical', 'anti-theatrical' or 'real' presence that stands outside these relations. Indeed, in returning, in the context of these practices, to other influential practitioners in theatre, art and performance whose work has engaged with the overt technological mediation of theatrical or performative acts, events and encounters, integrations with media have invariably been deployed towards the capturing, shaping and articulation of acts and experiences of presence. Thus, in reflecting on the Wooster Group's multimedia performances, which critical discourse in performance studies has frequently positioned as exemplifying the deconstruction and interruption of the authority of presence in performance, the company's artistic director Elizabeth LeCompte's own remarks have also implied a continuity with earlier theatrical foci on the amplification and experience of 'performer presence'. Here, too, LeCompte's remarks suggest that, with regard to her own work, 'presence' may be enacted in the very multiplication of the company's means of address rather than in the 'security' of the performer's 'place'. LeCompte has noted that:

> presence is something that I think is . . . always in conversation with the formal pattern. The formal pattern will tend to allow the performer to get lulled into feeling safe . . . the constant battle for me as a director is to find ways that an actor can be always present, always alive, always thinking this is the first and last moment that she's there – doing this thing
> –   [LeCompte in Kaye 1996: 257–8]

Consistently with this, associations of technology with experiences of 'presence' in art and performance form an important part of the history and lineage of avant-garde and 'postmodern' performative practices. Indeed, the convergence of media, technology, performance and performances of presence are reflected in the sources of contemporary visual art and performance work; in the values of experimental music, for example, which provide one of the influences shaping Gary Hill's engagement with video installation. It is a convergence of performance, technology and presence explicitly reflected, in this context, in John Cage's seemingly paradoxical claim that in the performance of his early electronic musical works 'live sounds really have a different quality . . . They have a presence, and this presence is intact' (Cage and Charles 1981: 137).

Evidently, too, a wide range of 'experimental' forms of art and performance with various relationships to media practices have deployed tactics towards the unfolding or irruption of experiences of presence within performance in ways analogous to the work foregrounded in this volume. In the UK, Forced Entertainment's theatre performances exemplify an engagement with performed presence through work that explicitly plays with the 'doubt' over the place and position of 'character' and 'performer', as well as liveness and mediation. In Italy, Societas Raffaello Sanzio overtly disrupt the representational frames of theatrical performance through the integration of animals, untrained performers and children into their work, to produce 'excessive' moments of performance that amplify and challenge the viewer's reading and experience of presence 'on stage'. In the United States, Robert Wilson and Richard Foreman's early work and, more recently, John Jesurun's multimedia theatre, at once multiply schemes for performance and amplify and modulate readings and experiences of performer presence. In this, and a wide range of other work, it is in the unfolding of phenomena of presence – of 'presence' as a 'medium' of the work in its emergence, modulation and variation – that the performance of presence is elaborated, interrogated and seen.

As the artwork and processes set at the core of this book suggests, the performative configuration, framing and enactment of technology and media has frequently been positioned as a root and means of the performance of presence: a mechanism in which the experiences and implications of presence may be felt, enacted and articulated. In turn, the deployment of these technologies with regard to presence, is not in any way in fundamental opposition or difference to 'liveness', to performance that eschews or evades electronic 'media'. Indeed, where presence is always already performed, so it cannot be resolved into the qualities or properties of any particular object or medium, but arises in temporary and relational acts, in time, as phenomena which, in being emergent, are also contingent and unstable. It is to the deeper connections between such histories of practice engaging with presence that the work examined here also implicitly directs attention. Indeed, it is in these developments of performative practices, and in connections and conflations between practices and discourses in new media, visual art, theatre and aspects of enquiry in computer science and virtual reality, that the most productive contemporary dialogues over phenomena of presence, and their implications for the contemporary performance of self and other, may be found. Seen in the broader contexts of performance practice and its histories, then, the interrogation and realization of the performance of presence through media and technology provide not so much a departure from 'live' performance and its 'presence' as a deeper elaboration of its mechanisms and meanings.

Finally, then, and linked to this history and broader connection of work, it is in the very movements across divisions, differences and multiplications of media, form, and position, too, that the production and reception of phenomena of presence may be most clearly seen to be realized and effected in performative acts. Indeed, such a performativity is implicit in the etymology of presence. As *prae-sens*, 'presence' precedes itself; it is that which is 'before' 'I am', occurring in a movement or in an act of unfolding across division or difference. It is also this movement, or performance of presence, that admits temporal and spatial complexities into the effects and acts of presence and in relation to which mechanisms of the sign and representation can be understood as motors for experiences of presence. It is in the performativity of presence, too, that the inter-subjective and social implications of 'being present' to and before the other are foregrounded and in which presence is revealed as a culturally contested site and experience, even as this phenomenon unfolds and gains ground. Such performative engagements with presence also contest simple oppositions between 'absence' and 'presence': between a property or quality of 'a' presence 'belonging' or manifest *in* the body, as a 'real' act, or as an immanent property of an object or thing, and the 'illusion' of presence effected in a staging of forms and modes of representation. By contrast, these works and investigations unfold through heterogeneous dynamics and processes, whereby the production and reception of 'presence' are performed and interrogated over time, in operations between unobtainable moments of 'absence' and 'presence', between the 'live' and the 'simulated', and so *in* the implication of the one in the other. Indeed, it is in these dynamics and interrogations that the work and processes considered in this volume gain their wider resonance, as they explore the constitution of *being before*, of identity, encounter, and the definition of self and other as *acts* of presence.

REFERENCES

Acconci, V. (2001 [1984]) 'Television, furniture and sculpture: the room with the American view' in G. Moure (ed.) *Vito Acconci: Writings, Works, Projects*, Barcelona: Polígrafa, 371–7.
Acconci, V. (2005) *Vito Hannibal Acconci Studio*, Barcelona: Museu d'art contemporani Barcelona.
Adams, M. (2005a) unpublished interview with Gabriella Giannachi, London, 11 April.
Adams, M. (2005b) 'Highlight: *Day of the Figurines*', IPerG *Newsletter*, August. Available online: www.pervasive-gaming.org/index_swf.html. Accessed 15 June 2006.
Adams, M., Benford, S. and Giannachi, G. (2008) 'Pervasive presence: Blast Theory's *Day of the Figurines*', *Contemporary Theatre Review*, 18:2, 218–33.
Albright, T. (n.d.) 'A Ghostly Hotel Room Tableau', Lynn Hershman papers, M452, BOX 18. Department of Special Collections, Stanford University Libraries, Stanford CA.
Ansty, J. and Pape, D. (1998) 'The growing thing: interactive story telling' in G. Stocker and C. Schöpf (eds) *InfoWar: Ars Electronica 1998*, Vienna and New York: Springer, 226–32.
Ardenne, P. (2005) 'Incommunicating bodies' in C.V. Assche (ed.) *Tony Oursler*, Helsinki: Salamancar, 41–5.
Ascott, R. (1990) 'Is there love in the telematic embrace?' *Art Journal*, 49:3, 241–7.
Auslander, P. (1992) *Presence and Resistance: Postmodernism and Cultural Politics in Contemporary American Performance*, Ann Arbor MI: University of Michigan Press.
Auslander, P. (1999) *Liveness*, London: Routledge.
Barfield, W. and Hendrix, C. (1995) 'The effect of update rate on the sense of presence in virtual environments', *Virtual Reality: Research, Development, Applications*, 1:1, 3–15.
Barfield, W. and Weghorst, S. (1993) 'The sense of presence within virtual environments: a conceptual framework' in G. Salvendy and M. Smith (eds) *Human Computer Interaction: Software and Hardware Interfaces*, Atlanta GA: Elsevier, 699–704.
Barfield, W., Hendrix, C. and Bystrom, K. (1997) 'Visualizing the structure of virtual objects using desktop virtual reality displays', *Proceedings of the IEEE Annual International Symposium on Virtual Reality '97*, Albuquerque NM, Piscataway

NJ: IEEE, 114–19. Available online: http://ieeexplore.ieee.org/xpl/tocresult. jsp?isnumber=12656&isYear=1997. Accessed 6 January 2010.

Barfield, W., Sheridan, T., Zeltzer, D. and Slater, M. (1995) 'Presence and performance within virtual environments', in W. Barfield and T. Furness III (eds) *Virtual Environments and Advanced Interface Design*, Oxford: Oxford University Press, 473–513.

Baudrillard, J. (1983) *Simulations*, translated by P. Foss, P. Patton and P. Beitchman, New York: Semiotext(e).

Baudrillard, J. (1993) *Symbolic Exchange and Death*, translated by I. H. Grant, London: Sage.

Baudrillard, J. (1995; [1991]) *The Gulf War Did Not Take Place*, translated by Power Institute and P. Patton, Sidney: Power Publications.

Baumgärtel, T. (2001a) [net.art 2.0] *Neue Materiale zur Netzkunst/New Materials towards Net Art*, Nuremberg: Verlag für moderne Kunst.

Baumgärtel, T. (2001b) 'On the history of artistic work with telecommunications media' in P. Weibel and T. Druckrey, (eds) *net_condition: art and global media*, Cambridge MA: MIT Press, 152–61.

Béar, L. (1974) 'Gordon Matta-Clark: splitting interview', *Avalanche*, December, 34–7.

Béar, L. and Sharp, W. (1996 [1970]) 'Discussions with Heizer, Oppenheim, Smithson' in J. Flam (ed.) *Robert Smithson: The Collected Writings*, California: University of California Press, 242–52.

Belting, H. (1995) 'Gary Hill and the alphabet of images' in T. Vischer (ed.) *Gary Hill: Imagining the Brain closer than the Eyes*, Basel: Museum fur Gegenwartskunst Basel, Cantz Verlag, 41–65.

Benford, S. (2006) 'WP12: City as Theatre Deliverable D12.4 Evaluation of the first City as Theatre Public Performance'. Version 2. Release date: 10 February. Available online: www.pervasive-gaming.org/downloadsub1.html. Accessed 27 December 2007.

Benford, S. and Capra, M. (2005) 'Deliverable D5: Design and Evaluation Literature Review'. Available online: http://iperg.sics.se/downloadsub2.html. Accessed 25 June 2007.

Benford, S. and Giannachi, G. (2008) 'Temporal trajectories in shared interactive narratives', *Proceedings ACM SIGCHI Conference on Human Factors in Computing Systems (CHI 2008)*, New York: ACM, 73–82.

Benford, S. and Giannachi, G. (2011) *Performing Mixed Reality*, Cambridge MA: MIT Press.

Benford, S., Greenhalgh, C., Reynard, G., Brown, C., and Koleva, B. (1998) 'Understanding and constructing shared spaces with mixed-reality boundaries', *ACM Transactions on Computer–Human Interaction*, 5:3, 185–223.

Biocca, F. (1997) 'The cyborg's dilemma: progressive embodiment in virtual environments', *Journal of Computer Mediated Communication*, 3:2. Available online: http://jcmc.indiana.edu/vol3/issue2/biocca2.html. Accessed 11 December 2009.

Biocca, F. (2001) 'Inserting the presence of mind into a philosophy of presence: a response to Sheridan and Mantovani and Riva', *Presence: Teleoperators and Virtual Environments*, 10:5, 546–56.

Birnbaum, D. (2008) *The Hospitality of Presence: Problems of Otherness in Husserl's Phenomenology*, Berlin: Sternberg Press.

Blanchot, M. (1999a) 'Literature and the right to death' in G. Quasha (ed.) *The Station Hill Blanchot Reader*, translated by L. Davis, P. Auster and R. Lamberton, Barrytown NY: Station Hill Press, 359–400.

Blanchot, M. (1999b) 'The absence of the book' in G. Quasha (ed.) *The Station Hill Blanchot Reader*, translated by L. Davis, P. Auster and R. Lamberton, Barrytown NY: Station Hill Press, 471–86.

Blanchot, M. (1999c) 'Two versions of the imaginary' in G. Quasha (ed.) *The Station Hill Blanchot Reader*, translated by L. Davis, P. Auster and R. Lamberton, Barrytown NY: Station Hill Press, 417–28.

Blast Theory (2002) *Desert Rain*, catalogue, company archive.

Blast Theory (2005) *Blast Theory*. Available online: www.blasttheory. Accessed 1 March 2005.

Blunk, A. (1998) 'Presence and representation in interactive works' in M. Buscher, J. Hughes, J. O'Brien, T. Rodden (eds) *Presence and Representation in Multimedia Art and Electronic Landscapes'*, *Escape*, 26–67. Available online: www.comp.lancs.ac.uk/computing/research/cseg/DIGITAL-LIBRARY/Escape/ Escape-D1.1.pdf. Accessed 17 September 2009.

Boehm, G. (1995) 'Time present: a perpetual coming to fruition' in T. Vischer (ed.) *Gary Hill: Imagining the Brain Closer than the Eyes*, Basel: Museum fur Gegenwartskunst Basel, Cantz Verlag, 25–40.

Brenton, H., Gillies, M., Ballin, D., and Chatting, D. (2005) 'The uncanny valley: does it exist?' Human animated characters interaction workshop, British HCI 2005, Edinburgh, 2005.

Broekmann, A. (2000) *Machine Times*, Rotterdam: V2 Publishing.

Bureaud, A. (2000) 'Eduardo Kac, pioneer and visionary' in A. Kostic and P.T. Dobrila (eds) *Eduardo Kac: Telepresence, Biotelematics, Transgenetic Art*, Ljubljana: Association for Culture and Education, 7–18.

Cage, J. (1965) *Variations V: Thirty-seven Remarks re an Audio-visual Performance*, New York: Henmar Press.

Cage, J. and Charles, D. (1981) *For the Birds: John Cage in Conversation with David Charles*, London: Marion Boyars.

Campanella, T.J. (2000) 'Eden by wire: webcameras and the telepresent landscape' in K. Goldberg (ed.) *The Robot in the Garden: Telerobotics and Telepistemology in the Age of the Internet*, Cambridge MA: MIT Press, 22–47.

Capra, M. and Benford, S. (2007) *Deliverable D12.7. Evaluation of Day of the Figurines II. Final Report from Touring Day of the Figurines. Version 3*. Available online: www. pervasive-gaming.org/downloadsub1.html. Accessed 18 June 2008.

Capra, M., Radenkovic, M., Benford, S., Oppermann, L., Drodz, A. and Flintham, M. (2005) 'The multimedia challenges raised by pervasive games' in *Proceedings of the Thirteenth Annual ACM International Conference on Multimedia*, New York: ACM, 89–95.

Castellucci, R. (2000) 'The Animal Being On Stage,' *Performance Research*, 5:2, 23–8.

Caudell, T. and Mizell, D. (1992) 'Augmented reality: an application of heads-up display technology to manual manufacturing processes' in *Proceedings of Hawaii International Conference on System Sciences*, 659–69.

Chalmers, J. (1999) 'A conversation about *Jet Lag*', *Performance Research*, 4:2, 57–60.

Cleater, J. and Kaye, N. (2007) 'John Cleater: *Presence* interview'. Available online: http:// presence.stanford.edu:3455/Collaboratory/50333. Accessed 11 December 2009.

Coen, E. (2005) '*Risonanze oscure*/Dark resonances' in E. Coen and G. Stella (eds) *Gary Hill, Resounding Arches/Archi risonanti*, Milan: Electa, 139–49.

Conrad, T. (2001) '"Who will give answer to the call of my voice?" Sound in the work of Tony Oursler' in E. Janus and G. Moure (eds) *Tony Oursler*, Barcelona: Poligrafa, 150–75.

Cooke, L. (2000 [1994]) 'Postscript. Re-embodiments in alter-space' in R.C. Morgan (ed.) *Gary Hill*, Baltimore MD: Johns Hopkins University Press, 135–48.

Cooke, L. and Oursler, T. (2008) 'Interview' in J.C. Welchman (ed.) *Tony Oursler: Works, 1997-2007*, Zurich: JRP Ringier.

de Certeau, M. (1984) *The Practice of Everyday Life*, Berkeley CA: University of California Press.

DeJong, C. and Conrad, T. (1995) 'A conversation between Constance DeJong and Tony Conrad' in F. Malsch (ed.) *Tony Oursler: Dummies, Clouds, Organs, Flowers, Watercolours, Videotapes, Alters, Performances and Dolls*, Frankfurt am Main: Portikus, 6–7.

Derrida, J. (1976) *Of Grammatology*, translated by G.C. Spivak, Baltimore MD and London: Johns Hopkins University Press.

Dinkla, S. (1997) *Pioniere interaktiver Kunst von 1970 bis Heute*, Karlsruhe: ZKM, Cantz Verlag.

Dinkla, S. (2001) 'Auf dem Weg zu einer performativen Interaktion' in M. Leeker (ed.) *Maschinen, Medien, Performances. Theater an der Schnittstelle zu digitalen Welten*, Berlin: Alexander, 126–41.

Dinkla, S. (2002) 'The art of narrative: towards the *Floating Work of Art*' in M. Rieser and A. Zapp (eds) *New Screen Media Cinema/Art/Narrative*, London: British Film Institute, 27–41.

Dix, A. *et al.* (2004) 'absenT Presence'. Available online: www.crg.cs.nott.ac.uk/~sdb/r&rworkshop/dix.pdf. Accessed 3 December 2009.

Donnis, J., Thorup, L. and Gade, M. (2007) *Lifelike*, Landsforeningen: Projektgruppen KP07, in conjunction with Knudepunkt.

Eisenman, P. (1986) *Moving Arrows, Eros and other Errors: An Architecture of Absence*, London: Architectural Association.

Elam, K. (2002) *The Semiotics of Theatre and Drama*, London: Routledge.

Erickson, J. (1998) *The Fate of the Object: From Modern Object to Postmodern Sign in Performance, Art, Poetry*, Ann Arbor MI: University of Michigan Press.

Féral, J. (1982) 'Performance and theatricality: the subject demystified', *Modern Drama*, 25, 170–81.

Fischer-Lichte, E. (2008) *The Transformative Power of Performance: A New Aesthetics*, translated by Saskya Iris Jain, London: Routledge.

Flintham, M., Benford, S., Anastasi, R., Hemmings, T., Crabtree, A., Greenhalgh, C., Tandavanitj, N., Adams, M. and Row-Farr, J. (2003) 'Where on-line meets on the streets: experiences with mobile mixed reality games' in *Proceedings of ACM CHI 2003 Conference on Human Factors in Computing Systems*, Vol. I, New York: ACM, 569–76.

Flintham, M., Giannachi, G., Benford, S. and Adams, M. (2007) 'Day of the figurines: supporting episodic storytelling on mobile phones', *International Conference on Virtual Storytelling, Proceedings*, 167–75.

Fontaine, G. (1992) 'The experience of a sense of presence in intercultural and international encounters', *Presence: Teleoperators and Virtual Environments*, 1:4, 482–90.

Freud, S. (2003) *The Uncanny*, translated by D. McLintock, London: Penguin Books.

Fuchs, E. (1985) 'Presence and the revenge of writing: rethinking theatre after Derrida', *Performing Arts Journal*, 26–7, 163–73.

Furlong, L. (2000 [1993]) 'A manner of speaking' in R.C. Morgan (ed.) *Gary Hill*, Baltimore MD: Johns Hopkins University Press, 181–205.

Garau, M. Slater, M., Pertaub, D-P. and Razzaque, S. (2005) 'The responses of people to virtual humans in an immersive virtual environment', *Presence: Teleoperators and Virtual Environments*, 14:1, 104–16.

Gary Hill Studio (2002) letter to Nick Kaye and covering material, 13 November.

Gaver, W., Beaver J. and Benford S. (2003) 'Ambiguity as a resource for design' in *Proceedings of ACM CHI 2003 Conference on Human Factors in Computing Systems*, Vol. I, New York: ACM, 233–40.

Giannachi, G. and Benford, S. (2008) 'Temporal expansion in Blast Theory's *Day of the Figurines*', *PAJ: A Journal of Performance and Art*, 30:3, 60–9.

Giannachi, G. and Kaye, N. (2002) *Staging the Post-Avant-Garde: Italian Experimental Performance after 1970*, Oxford: Peter Lang.

Giannachi, G. and Kaye, N. (2006) 'Tim Etchells interviewed by the Presence project'. Available online: presence.stanford.edu:3455/Collaboratory/646. Accessed 10 December 2009.

Gibbs, J. (2008a) unpublished interview with Nick Kaye, New York City, February.

Gibbs, J. (2008b), artists in conversation, Brooklyn Academy of Music, November.

Goldberg, K. (ed.) (2000) *The Robot in the Garden: Telerobotics and Telepistemology in the Age of the Internet*, Cambridge MA: MIT Press.

Goodman, C. (1998) 'Art and technology: the ineluctable liaison' in C. Sommerer and L. Mignonneau (eds) *Art @ Science*, Vienna and New York: Springer, 240–61.

Graham, D. (1979) *Dan Graham: Video/Architecture/Television*, edited by B.H.D. Buchloch, New York: New York University Press.

Grau, O. (2000) 'The history of telepresence: automata, illusion and the rejection of the body' in K. Goldberg (ed.) *The Robot in the Garden: Telerobotics and Telepistemology in the Age of the Internet*, Cambridge MA: MIT Press, 226–45.

Hayles, K.N. (1996a) 'Virtual bodies and flickering signifiers' in T. Druckrey (ed.) *Electronic Culture: Technology and Visual Representation*, New York: Aperture, 259–76.

Hayles, K.N. (1996b) 'Embodied virtuality: or, How to put bodies back in the picture' in M.A. Moser and D. MacLeod (eds) *Immersed in Technology*, Cambridge MA: MIT Press, 259–76.

Heeter, C. (1992) 'Being there: the subjective experience of presence', *Presence: Teleoperators and Virtual Environments*, 1:2, 262–72.

Heidegger, M. (1971) *On the Way to Language*, New York; London: Harper & Row.

Heidegger, M. (1992) *The Concept of Time*, translated by W. McNeill, Oxford: Blackwell.

Heim, M. (1995) 'The design of virtual reality' in M. Featherstone and R. Burrows (eds) *Cyberspace, Cyberbodies, Cyberpunk*, London: Sage, 65–78.

Hershman, L. (n.d. a) '19. Reprinted from Forming a Sculpture/Drama in Manhattan', Lynn Hershman papers, M452, BOX 19. Department of Special Collections, Stanford University Libraries, Stanford CA.

Hershman, L. (n.d. b) 'New York Hotels'. Box 24. Lynn Hershman papers, M452, BOX 24. Department of Special Collections, Stanford University Libraries, Stanford CA.

Hershman, L. (n.d. c) 'Audio Timelapse Record . . . Playback' Box 33. Lynn Hershman papers, M452, BOX 24. Department of Special Collections, Stanford University Libraries, Stanford CA.

Hershman, L. (1973a) 'Fragmented Journal from 1973: A Partial Chronicle of Events', Lynn Hershman papers, M452, BOX 4. Department of Special Collections, Stanford University Libraries, Stanford CA.

Hershman, L. (1973b) 'October 1972–July 1973. The Dante Hotel', Lynn Hershman papers, M452, BOX 18. Department of Special Collections, Stanford University Libraries, Stanford CA.

Hershman, L. (1975) 'Re-forming Familiar Environments, May 16 1975'. Lynn Hershman (with Eleanor Coppola) Box 22. Lynn Hershman papers, M452. Department of Special Collections, Stanford University Libraries, Stanford CA.

Hershman Leeson, L. (ed.) (1996) *Clicking in: Hot Links to a Digital Culture*, Seattle WA: Bay Press.

Hershman Leeson, L. (2003) www.lynnhershman.com/. Accessed 5 February 2003.

Hershman Leeson, L. (2009) *Life*[n], San Francisco: Hotwire Productions.

Hill, G. (2000a [1991]) 'Site re:cite' in R.C. Morgan (ed.) *Gary Hill*, Baltimore MD: Johns Hopkins University Press, 301–8.

Hill, G. (2000b [1992]) 'Inter-view' in R.C. Morgan (ed.) *Gary Hill*, Baltimore MD: Johns Hopkins University Press, 290–8.

Hill, G. (1994) *Gary Hill*, Seattle WA: Henry Art Gallery, University of Washington.

Hill, G. (2002) *Selected Works/Catalogue raisonné*, Cologne: DuMont.

Hobbs, R. (ed.) (1981) *Robert Smithson: Sculpture*, London: Cornell University Press.

Huizinga, J. (1971) *Homo Ludens*, Boston MA: Beacon Press.

Humphries, J. (2007) 'Jacqueline Humphries interviews Tony Oursler on his newest piece: *Seven Months of my Aesthetic Education plus Some . . .*' Tony Oursler Online. Available at: http://tonyoursler.com/tonyourslerv2/main.html. Accessed 7 July 2007.

Janko, S., Leopoldseder, H. and Stocker, G. (eds) (1996) *Ars Electronica Center Linz, Museum of the Future*, Linz: AEC Verein, Orf.

Janus, E. (1999) 'Talking back: a conversation with Tony Oursler' in D. Rothschild (ed.) *Tony Oursler, Introjection: Mid-career Survey, 1976–1999*, Williamstown MA: Williams College Museum of Art, 70–95.

Kac, E. (2000) 'Dialogical telepresence and Net ecology' in K. Goldberg (ed.) *The Robot in the Garden: Telerobotics and Telepistemology in the Age of the Internet*, Cambridge MA: MIT Press, 180–97.

Kac, E. (2002) www.ekac.org. Accessed 2 December 2002.

Kaye, N. (1996) *Art into Theatre: Performance Interviews and Documents*, London: Routledge.

Kaye, N. (2000) *Site-specific Art: Performance, Place and Documentation*, London; New York: Routledge.

Kaye, N. (2007a) *Multi-media: Video – Installation – Performance*, London: Routledge.

Kaye, N. (2007b) 'Screening presence: The Builders' Association and dbox, SUPER VISION (2005)' in *Contemporary Theatre Review*, 17:4, 557–76.

Kaye, N. and Weems, M. (2005) 'Marianne Weems, SUPER VISION interview'. Available online: http://presence.stanford.edu:3455/Collaboratory/831. Accessed 11 December 2009.

Kelley, M. (1999) 'An endless script: a conversation with Tony Oursler,' in D. Rothschild (ed.) *Tony Oursler, Introjection: Mid-career Survey, 1976–1999*, Williamstown MA: Williams College Museum of Art, 38–55.

Kermode, F. (1987) 'Endings, continued', in S. Budick and W. Ider (eds) *Languages of the Unsayable: The Play of Negativity in Literature and Theory*, Stanford CA: Stanford University Press, 71–94.

Kern, S. (1983) *The Culture of Time and Space, 1880–1918*, Cambridge MA: Harvard University Press.

Komparu, K. (2006) *The Noh Theater: Principles and Perspectives*, Warren CT: Floating World.

Kozel, S. (1994a) 'Virtual reality: choreographing cyberspace', *Dance Theater Journal*, 11:2, 34–7.

Kozel, S. (1994b) 'Spacemaker: experiences of a virtual body', *Dance Theater Journal*, 11:3, 12–13 and 46–7.

Lanier, J. (1992) 'Virtual reality: a status report' in L. Jacobson (ed.) *CyberArts: Exploring Art and Technology*, San Francisco: Miller Freeman, 272–9.

Lestocart, J-L. (2000 [1996]) 'Surfing the medium' in R.C. Morgan (ed.) *Gary Hill*, Baltimore MD: Johns Hopkins University Press, 232–9.

Levinas, E. (1969) *Totality and Infinity: An Essay on Exteriority*, translated by A. Lingis, Pittsburgh PA: Duquesne University Press.

Lippard, L.R. and Smithson, R. (1996 [1973]) 'Fragments of an interview with P.A. [Patsy] Norvell' in J. Flam (ed.) *Robert Smithson: The Collected Writings*, Berkeley CA and Los Angeles: University of California Press, 192–5.

Lombard, M. and Ditton, T. (1997) 'At the heart of it all: the concept of presence', *Journal of Computer Mediated Communication*, 3:2. Available online: http://jcmc.indiana.edu/vol3/issue2/lombard.html. Accessed 4 December 2008.

Magerkurth, C., Cheok, A.D., Mandryk, R. and Nilsen, T. (2005) 'Pervasive games: bringing computer entertainment back into the real world', *ACM Computers in Entertainment*, 3:3, 1–19 (article 4A).

Malsch, F. (ed.) (1995) *Tony Oursler: Dummies, Clouds, Organs, Flowers, Watercolours, Videotapes, Alters, Performances and Dolls*, Frankfurt am Main: Portikus.

Manovich, L. (2001) *The Language of New Media*, Cambridge MA: MIT Press.

Manovich, L. (2000) 'To lie and to act: Potemkin's villages, cinema and telepresence' in K. Goldberg (ed.) *The Robot in the Garden: Telerobotics and Telepistemology in the Age of the Internet*, Cambridge MA: MIT Press, 164–79.

Mantovani, G. and Riva, G (1999) '"Real" presence: how different ontologies generate different criteria for presence, telepresence, and virtual presence', *Presence: Teleoperators and Virtual Environments*, 8:5, 540–50.

Mauss, M. (2000 [1954]) *The Gift: Forms and Functions of Exchange in Archaic Societies*, translated by W.D. Halls, New York: Norton.

McMillan, D. and Fehsenfeld, M. (1988) *Beckett in the Theatre*, London: John Calder; New York: Riverrun Press.

Milgram, P. and Kishino, F. (1994) 'A taxonomy of mixed reality visual displays', *IEICE Transactions on Information Systems E77-D* (12), 1321–9.

Minsky, M. (1980) 'Telepresence', *Omni*, June, 45–51.

Minton, J. (n.d.) 'Trespassing at the Dante', Lynn Hershman papers, M452, BOX 18. Department of Special Collections, Stanford University Libraries, Stanford CA.

Montola, M. (2003) 'Role-playing as interactive construction of subjective diegesis' in M. Gade, L. Thorup and M. Sander (eds) *As Larp Grows up: Theory and Methods in Larp*, Projektgruppen KP03, 34–9. Available online: www.laivforum.dk/kp03.pdf. Accessed 1 July 2007.

Montola, M. (2005) 'Exploring the edge of the magic circle: defining pervasive games', *Proceedings of Digital Experience: Design, Aesthetics, Practice Conference*, Copenhagen. Available online: http://users.tkk.fi/mmontola/exploringtheedge.pdf. Accessed 6 January 2010.

Montola, M. and Stenros, J. (2004) *Beyond Role and Play*, Helsinki: Ropeconry.

Mulder, A. and Post, M. (2000) *Book for the Electronic Arts*, Rotterdam: De Balie.

Murray, C. (1998) 'Conceptualising and explicating presence' in M. Buscher, J. Hughes, J. O'Brien and T. Rodden (eds) 'Presence and representation in multimedia art and electronic landscapes', *Escape*, 211–32. Available online: http://www.comp.lancs.ac.uk/computing/research/cseg/DIGITAL-LIBRARY/Escape/Escape-D1.1.pdf. Accessed 23 September 2009.

Nemser, C. (1971) 'An interview with Vito Acconci', *Arts Magazine*, March, 20–3.

Neri, L. (2001) 'Smoke and mirrors: Tony Oursler's influence machine: a conversation between Tony Oursler and Louise Neri,' in T. Oursler, *Tony Oursler: The Influence Machine*, London and New York: Artangel/ Public Art Fund, 2001, 56–62.

Nyman, M. (1999) *Experimental Music: Cage and Beyond (Music in the Twentieth Century)* (2nd edition), Cambridge: Cambridge University Press.

OED (2009) *Oxford English Dictionary Online*. Available at: http://0-dictionary.oed.com.lib.exeter.ac.uk:80/. Accessed 15 December 2009.

Oursler, T. (1991) 'Conversation about some recent work'. Available online: http://tonyoursler.com/tonyourslerv2/main.html. Accessed 27 November 2009.

Oursler, T. (1994) 'Proposal for Judy an installation at Salzberg Kunstverein'. Available online: http://tonyoursler.com/tonyourslerv2/main.html. Accessed 27 November 2009.

Oursler, T. (1995) 'Window Project, 1993' in F. Malsch (ed.) *Tony Oursler: Dummies, Clouds, Organs, Flowers, Watercolours, Videotapes, Alters, Performances and Dolls*, Frankfurt am Main: Portikus, 52–7.

Oursler, T. (1997) 'Sketches at twilight,' in T. Oursler, *My Drawings, 1976-1996*, Kassel: Oktagon, 1997, pages unnumbered.

Oursler, T. (2001) 'Timestream: "I hate the dark, I love the light"' in T. Oursler, *Tony Oursler: The Influence Machine*, London and New York: Artangel/Public Art Fund, 79–103.

Oursler, T. (2002) 'Pop dead pictures', in E. Janus (ed.) *Tony Oursler*, Milan: Electa, 156–71.

Oursler, T. (2005) 'Blob'. Available online: http://tonyoursler.com/tonyourslerv2/main.html. Accessed 3 July 2007.

Paik, N.J. (1993) *Nam June Paik. Eine Data Base*, Stuttgart: Cantz.

Pearson, M. and Shanks, M. (2001) *Theatre/Archaeology*, London: Routledge.

Pfister, M. (1991 [1977]) *The Theory and Analysis of Drama*, translated by J. Halliday, Cambridge: Cambridge University Press.

Phelan, P. (1993) *Unmarked: The Politics of Performance*, London: Routledge.

Pontbriand, C. (1982) 'The eye finds no fixed point on which to rest', *Modern Drama*, 25, 154–62.

Popper, F. (1993) *Art of the Electronic Age*, London: Thames & Hudson.

Quasha, G. and Stein, C. (1997a) *Viewer: Gary Hill's Projective Installations, Number 3*, Barrytown NY: Station Hill Press.

Quasha, G. and Stein, C. (1997b) *Tall Ships: Gary Hill's Projective Installations, Number 2*, Barrytown NY: Station Hill Press.

Quasha, G. and Stein, C. (2000 [1998]) '*Liminal Performance:* Gary Hill in dialogue' in R. C. Morgan (ed.) *Gary Hill*, Baltimore MD: Johns Hopkins University Press, 243–70.

Quasha, G. and Stein, C. (2001) 'Performance itself' in G. Quasha and C. Stein (eds) *Around and About: A Performative View*, Paris: Du Regard, 1–24.

Robins, K. (1996) *Into the Image: Culture and Politics in the Field of Vision*, London and New York: Routledge.

Roth, M. (n.d.) 'Leaping the Fence: An Introduction to the Work of Lynn Hershman', Lynn Hershman papers, M452, BOX 19. Department of Special Collections, Stanford University Libraries, Stanford CA.

Rothschild, D. (1999) '*Introjection:* in Oursler's world, no one escapes its unbidden influences, in D. Rothschild (ed.) *Tony Oursler, Introjection: Mid-career Survey, 1976–1999*, Williamstown MA: Williams College Museum of Art, 1999, 12–37.

Royle, N. (2003) *The Uncanny*, Manchester: Manchester University Press.

Rubin, B. (2007) unpublished interview with Nick Kaye, New York City, November.

Salen, K. and Zimmerman E. (2004) *Rules of Play: Game Design Fundamentals*, Cambridge MA: MIT Press.

Salz, D. Z. (2001) 'The collaborative subject: telerobotic performance and identity', *Performance Research*, 6:3, 70–83.

Sans, J. (1999) 'Gary Hill interviewed by Jérôme Sans' in A. Kold (ed.) *Gary Hill*, Aarhus: Aarhus Kunstmueum, 71–4.

Sarrazin, S. (2000 [1992]) 'A discussion with Gary Hill' in R.C. Morgan (ed.) *Gary Hill*, Baltimore MD: Johns Hopkins University Press, 206–23.

Schechner, R. (1966) 'Approaches to theory/criticism', *Tulane Drama Review*, 10:4, 20–53.

Schwartz, I. (1997) www.archis.org/archis_art_e_1997/archis_art_9709_ENG.html. Accessed 5 December 2000.

Schwarz, H-P. and Shaw, J. (1996) *Perspektiven der Medienkunst*, Karlsruhe: ZKM, Cantz Verlag.

Sermon, P. (2003) www.artdes.salford.ac.uk/sermon/vision/tv_a.html. Accessed 6 January 2003.

Shanks, M. *et al.* (2009) *Life Squared*. Available online: http://documents.stanford.edu/michaelshanks/36. Accessed 8 December 2009.

Sheridan, T.B. (1992b) 'Defining our terms', *Presence: Teleoperators and Virtual Environments*, 1:2, 272–4.

Sheridan, T. B. (1992a) 'Musings on telepresence and virtual presence', *Presence: Teleoperators and Virtual Environments*, 1:1, 120–5.

Shorter OED (1975) *Shorter Oxford English Dictionary*, edited by C.T. Onions, Oxford: Clarendon Press.

Simon, J. (2007) 'Motion pictures: Gordon Matta-Clark' in E. Sussman (ed.) *Gordon Matta-Clark: You are the Measure*, New Haven CT: Yale University Press; New York: Whitney Museum of American Art, 124–35.

Slater, M. (1997) 'Introduction to special issue. Framework for Immersive Virtual Environments Conference of the FIVE Working Group, London, December 1995', *Presence: Teleoperators and Virtual Environments*, 6:6, iii–iii.

Slater, M. (2002) 'Presence and the sixth sense', *Presence: Teleoperators and Virtual Environments*, 11:4, 435–9.

Slater, M. (2003) 'A note on presence terminology', *Presence Connect*, 3. Available online: presence.cs.ucl.ac.uk/presenceconnect/articles/Jan2003/melslaterJan27200391557/melslaterJan27200391557.html. Accessed 4 December 2008.

Slater, M., Brogni, A. and Steed, A. (2003) 'Physiological responses to breaks in presence: a pilot study', *Presence 2003: the Sixth Annual International Workshop on Presence*. Available online: www.cs.ucl.ac.uk/staff/m.slater/Papers/physbips.pdf. Accessed 6 January 2010.

Slater, M., Usoh, M., and Steed, A. (1994), 'Depth of presence in virtual environments', *Presence: Teleoperators and Virtual Environments*, 3:2, 130–44.

Slater, M. and Usoh, M. (1994) 'Representation systems, perceptual position, and presence in immersive virtual environments', *Presence: Teleoperators and Virtual Environments*, 2:3, 221–33.

Slater, M. and Wilbur, S. (1995) 'Through the looking-glass world of presence: a framework for immersive virtual environments' in M. Slater (ed.) *FIVE '95 Framework for Immersive Virtual Environments*, London: Queen Mary and Westfield College, University of London.

Smithson, R. (1996 [1972]) 'The spiral jetty' in J. Flam (ed.) *Robert Smithson: The Collected Writings*, Berkeley CA and Los Angeles: University of California Press, 143–53.

Steed, A. and Parker, C. (2005) 'Evaluating effectiveness of interaction techniques across immersive virtual environments systems', *Presence: Teleoperators and Virtual Environments*, 14:5, 511–27.

Stella, G. (2005) '*Archi risonanti*/Resounding arches' in E. Coen and G. Stella (eds) *Gary Hill, Resounding Arches/Archi risonanti*, Milan: Electa, 12–31.

Steuer, J. (1992) 'Defining virtual reality: dimensions determining telepresence', *Journal of Communications*, 42, 73–93.

Stocker, G. (2000) 'Uprising' in A. Kostic and P.T. Dobrila (eds) *Eduardo Kac: Telepresence, Biotelematics, Transgenetic Art*, Ljubljana: Association for Culture and Education, 7–18.

Sutherland, E. (1968) 'A futures market in computer time', *Communications of the ACM*, 11:6, 449–51.

Thomson, P. (1970) 'Games and plays: an approach to Ionesco', *Educational Theatre Journal*, 22:1, 60–70.

Tomlinson, B. (2000) 'Dead technology', *Style*, 33, 316–35.

Triesman, A.M. (1963) 'Verbal cues, language and meaning in selective attention', *American Journal of Psychology*, 77, 206–19.

Tromble, M. (ed.) (2005) *The Art and Films of Lynn Hershman Leeson*, Berkeley CA and Los Angeles: University of California Press.

Tschumi, B. (1987) *Cinégram folie: le parc de la Villette*, Princeton NJ: Princeton Architectural Press.

Tschumi, B. (1994a) *Architecture and Disjunction*, London: MIT Press.

Tschumi, B. (1994b) *The Manhattan Transcripts*, London: Architectural Association.

Tice, S. and Laurel, B. (1992) 'The art of building virtual reality' in L. Jacobson (ed.) *CyberArts: Exploring Art and Technology*, San Francisco: Miller Freeman, 280–91.

V2 (1997) *Technomorphica*, Rotterdam: Naj.

Valentini, V. (ed.) (1995) *Percorsi tra video, cinema e teatro*, Milan: Electa.

Varela, F. J. (1999) 'The specious present: a neurophenomenology of time consciousness' in J. Petiot *et al.* (eds) *Naturalizing Phenomenology: Issues in Contemporary Phenomenology and Cognitive Science*, Stanford CA: Stanford University Press. Available online: http://www.franzreichle.ch/images/Francisco_Varela/Human_ Consciousness_Article02.htm. Accessed 8 December 2009.

Virilio, P. (2000 [1990]) *Polar Inertia*, translated by P. Camiller, London: Sage.

Virilio, P. (1995) 'Speed and information: cyberspace alarm!' *CTHEORY*. Available online: www.ctheory.net/articles.aspx?id=72. Accessed 3 December 2009.

Wærn, A., Benford, S., Goetcherian, V., Åkesson, K.P., Söderlund, T., Björk, S., Mäyrä, F., Holopainen, J., Schäfer, L. and Ghellal, S. (2004) 'IPerG position paper. Workshop on Gaming Applications in Pervasive Computing Environments, Second International Conference on Pervasive Computing' *Pervasive 2004*, Vienna. Available online: www. ipsi.fraunhofer.de/ambiente/pervasivegaming/. Accessed 24 September 2005.

Wardrip-Fruin, N. and Harrigan, P. (eds) (2004) *First Person: New Media as Story, Performance, and Game*, Cambridge MA and London: MIT Press.

Weber, S. (1996) *Mass Mediauras: Form, Technics, Media*, edited by A. Cholodenko, Stanford CA: Stanford University Press.

Wehle, P. (1999) 'Overlapping worlds: The Builders' Association and *Jump Cut* (*Faust*)', *TheaterForum*, 14, 4–9.

Weibel, P. and Druckrey, T. (eds) (2001) *net_condition: art and global media*, Cambridge MA: MIT Press.

Wilson, S. (2002) *Information Arts: Intersections of Art, Science, and Technology*, Cambridge MA: MIT Press.

Witmer, B. and Singer, M. (1998) 'Measuring presence in virtual environments: a presence questionnaire', *Presence: Teleoperators and Virtual Environments*, 7:3, 225–4.

INDEX

Page numbers in italics indicate illustrations, following references in the text.
Art and literary works are listed as sub-entries to the relevant author.